NEGATIVE ACTIONS

Negative actions, like intentional omissions or refrainments, seem to be genuine actions. The standard metaphysical theories of action are event-based: they treat actions as events of a special kind. However, it seems that many (and perhaps all) negative actions are not events, but absences thereof. This is the first book-length treatment of the problem of negative action. It surveys the recent literature, and shows how the problem is rooted in interconnected issues in metaphysics, the philosophy of action, and the philosophy of language. In particular, it connects competing views of the ontology of negative actions to competing views of the semantics of 'negative action sentences', and develops unique ontological and semantic theories to solve the problem. It provides a comprehensive picture of the nature of negative actions, our thought and talk about them, and their place in a theory of action.

JONATHAN D. PAYTON is Assistant Professor of Philosophy at Bilkent University, Turkey. He has published numerous articles on metaphysics, the philosophy of action and the philosophy of language in journals including the *Australasian Journal of Philosophy*, the *Canadian Journal of Philosophy*, *Erkenntnis* and *Synthese*.

T0370823

NEGATIVE ACTIONS

Events, Absences, and the Metaphysics of Agency

JONATHAN D. PAYTON

Bilkent University

CAMBRIDGE
UNIVERSITY PRESS

Shaftesbury Road, Cambridge CB2 8EA, United Kingdom

One Liberty Plaza, 20th Floor, New York, NY 10006, USA

477 Williamstown Road, Port Melbourne, VIC 3207, Australia

314–321, 3rd Floor, Plot 3, Splendor Forum, Jasola District Centre, New Delhi – 110025, India

103 Penang Road, #05–06/07, Visioncrest Commercial, Singapore 238467

Cambridge University Press is part of Cambridge University Press & Assessment, a department of the University of Cambridge.

We share the University's mission to contribute to society through the pursuit of education, learning and research at the highest international levels of excellence.

www.cambridge.org
Information on this title: www.cambridge.org/9781108813730

DOI: 10.1017/9781108885157

First published 2021
First paperback edition 2022

A catalogue record for this publication is available from the British Library

ISBN   978-1-108-83979-2   Hardback
ISBN   978-1-108-81373-0   Paperback

Contents

v

Acknowledgements

My work on negative actions began with my dissertation, written at the University of Toronto roughly between September 2013 and December 2015. Thanks to the members of my dissertation committee – Phil Clark, Michela Ippolito, Sergio Tenenbaum, and Jessica Wilson – for all their guidance and support throughout this period and beyond. Thanks also to Gurpreet Rattan and Helen Steward, who served as external referees and who have both continued to provide support in the intervening years. Thanks, finally, to the Social Sciences and Humanities Research Council of Canada (SSHRC) for a Joseph-Armand Bombardier Doctoral Scholarship which funded my research.

This book was written between September 2018 and March 2020, while I was a SSHRC Postdoctoral Fellow at the University of Calgary. Special thanks are due to my postdoctoral supervisor, David Liebesman, who provided invaluable feedback and advice on this and other philosophical projects, as well as support in matters philosophical and otherwise; I couldn't have asked for a better supervisor. Special thanks also to Ishtiyaque Haji, who provided great advice as I prepared the original proposal. Thanks, finally, to SSHRC for the Postdoctoral Fellowship which funded my research, and without which this book wouldn't have been possible.

Thanks to Hilary Gaskin at Cambridge University Press for encouraging me to submit the original proposal for this book, and to both her and Hal Churchman for all their help along the way. Thanks also to two anonymous referees for Cambridge University Press for their careful, judicious reading and valuable feedback.

I owe a debt of gratitude to the entire Department of Philosophy at the University of Calgary (both faculty and graduate students) for providing a welcoming and productive environment over the past two years. In addition to Dave and Ish, I want to single out Noa Latham and Mark Migotti for feedback on various chapters, as well as David Dick, Jeremy Fantl,

Christopher Framarin, Allen Habib, Joe Kadi, Yoshiki Kobasigawa, Ann Levey, C. Kenneth Waters, and Nicole Wyatt for helpful conversations both philosophical and otherwise.

This book includes revised and expanded material from my articles, 'The logical form of negative action sentences' (*Canadian Journal of Philosophy* 46(6):855–876, 2016) and 'How to identify negative actions with positive events' (*Australasian Journal of Philosophy* 96(1):87–101, 2018); thanks to the Taylor and Francis Group for the relevant permissions. Since I began writing, I've presented ideas and arguments from the book at the Apeiron Society for the Practice of Philosophy (at the invitation of Mark Migotti), the Banff Workshop on Language and Metaphysics (at the invitation of David Liebesman and Rachel Sterken), and a colloquium run by the graduate students in the Department of Philosophy at the University of Calgary (at the invitation of Nima Khodabandeh). Thanks to all those audiences. Thanks also to Sara Bernstein, Andrei A. Buckareff, Herman Cappellen, Randolph Clarke, Josh Dever, Matti Eklund, Kim Frost, Benj Hellie, Paul Henne, Jennifer Hornsby, John Hyman, Nicky Kroll, Nicholas Leonard, Lawrence Lombard, Kirk Ludwig, Jeff Pelletier, Garrett Pendergraft, Carolina Sartorio, Neil E. Williams, and Stephen Yablo for discussion of various issues related to negative actions.

Last, but not least, thanks to my parents and to Theresa and Laura, for all their love and support over the years.

Introduction

The aim of this book is to solve a problem facing contemporary meta-physical theories of action and agency.

The central task of a theory of action is to explain the difference between action and mere behaviour. When I raise my arm in order to hail a passing cab, the raising of my arm isn't something that merely happens to me; rather, I exercise control over my behaviour, and thereby exercise my agency. By contrast, when my arm rises as the result of an involuntary spasm, the rising of my arm is something that merely happens to me; I don't exercise control over my behaviour, and so I don't exercise my agency. The central task of a theory of action is to explain what the difference between these different sorts of behaviour consists of. For instance, according to the Causal Theory of Action defended by Donald Davidson and others, the difference between actions and mere behaviours is a difference in their causal histories. When I raise my arm in order to hail a passing cab, the rising of my arm is caused (in the right way) by certain mental states of mine, namely, intentions, beliefs, and desires which rationalize my behaviour. Because it is caused in this way, the rising of my arm counts not merely as an arm-*rising*, but as an arm-*raising*. By contrast, when my arm rises as the result of a spasm, it lacks the sort of causal history that an arm-raising has, and so it is merely an arm-rising. The hope, of course, is that a similar story can be told for all sorts of actions, not just arm-raisings.

Now, it's an important fact about our agency that we can exercise it both by doing things and by not doing things. If I intentionally omit to pick up a friend at the airport, or refrain from having a second helping of dessert, I thereby exercise my agency, just as when I raise my arm in order to hail a passing cab. When I intentionally omit to do something, or refrain from doing it, I thereby exercise control over my own behaviour, and so it seems that I've *acted*, in omitting or refraining. By contrast, if I simply forget to pick up my friend at the airport, or fail to have a second helping of dessert simply because it doesn't occur to me to take seconds, I haven't exercised my agency; I have simply not done something.

A satisfactory theory of action and agency must accommodate 'negative actions' – i.e. exercises of agency which seem to consist primarily in an agent not doing a certain thing. Such behaviours are precisely the sort of thing that a theory of action is supposed to be a theory *of*.

However, negative actions present a metaphysical problem for the dominant theories. These theories – including the Causal Theory – are 'event-based': they are built on the assumption that actions are events, i.e. occurrences or happenings. With this assumption in place, the central task of a metaphysical theory of action becomes the task of distinguishing actions from other events, i.e. explaining what distinguishes actions as a subset of the larger category of events. The problem is that, according to many philosophers of action, negative actions (with perhaps a few exceptions) are *not* events. For, it seems, if doing something is a matter of the occurrence of an event, then *not* doing that thing is a matter of the *absence* of an event: if I intentionally omit to raise my arm, what's happened isn't that an event of a special kind, an *omission to raise my arm*, has occurred; rather, what's happened is simply that *no* event of the kind *raising of my arm* has occurred. The problem is clear. If all actions are events, but many (and perhaps all) negative actions aren't, then so-called negative actions aren't really *actions* at all, but *absences* of action. The dominant, event-based theories of action seem incapable of accommodating an important class of actions, and hence incapable of accommodating an important aspect of our agency.

Call this 'the problem of negative action'. It can be presented as an inconsistent triad. Let 'NEG' be a schematic verb for negative behaviours, e.g. omitting and refraining, which can be combined with another verb, 'φ', to generate a negative verb phrase, 'NEG-φ', whose instances include 'omit to φ', 'refrain from φ-ing', and the like. Then, each of the following propositions is deeply intuitive, or widely held among philosophers of action for theoretical reasons, or both, but they can't all be true.

(PNA 1)   Negative actions – in the sense of things done – are genuine actions; necessarily, if NEG-φ is a negative action for x at t, then if x NEG-φ-s at t, then x acts by NEG-φ-ing at t.

(PNA 2)   Necessarily, if x acts by φ-ing at t, then there exists an event that is x's token φ-ing at t.

(PNA 3)   Possibly, x NEG-φ-s at t, and there exists no event that is x's token NEG-φ-ing at t.

One or more of these propositions must be rejected.

To reject (PNA 1) is to deny the appearances and insist that so-called negative actions aren't really actions at all. If we go this way, then we needn't revise or reject the dominant event-based theories in light of the alleged counterexamples of intentional omissions, refrainments, and the like. If these behaviours aren't actions, then they aren't the sort of thing that a theory of action is meant to be a theory *of*, and so they can't be counterexamples to event-based theories.

To reject (PNA 2), by contrast, is to take on the burden of revising the dominant event-based theories so as to free them from the assumption that actions are events – e.g. in the case of the Causal Theory, providing an account of how there can still be a causal process of the right kind when there is no such behaviour as my omission to raise my arm, to which mental states of mine can stand in the relation of singular causation – or rejecting those theories altogether.

The solution I prefer is to reject (PNA 3): negative actions are events, not absences. If we go this way, then we get the benefit of the first solution: we needn't revise or reject the dominant event-based theories in order to accommodate negative actions; since negative actions are events, rather than absences thereof, then they pose no metaphysical problem for event-based theories. And we do so without having to deny what seems *prima facie* obvious, that intentional omissions, refrainments, and the like are exercises of agency, and that a theory of action should be able to explain the difference between intentionally omitting to do something, or refraining from doing it, on one hand, and merely not doing it, on the other.

Despite these attractions, my preferred solution has few defenders. The bulk of the book will be dedicated to addressing the motivations behind (PNA 3), showing that they fail, and developing an account of negative actions as events which will answer the standard worries one finds in the literature.

In defending my solution, I appeal in part to ideas and arguments from the philosophy of language. The major motivation for (PNA 2) comes from the 'Neo-Davidsonian' approach to the analysis of action sentences. According to this approach, ordinary action sentences such as 'I raised my arm' are existential quantifications over events: the logical form of 'x φ-s' is 'There exists an event, e, that is x's φ-ing'. Thus, these sentences are true just in case those events exist. The major motivation for (PNA 3) is that the same is not true for negative action sentences. According to a widely-assumed view which I call 'Deflationism', negative action sentences are simply the negations of corresponding positive action sentences, and hence they express negative existentials: the logical form of 'x NEG-φ-s' is 'There

exists *no* event, *e*, which is *x*'s φ-ing'. There's no requirement that there be
any such event as *x*'s NEG-φ-ing in order for this sentence to be true;
what's required is the *absence* of a certain kind of event, not the presence of
one. Hence (PNA 3) and the idea that negative actions are not events but
absences thereof.

I argue that Deflationism is false. The best account of the logical form of
negative action sentences is a Neo-Davidsonian one, according to which they
report the occurrence of negative actions *qua* events. Thus, the motivation for
thinking that ordinary actions are events extends to negative ones as well.

This style of argument relies on a Quinean criterion of ontological
commitment. According to this criterion, you're ontologically committed
to the entities which are quantified over in the sentences you accept: if you
accept a sentence '*S*' (equivalently: if you think that *S* is the case) and '*S*'
has the form '∃*xFx*' (and so, '*S*' is true just in case there are *F*s), then you're
ontologically committed to *F*s. Thus, if negative action sentences quantify
over negative actions *qua* events, and you think those sentences are
sometimes true (that is, if you think that people sometimes omit to do
things, refrain from doing things, etc.), then you ought to think that
negative actions are events, not absences.

This criterion, and this style of argument, are unpopular these days.
Many metaphysicians reject the Quinean criterion, and even deny that we
can appeal to considerations of language and logical form at all when
engaging in properly metaphysical argument. I defend the Quinean criterion in more detail in Section 1.3.2, but some remarks about it, and the
style of argument I'll be giving in later chapters, are in order here.

It's often thought that if we appeal to considerations of language and logical
form when arguing for a metaphysical conclusion then we fail to do justice to
the metaphysician's conception of herself as inquiring into the nature of reality,
rather than into how we happen to talk about it. Worse, it's often thought that
to appeal to considerations of this sort is to attempt to 'read off' facts about how
things are from facts about how we talk, or to engage in a shaky inference from
'We speak as if *p*' to *p*. But we needn't reduce metaphysics to 'mere' linguistics
or take how we happen to talk as an infallible guide to how things are in order
to make the kind of argument I'll be making in this book.

Consider the following argument form:

(α) '*S*' is true ≡ *S*.
(β) '*S*' is true ≡ *p*.
(γ) ∴ *S* ≡ *p*.

(α) is simply the T-schema, according to which you can give the truth-
conditions for a sentence by using that sentence – e.g. 'Snow is white' is

true just in case snow is white. (β) is a schema for giving the truth-conditions for a sentence without using that very same sentence. '*p*' names the propositional content of '*S*' and needn't be structurally equivalent to '*S*' – e.g. using the resources of first-order formal languages we might say that 'Snow is white' is true just in case *White* (snow). If both (α) and (β) are true, then (γ) follows by elementary reasoning: the state of affairs reported by '*S*' obtains just in case the state of affairs reported by '*p*' obtains.

(α) and (β) are framed in meta-linguistic terms, and so there's a clear sense in which they are claims about language. By contrast, unless '*S*' itself is a meta-linguistic sentence, (γ) isn't about language in any obvious sense; it reports that one state of affairs obtains just in case another state of affairs obtains. Nonetheless, since the argument is valid, there's no reason to think that (γ) *can't* follow from (α) and (β), simply because they explicitly concern our language while (γ) doesn't.[1]

To appeal to the Quinean criterion of ontological commitment is to make an argument of this form. In particular, it's to make an argument of this form where *p* is existentially quantified: 'Given that the truth-condition of "*S*" is "∃*xFx*", *if* you accept that *S*, *then* you must accept that there are *Fs*'. Thus, my main argument that negative actions are events goes like this:

(1) '*x* NEG-φ-s' is true ≡ *x* NEG-φ-s.
(2) '*x* NEG-φ-s' is true ≡ There exists an event that is *x*'s token NEG-φ-ing.
(3) ∴ *x* NEG-φ-s ≡ There exists an event that is *x*'s token NEG-φ-ing.

Regarding (1), I assume that the T-schema applies unproblematically to negative action sentences. It's well known that the schema can't apply in full generality, on pain of paradox (let '*S*' be '*S* is false'). But all the solutions to this problem of which I'm aware aim to recover as many instances of the schema as possible. Since I'm not aware of any reason to think that applying the schema to negative action sentences leads to paradox, I assume it applies unproblematically to them. Point (2) is the Neo-Davidsonian claim I'll be defending in detail in the central chapters of the book. Given (1) and (2), (3) follows unavoidably: an agent performs a negative action (i.e. she omits to do something, refrains from doing it, etc.) just in case there exists an event which is her token negative action (an omission, a refrainment, etc.).

Now, it doesn't follow from (3) that there actually are such events as negative actions: the opponents of the Quinean criterion are right that we

---

[1] Thanks to David Liebesman for discussion.

can't simply read the existence of *F*s off the fact that some sentences in our language quantify over *F*s. (As I note in Section 1.3.2, Quine himself was quite clear on this.) What follows from (3) is that *if* agents ever omit to do things, refrain from doing them, etc., *then* there are such as events as their token negative actions. You're free to reject an ontology which includes such events if you find them problematic. But if you do, then you must deny that negative action sentences are ever true, and hence deny that agents ever perform negative actions.

As I said, I'll defend this style of argument in more detail in Section 1.3.2, I turn now to sketching the argument of the book as a whole.

In Chapter 1, I lay out some preliminary doctrines regarding action and ontology, including an account of the ontological distinction between *the things we do* and *our doings of those things*, which will be important at various points throughout the book.

In Chapter 2, I discuss the phenomenon of negative action in more detail. I also provide a more detailed presentation of the motives behind each of (PNA 1)–(PNA 3), and show that the widespread acceptance of (PNA 3) can be traced to widespread acceptance of Deflationism about negative action sentences.

In Chapter 3, I consider and reject a popular solution to the problem, which is to reject (PNA 1) and insist that, while so-called negative actions are an important aspect of our *agency*, they nonetheless aren't *actions*, strictly speaking. I argue that it's more difficult than it might seem to draw the requisite distinction between actions and 'mere manifestations of agency', and to justify placing intentional omissions, refrainments, and the like in the latter category. If we want to do justice to the importance these behaviours have for our agency, we're better off treating them as actions proper.

In Chapter 4, I turn my attention to (PNA 2), (PNA 3), and their linguistic motivations. Although Deflationism is widespread, both the thesis itself and the linguistic evidence for it are often left implicit or underdeveloped. In this chapter, I build an explicit case for Deflationism on behalf of its proponents. In brief, there's a range of linguistic data which is typically used to motivate the Neo-Davidsonian approach to ordinary action sentences; however, the same kind of linguistic data undermines a simple Neo-Davidsonian approach to *negative* action sentences, and favours the Deflationist approach.

If we want to reject Deflationism, and with it (PNA 3), we need an alternative semantics for negative action sentences. I develop this alternative – which I call 'the sophisticated Neo-Davidsonian approach' – in

Chapter 5. On this approach, negative action sentences are existential quantifications over events which play what I call 'the ensuring role': to say that *x* NEG-φ-s at *t* is to say that some behaviour of hers ensures (in a semi-technical sense, which I explain in detail) that *x* doesn't φ at *t*. Thus, to say that *x* NEG-φ-s is to report the occurrence of a token NEG-φ-ing, now understood as an event which plays the ensuring role. This approach accommodates the linguistic data which scuttles the simpler Neo-Davidsonian approach discussed in Chapter 4.

By the end of Chapter 5, Deflationism and the Neo-Davidsonian approach are at a stalemate. In Chapter 6, I introduce a new range of linguistic data which my Neo-Davidsonian approach can accommodate but which the Deflationist approach can't. Thus, taking all the linguistic evidence into account, my approach is to be preferred. We ought to think that negative action sentences are existential quantifications over ensuring-events, and hence (by the Quinean argument form sketched above) that if agents ever perform negative actions, there are such ensuring-events.

In Chapter 7, I turn to more robustly metaphysical issues. In my view, negative actions aren't negative in a metaphysically deep sense. The 'negativity' of negative actions resides in the description of the ensuring role (*x*'s NEG-φ-ing at *t* is whatever event ensures that no event is a φ-ing by *x* at *t*), while negative actions themselves are token-identical to ordinary, positive events. The reason is simple: negative actions are events which play the ensuring role; positive events play the ensuring role; therefore, negative actions are these positive events. This view is an analogue of 'token realizer functionalism' in the philosophy of mind, according to which a token mental state is whatever plays the functional role associated with that state (and hence, if that role is played by a token *physical* state, the mental and physical states are token-identical).

As I go on to show in Chapter 7, this realizer functionalist view is *prima facie* in conflict with the popular property-exemplification theory of events. Thus, it seems that if we want to endorse that theory of events, we must adopt a view on which negative actions aren't *identical* to positive events, but are perhaps *realized* or *constituted* by them. However, I argue that we have independent reason to revise the theory in such a way that it's consistent with realizer functionalism.

Finally, in Chapter 8, I consider a range of popular objections to the claim that negative actions are token identical to ordinary, positive events. Drawing on the details of my theory of negative actions, as well as the ontological framework defended in Chapter 1, I show that all these arguments fail.

In this book, I draw on ideas and arguments in the philosophy of action, the philosophy of language, and general metaphysics, in order to present a unified account of the nature of negative actions, our thought and talk about them, and their place in a theory of agency. On this account, negative actions can take their place alongside ordinary actions in event-based theories, and so we can retain those theories while recognizing the importance of negative actions to the fabric of human agency.

Action and Ontology

1.1 Introduction

In this chapter, I lay out some doctrines regarding action and ontology which will be important for understanding the problem of negative action and my solution to it. In Section 1.2, I explain the task of a metaphysical theory of action, draw a distinction between two kinds of action – the things we do and our particular doings of those things – and make clear what I will and won't be assuming about the scope of a theory of action. In Section 1.3, I turn to the ontology of action, specifically the ontology of doings and things done. I defend the view that doings are events while things done are properties of agents, and defend commitment to entities of both kinds on Quinean grounds.

1.2 Action

1.2.1 The Task of a Theory of Action

Agents can behave in many different ways. I can raise my arms, kick my legs, run, jump, sing, and dance. I can also bump into doors, fall down stairs, and fall asleep. Some of these things aren't like the others. Although all of these are things that I do, in some sense of the word 'do', there seems to be a more restricted sense of the word on which only some of them count as things I do, while the others are relegated to the category of 'things that happen to me'. In some sense, raising my arms, kicking my legs, running, jumping, singing, and dancing are things I do, while bumping into doors, falling down stairs, and falling asleep are things that merely happen to me (Davidson 1971: 43). What's the difference?

At its most abstract, the difference is between those things I do which are *actions* – i.e. those things in doing which I exercise my agency – and those which aren't. The distinction between actions and non-actions is of great importance for our understanding of ourselves and how we fit into the natural world. Agents, we think, have a kind of control over their behaviour that non-agents don't, and which they exercise whenever they act.[1]

The task of a theory of action is to explain the difference between action and 'mere behaviour'. Not all ways of behaving can be classified one way or the other for all agents, or even for a single agent at all times. Breathing, for instance, is something I typically do automatically, and is not clearly a candidate for a behaviour through which I exercise my agency. However, I can take control of my breathing, and so breathing is *sometimes* a way of acting for me. Thus, action theorists focus on specific cases involving specific agents behaving in specific ways at specific times: the task of a theory of action is to explain the difference between cases in which agents exercise their agency and cases in which this isn't so.

The task isn't, in the first instance, to provide an *extensional* account of the distinction between cases of action and cases of non-action, i.e. an inventory of which cases are which. We already have (or think we have) a good sense of which cases are which (e.g. a case in which I raise my arm to signal a passing cab is a case of action; a case in which my arm rises as the result of an involuntary spasm isn't), and a theory of action is to be judged, in part, by how well its dictates accord with our firmer judgments (e.g. a theory which says that I act when my arm rises due to a spasm but not when I raise my arm to hail a cab is in trouble). Rather than telling us which behaviours are actions and which aren't, the task of a theory of action is primarily to tell us what the difference between action and mere behaviour consists in, and *why* any given case belongs in the category it does.

I say we have a *good* sense of which cases are which, not that we have a *perfect* sense. As in other areas of philosophy, disagreement is always possible about particular cases. Consider, for instance, alleged mental actions – roughly, actions which don't involve an agent moving, positioning, or otherwise affecting those parts of her body that are visible to an outside observer. It certainly seems that some of the mental things I do are exercises of agency while others aren't: making a decision seems to be something I *do*, while remembering seems to be something that merely

---

[1] Bishop (1989: ch. 1), Shepherd (2014a), and Steward (2012a: chs. 1–3) explicitly tie agency to control over one's behaviour. Bishop and Steward both stress the importance of control to our conception of ourselves, not only as agents, but as free and responsible ones. On the connection between agency, freedom, and responsibility, see also the introduction to Moya (1990).

happens to me (although I can often do many *other* things in order to *bring it about* that I remember something). But philosophers of action are thoroughly divided over where to draw the line between mental action and mere mental behaviour, with some even arguing that there really *aren't* any mental actions.[2] Thus, while a theory of action is to be judged, in part, by how well it accords with our firmer judgments, there are cases which may have to be decided by appeal to such a theory: if a theory which is satisfying in other respects, and which performs better than its rivals, says that a case of decision-making is a case of action, then we may have to declare it to be so, regardless of the reservations we may have.

Likewise, we may have to sacrifice even some of our firmer intuitions on the altar of an otherwise successful theory. If a particular theory of action does a better job than its rivals of systematizing a large number of pre-theoretical judgments, is simpler than its rivals, relying on fewer contentious assumptions or posits, and faces fewer problems in explication and application, then we may have to accept its dictates about what is, or isn't a case of action, regardless of firm intuitions to the contrary.

Not everything that philosophers of action do contributes to the development of a theory of the sort I've described. Philosophers of action are interested in many different issues, including: the nature and possibility of free will; the nature and possibility of moral responsibility for our actions; the nature of certain mental states, like desire and intention, and their roles in practical deliberation and the production of action; the constraints on good practical reasoning; the conditions under which an agent can be said to possess a reason to do something; the difference between a reason that justifies your action and a reason that motivates it; the nature and possibility of *akratic* action, or weakness of will; the logical analysis of action sentences; speech act theory; and many more. Confronted with this fact, you might worry that my description of the task of a theory of action is myopic. However, I can easily acknowledge that to pursue any of these topics is to pursue a project in the philosophy of action. I simply insist on using the phrase 'theory of action' to describe a theory of what action *is*, and how it differs from mere behaviour.

1.2.2 *Doings, Things Done, and Doing-Types: Preliminary Remarks*

Hornsby (1980: 3–5) distinguishes two kinds of action, and hence two things we might have in mind, when talking about someone's 'actions'. In

---

[2] See, e.g. the various essays in O'Brien & Soteriou (2009).

one sense, an 'action' is a *thing done*, a way of acting. To talk about my actions, in this sense, is to talk about the things I have done, or am doing, or will do. In the other sense, an 'action' is a *doing* of something, a particular agent's acting in a certain way. To talk about my actions, in this sense, is to talk about past, present, or future doings of mine.[3] Of course, the distinction between doings and things done can be drawn for behaviours in general, and not just for actions: in one sense, a 'behaviour' is a thing done, a way of behaving; in another sense, a 'behaviour' is a doing, a particular agent's behaving in that way.

So far, I've only been concerned with things done: the primary task of a theory of action, I've said, is to distinguish cases in which an agent exercises her agency by doing a certain thing from cases in which this isn't so. But a comprehensive metaphysical theory of action should also be concerned with doings. It should tell us whether there are such things – since, as Lowe (2010a: 3) notes, we shouldn't simply *assume* that there are – and to what ontological category they belong. And it should explain the difference between actions and 'mere behaviours' – i.e. the difference between those doings that are exercises of agency and those that aren't.

The distinction between doings and things done will also be important at various points in the rest of this book. We'll see in Chapter 7 that a proper understanding of the ontological status of things done allows us to reconcile my view of negative actions with the property-exemplification theory of events. And we'll see in Chapter 8 that a proper understanding of the distinction undermines some popular arguments against views like mine. I'll discuss the metaphysics of doings and things done in detail in Section 1.3, but it will be useful to have in place a preliminary understanding of the distinction.

The distinction between doings and things done is, *prima facie*, an instance of the more general distinction between particulars and universals. The things we do are, *prima facie*, universals, in the sense that they are shareable, repeatable things. If you and I each go for a walk on our own, then there is something we've each done (although we haven't done it together), and if I go for a walk today and tomorrow, then there is something I've done more than once. If we take reference to, and quantification over, things done ontologically seriously, then we seem to be referring to and quantifying over universals.[4]

---

[3] For further discussion, see Hornsby (1997: 87–92; 1999: 623–626) and Sandis (2012: 142–154).

[4] Following Hornsby (1980: 4n.4; 1999: 625), I say only that things done are *prima facie* universals. You might think that universals can, quite generally, be eliminated in favour of, or reduced to, classes

By contrast, doings are, *prima facie*, particulars in the sense that they aren't shareable or repeatable. If you and I each go for a walk on our own, then although we do the same thing, our doings of that thing aren't the same. Likewise, if I go for a walk every day, then although I do the same thing each day, my doings of that thing aren't the same. If we take reference to, and quantification over, doings ontologically seriously, then we seem to be referring to and quantifying over particulars.

This metaphysical distinction is roughly tracked by a grammatical distinction. The things we do are typically denoted by verb phrases: if I go for a walk, and so the verb phrase 'go for a walk' is true of me, then what I've done is *go for a walk*. By contrast, our doings are typically denoted by a special kind of noun phrase. Borrowing Bennett's (1988: 4–5) example, consider the sentence (1), and the derived nominals (2) and (3):

(1) Quisling betrayed Norway.
(2) Quisling's betraying Norway.
(3) Quisling's betrayal of Norway.

Notice that, in (3), we can replace the possessive 'Quisling's' with a definite or indefinite determiner phrase – 'The betrayal of Norway', 'A betrayal of Norway' – whereas we can't do this with (2). Moreover, the phrase, 'betrayal of Norway' can be count-quantified – 'One betrayal of Norway', 'Two betrayals of Norway', 'Some betrayal of Norway', 'All betrayals of Norway' – while count-quantification of 'betraying Norway' is strained, at best. Finally, notice that 'betrayal of Norway' can be modified using adjectives – 'Quisling's treacherous betrayal of Norway' – while 'betraying Norway' can only be modified using adverbs – 'Quisling's treacherously betraying Norway'. These facts, and others, lead Bennett – and, before him, Vendler (1967) – to classify derived nominals like (2) and (3) in different ways. (2) is an 'imperfect nominal'. The word 'betraying' has the character of a verb – it can be modified adverbially, but not adjectivally – and so (2) isn't perfectly a noun phrase. According to Bennett and Vendler, its job is to refer to a fact or state of affairs, the fact or state of affairs of Quisling's betraying Norway. By contrast, (3) is a 'perfect nominal'. The word 'betrayal' has the character of a noun – it can be modified adjectivally, but not adverbially – and so (3) is perfectly a noun phrase. According to Bennett and Vendler, its job is to refer to an

of particulars, e.g. classes of substances (Rodriguez-Pereyra 2002) or classes of tropes (Ehring 2011). I won't deal with this general issue in this book, and nothing in what follows will hinge on the assumption of realism about universals.

event, the event of Quisling's betrayal of Norway. When we attempt to refer to particular doings, rather than things done, we typically use perfect nominals, not imperfect ones.

Perfect nominals contain noun phrases, derived from verbs, which seem to stand for types of events. For example, from 'explode' we derive 'explosion', a noun which applies to all events in which something explodes; from 'marry' we derive 'marriage', a noun which applies to all events in which someone gets married; and from 'die' we derive 'death', a noun which applies to all events in which someone, or something, dies (Bennett 1988: 2–3). Thus, in addition to doings and things done, we can add a category of doing-types, denoted by derived nouns of this sort, the latter of which form a subclass of 'event sortals'.[5]

Like things done, doing-types are *prima facie* universals. (Indeed, some philosophers think that things done and doing-types are the *same* universals. I'll consider that view in Section 1.3.3.) If you and I each go for a walk, or if I go for a walk on two different occasions, then there is something that multiple doings are: they are *walks*. Since doings are instances of these types, I'll often refer to the former as 'token actions' or 'token behaviours', in what follows.

Ordinary English doesn't contain a derived event sortal corresponding to every verb phrase – e.g. there is no derived noun that stands to 'raising' as 'betrayal' stands to 'betraying', and so the only English phrase we might use to refer to my act of raising my arm is the imperfect nominal, 'My raising of my arm'. We shouldn't exaggerate the metaphysical consequences of this fact, and conclude that there are no such events as arm-raisings. If English contains no event sortal for a certain kind of doing, we're always free to introduce one – that is, for any verb phrase, we're free to introduce a new noun phrase with the stipulation that the latter stands to the former as 'betrayal' stands to 'betray'.

In the remainder of this book, I'll largely rely on the grammatical distinction between perfect nominals, verb phrases, and event sortals – together with contextual cues – to keep track of what kind of action or behaviour is being talked about at any given point, i.e. a doing, a thing done, or a doing-type. Whenever confusion may arise, I'll be more explicit.

1.2.3   *The Scope of a Theory of Action*

There are some things that I do only by doing other things – e.g. I type this sentence by pressing down on the computer keys, which, in turn, I do

---

[5] In Section 1.3.3, I'll consider whether doing-types might be identified with things done.

by moving my fingers in certain ways. Other things, I simply do, without doing them by doing anything else – e.g. as I type this sentence, I don't move my fingers by doing anything else; I simply move them. When x φ-s by ψ-ing at t, but not vice-versa, say that ψ is 'more basic than' φ for x at t. If x φ-s at t by doing some more basic ψ, say that φ is 'non-basic' for x at t. If x φ-s at t without doing any more basic ψ, say that φ is 'basic' for x at t.[6]

Not all senses of the crucial word 'by' will license the claim that I don't move my fingers by doing anything else. For instance, there's a causal reading of 'by' on which x φ-s by ψ-ing just in case x's ψ-ing causes x's φ-ing. On that reading, it's at least arguable that I *do* move my fingers by doing something else, namely by contracting the muscles in my fingers. The relevant sense of 'by', it seems, is not a causal one, but a teleological one: x φ-s by ψ-ing just in case x ψ-s in order to φ; that is, just in case x desires or intends to ψ, and relies on her practical knowledge of how to ψ, to bring it about that she φ-s (Enç 2003: ch. 2; Ruben 2003: 60–70). With this teleological sense of 'by' in place, we can give an account of basic actions, both in the sense of things done and in the sense of doings:

Basic Actions (Things Done)
φ is basic for x at t iff (i) x φ-s at t and (ii) for all ψ, x φ-s without relying on practical knowledge of how to ψ in order to φ.

Basic Actions (Doings)
x's φ-ing at t is basic iff there is some ψ such that x's φ-ing is a ψ-ing, and ψ is basic for x at t.

This account yields the result that pressing the keys is non-basic while moving my fingers is basic: I rely on my knowledge of how to move my fingers in order to press down on the keys, but I don't rely on my knowledge of how to do anything else in order to move my fingers; certainly, I don't rely on knowledge of how to contract my muscles.[7]

Many ways in which I move or position my body at a given time are basic. However, not all ways of moving or positioning my body need to be basic, at any given time. If my right arm becomes paralysed, I may only be able to raise it, bend it, shake it, and so on, by first grasping it with my left hand and then using my left arm to produce the desired movements in my

---

[6] For early and influential discussion of basic actions, see Danto (1965, 1973).

[7] If I knew enough about how my muscles and tendons worked, I might be able to rely on knowledge of how to contract my muscles, in order to move my fingers. In such a case, moving my fingers would count as basic. The account allows that I can do the very same thing basically and non-basically. Thanks to Ishtiyaque Haji and David Liebesman for discussion on this point.

right. In such a case, I only move or position my right arm by relying on practical knowledge of how to move or position my left.

Might it nonetheless be that all basic actions are ways of moving or positioning one's body? Davidson thinks so. He writes,

> We must conclude, perhaps with a shock of surprise, that our primitive actions, the ones we do not do by doing something else, mere movements [and positionings] of the body – these are all the actions there are. We never do more than move [or position] our bodies: the rest is up to nature. (Davidson 1971: 59)[8]

Davidson's conclusion may not be as shocking as he suggests. From the supposition that all basic actions are ways of moving or positioning one's body, it simply doesn't follow that we never do more than move or position our bodies. To draw that conclusion is simply to forget about the category of non-basic actions. It's also misleading to suggest that any happenings beyond the boundaries of our bodies are 'up to nature', as opposed, presumably, to being at least partly up to *us*. The claim that all basic actions are ways of moving or positioning one's body is perfectly consistent with the claim that, as agents, we have some control over the world around us. The point is simply that the only way we can affect the world around us is by moving or positioning our bodies.

Nonetheless, there are reasons to be dissatisfied with the restriction. The first worry arises on the supposition that, when we talk about an agent 'moving or positioning her body', we mean to talk *only* of overt movements and positionings of her limbs – e.g. arm-raisings. Since mental actions don't consist in an agent moving or positioning her limbs, the restriction threatens to rule out the possibility of basic mental actions. But, surely, some mental actions *are* basic: when I make a decision, there's nothing else that I do in order to make it, I simply *make* it.

Davidson himself doesn't restrict 'bodily movements' to overt movements of one's limbs, explicitly allowing his term to cover mental actions like making a decision (1971: 49). But it's not clear that that phrase – or my preferred 'bodily movement or positioning' – can be happily used in that way. Certainly, *something* happens in my body – specifically, in my brain – when I make a decision, but it's not clear in advance that this

---

[8] Davidson use 'movement' to cover cases in which we would ordinarily say an agent *doesn't* move her body; that is, he uses it as a catch-all which covers movements and positionings (1971: 49). Some philosophers of action – e.g. Smith (2010: 45–46) – are willing to follow Davidson in this, but I think that referring to non-movements as movements is far too likely to introduce unnecessary confusion. Hence the interpolations.

something is happily described as some part(s) of my brain moving or remaining in a certain position.

Fortunately, we can rephrase Davidson's claim to accommodate mental actions. Our basic actions are all *bodily* actions, in the sense that to do any of these things is to affect one's body in some way, whether moving or positioning one's limbs in a certain way, or affecting one's brain in some way. The corollary of this claim is that we can only affect the world around us by affecting our bodies in one of these ways. That corollary isn't something to be met 'with a shock of surprise'; it's simply a denial of the existence of a particularly spooky sort of psychokinesis, a kind in which an agent can affect the world around her without even affecting her brain in order to do so.[9]

If all basic actions in the sense of *things done* are bodily actions, then all basic actions in the sense of *doings* are bodily events, i.e. events which entirely consist in an agent moving, positioning, or otherwise affecting some part(s) of her body, and don't involve the movement, positioning, or affection of any object beyond the boundaries of the agent's body.

Some philosophers of action go further, and insist that *all* token actions are bodily events, involving no objects beyond the boundaries of an agent's body. They do so by appealing to the following principle:[10]

By-Action Identity
If x φ-s by ψ-ing, where 'by' is understood in the sense relevant to the notion of basic action, then x's φ-ing = x's ψ-ing.

This principle is plausible when ψ is a purely bodily action and when φ intuitively involves nothing beyond the bodily movements, positionings, or affections involved in ψ-ing. Snapping my fingers is something I do *by* moving my thumb and middle finger in a certain way, and seems to involve nothing *more* than this, and so my snapping of my fingers just seems to *be* my movement of my thumb and middle finger. The principle is also plausible for some action pairs where ψ-ing doesn't *always* amount to, or result in, φ-ing, but does so only thanks to contingent features of the context in which one ψ-s. Suppose that I'm in a department meeting, and a vote is called for by a show of hands. If I raise my arm, I thereby count as having voted. This is so only thanks to contingent features of the context

---

[9] Of course, this strategy for accommodating mental actions can only succeed if a certain kind of substance dualism is false – i.e. only if to perform a mental action is *not* to affect an immaterial substance, like a soul. I proceed on the assumption that this kind of substance dualism *is* false.

[10] See, e.g. Davidson (1971) and Hornsby (1980: ch. 3; 1986). The view is sometimes attributed to Anscombe, but it seems that what Anscombe has in mind when she says that one action *just is* another, are things done rather than doings (see Section 1.3.4).

in which I raise my arm. Nonetheless, it seems, since voting in this context requires nothing more than that I raise my arm – my vote doesn't need to be recognized or counted, in order for it to be true that I've voted – my voting just *is* my raising of my arm.

These examples, however, don't justify *By-Action Identity* in full generality. First, the reasoning behind the identifications made in the previous paragraph doesn't rely on the claim that I do one thing *by* doing the other. Rather, the reasoning relies on the claim that doing one thing *involves nothing more than* doing the other. To say that φ-ing involves nothing more than ψ-ing isn't to say that *x* φ-s by ψ-ing: moving one's thumb and middle finger involves nothing more than snapping one's fingers but, in the imagined case, I snap my fingers by moving my thumb and middle finger, not *vice-versa*; likewise, raising one's arm, in the right context, involves nothing more than voting but, in the imagined case, I vote by raising my arm, not *vice-versa*.

Second, *By-Action Identity* has counterintuitive consequences for action pairs where ψ is a purely bodily action and φ intuitively *does* involve something beyond the bodily movements, positionings, or affections involved in ψ-ing. For instance, when I raise my coffee cup, I do so by raising my arm. My raising of my arm, it seems, is a bodily event, consisting entirely in me moving my arm, and doesn't involve any objects beyond the boundaries of my body. If *By-Action Identity* is true, and my raising of my coffee cup is identical to my raising of my arm, then my raising of my coffee cup consists entirely of me moving my arm, and doesn't involve the cup at all. That seems odd.

There may be responses to these objections, but I won't consider the matter in more detail. My aim has been not to refute *By-Action Identity*, but to justify not assuming it in what follows. I allow that *By-Action Identity* may be false, and so I allow that token actions may not all be purely bodily events, and that some may involve the behaviour of objects beyond the boundaries of the agent's body.

Summing up, I don't assume, in what follows, that the scope of a theory of action is restricted either to actions involving the overt movement, positioning, or affection of the agent's limbs (which apparently rules out mental actions) or to actions which consist entirely in the movement, positioning, or affection of some part(s) of the agent's body (which may rule out certain non-basic actions).

1.2.4   *Some Contemporary Theories of Action*

So far, I've discussed the nature and scope of theories of action, without giving any concrete examples. To some extent, this degree of abstraction is justified. I won't be concerned, in this book, to develop or defend a general theory of action. The problem of negative action sketched in the Introduction affects many theories, and my solution to the problem is intended to be consistent with all of them. However, it will be useful in what follows for us to have some concrete examples to work with.

Perhaps the most prominent theory of action is the Event-Causal Theory of Action (CTA), defended by Davidson, among others.[11] This theory begins from the claim that an agent exercises her agency, by φ-ing, just in case she φ-s intentionally. Applied to token actions, the claim is that x's φ-ing is an action just in case it is a doing of something x does something intentionally. This 'something' needn't be to φ. For, on a plausible view of act-individuation, x's φ-ing might be identical to x's ψ-ing, even if x only does one of these things intentionally. Suppose, again, that I'm in a meeting where a vote is called for by a show of hands. I haven't been paying attention, so I don't know that a vote has been called. I raise my arm in an attempt to stretch my muscles, and I thereby unintentionally cast a vote. It's plausible that my raising of my arm *is* my casting of a vote, so we have a single event which is *both* a doing of something that I do intentionally (raise my arm) *and* a doing of something that I do unintentionally (cast a vote). Thus, x's φ-ing is an action just in case there is some ψ such that x ψ-s intentionally and x's φ-ing is identical to x's ψ-ing (or, to use Davidson's terminology, just in case x's φ-ing is intentional 'under some description'[12]).

The claim that token actions are intentional behaviours isn't unique to CTA. What distinguishes CTA from other 'intentionalist' theories is the claim that a token behaviour is intentional only if the bodily event that (perhaps partly) constitutes it is caused (in the right way[13]) by the right sorts of mental states (or their realizers): x's φ-ing is intentional under that description only if it is caused either by an intention with some relevant content[14] or by beliefs and desires which rationalize φ, and to which x might appeal when explaining why she φ-ed.[15]

---

[11] Davidson (1963, 1971); see also Bishop (1989) and Enç (2003). This theory is often referred to as 'the standard story of action' – see, e.g. Hornsby (2004, 2010) and (Smith 2010).

[12] Davidson (1963: 4; 1971: 45–47). Davidson prefers this terminology because he is skeptical of the existence of things done, but thinks that talk of the things we do can be replaced with talk of the descriptions under which doings fall. See Section 1.3.4 for further discussion.

[13] The qualification 'in the right way' is required due to the possibility of 'deviant' causal chains, which don't intuitively render behaviour intentional – see Bishop (1989: chs. 4 and 5), Davidson (1971), and Enç (2003: ch. 4).

[14] The most obvious candidate is an intention to φ, but other intentions, such as the intention to *try* to φ, may be suitable (Bratman 1987).

[15] I discuss this kind of 'rationalizing explanation' in more detail in Section 3.3.

The main contender to CTA is the Agent-Causal Theory of Action (ACT).[16] ACT begins from the thought that agents possess some causal power (or powers) which allows them to affect the going-on in their bodies, and that to exercise such a power is to exercise one's agency. Crucially, the thought is that agents *qua* substances can affect these goings-on – e.g. when I raise my arm, it is *I*, not some of my mental states, who causes my arm to rise. Generalizing, x's φ-ing is an action only if x, *qua* substance, causes the bodily event that (perhaps partly) constitutes it.

Both CTA and ACT give an account of action in terms of the causation of bodily events. According to traditional versions of these theories, basic actions, at least, are identified with these bodily events so-caused – e.g. when I raise my arm, the raising of my arm *is* the rising of my arm, and it's distinguished as a raising (as opposed to a 'mere rising') by being caused in the right way.[17] (If a proponent of such a theory also accepts *By-Action Identity*, then all actions are bodily events, distinguished from 'mere events' by their causal histories.)

On an alternative way of developing these theories, basic actions aren't identified with the bodily events that are appropriately caused. Rather, basic actions are caus*ings* of bodily events: when I raise my arm, the raising of my arm consists in a rising of my arm being caused in the right way; the rising is a constituent of the arm-raising but not identical to it.[18] (If a proponent of such a theory also accepts *By-Action Identity*, then *all* actions are causings of bodily events.)

1.3   Ontology

1.3.1   Doings as Events

We encountered the claim that token doings are events in Section 1.2.2. This claim has some intuitive support. At the highest level of abstraction, events are happenings, or occurrences: whenever something happens, or occurs, there's an event that is that thing's happening, or occurring. It seems that, if an agent behaves in a certain way, then something has

---

[16] For some recent proposals and discussion, see Alvarez (2013), Alvarez and Hyman (1998), Hornsby (2004), Hyman (2015), Mayr (2011), and Steward (2012a).

[17] See Davidson (1963, 1971) for an event-causal theory of this sort, and Taylor (1966) for an agent-causal theory of this sort.

[18] See Moore (1993) for an event-causal theory of this sort, and Alvarez and Hyman (1998) and Steward (2012a) for agent-causal theories of this sort.

happened, or occurred. Therefore, whenever an agent behaves in a certain way, there's an event that is that agent's doing of that thing.[19]

It's sometimes claimed that events are changes: for an event to occur, one of two conditions must obtain: either some object x changes from possessing property P at time t_1 to lacking P at t_2; or some x changes from lacking property P at t_1 to possessing P at t_2; if neither condition obtains, then no event occurs (Alvarez 2013: 103; Hyman 2015: 61; Lombard 1986). I won't assume this, since there seem to be cases in which agents act even though no relevant change occurs in the agent's body. Consider a soldier who stands at attention. Standing at attention requires that the soldier remain in a very specific position, without moving. Thus, during the time which the soldier stands at attention, there seems to be no relevant change in her body in which her act of standing at attention could consist, even in part.[20] Nonetheless, when she stands at attention, something *happens*, and so not all events are changes.[21]

Recall, on some versions of both the Event-Causal Theory and the Agent-Causal Theory, basic actions are causings of bodily events. The claim that all token doings are events may seem to conflict with these theories, since some philosophers have argued that causings aren't events.

Lowe (2002: 222–223) and Ruben (2003: 166–171) argue that causings aren't events on the ground that they can't be located in space and time the way events can.[22] Borrowing Lowe's example, suppose that Alice

---

[19] Steward (2012b, 2013) argues that the category of happenings/occurrences includes entities of two distinct kinds, namely events and processes, and that actions are better understood as processes than as events. A full treatment of the distinction between events and processes is beyond the scope of this book. I'll proceed on the assumption that nothing of great importance for my purposes hinges on the distinction: if actions are best conceived as processes rather than events, then negative actions must themselves be processes; but whatever motivates the thought, canvassed in the Introduction, that negative actions are absences of events, could presumably also be used to motivate the thought that they are absences of processes.

[20] Of course, in any realistic case, there will still occur many small, involuntary changes in the position of the soldier's body – no actually-existing soldier can stand *completely* still. But the argument can be revised to accommodate this point. Although no *actual* soldier can stand completely still, it's metaphysically *possible* for a soldier to do so – having the ability to stand completely still could hardly preclude you from standing at attention.

[21] Steward (1997: 69) offers another example: a vigil is an event, but there are no changes which need to occur for a vigil to exist; indeed, '[t]he whole idea is that everyone should be still and silent' (p. 69). Of course, in any realistic case, there will be many small, involuntary changes in the positions of the bodies of the participants. But as long as it's metaphysically possible for a group of people to remain completely still and silent during a vigil, the point stands.

[22] Lowe, who believes in causings, takes the argument to show something interesting about the ontology of causings. Ruben uses the argument to motivate skepticism about causings. Note that, while Lowe and Ruben are primarily concerned with the question of whether causings of events by *substances* can be events, their arguments don't seem to hinge on this specification, and can be applied to the view that actions are causings of events by states, or by other events.

administers a slow-acting poison to Beth on Monday, and Beth dies on Tuesday. Where and when does Alice's killing of Beth occur? At the time and place that the poison was administered? At the time and place that Beth dies? Partly at one location and partly at the other? There's no clear answer, and so Lowe concludes that the killing isn't located in space and time at all.[23]

Lowe's conclusion is unwarranted. True, we're faced with competing answers to the question of where and when Alice's killing of Beth is located. But each answer locates the killing *somewhere*, and so each answer is consistent with the claim that the killing is an event.

Lowe has a more direct argument.

> Where an action consists in an agent's causing some event by means of causing various other, intermediary events, then the question of where and when the action was performed can, I suggest, only be answered by saying where and when all of these constituent events occurred – which implies that there is no such time as 'the' time at which the action [occurred] and no such place as 'the' place at which it [occurred]. (Lowe 2002: 223, slightly modified)[24]

Here, Lowe is suggesting that, if we locate the killing in space and time at all, the best we can do is to locate it at several disconnected regions of space and time, with each region occupied by some constituent of the killing. Evidently, he thinks that events can't be scattered in this way, but I see no reason to think this. If I give my class a ten-minute break in the middle of a lecture, then the lecture occupies two disconnected regions of time, with a ten-minute gap between them; and if I need to hold the second half of the lecture in a different room than the first, then the lecture occupies two disconnected regions of space.

A final note on causings and events. The claim that actions *qua* causings aren't events is more common among agent-causalists than event-causalists. However, attention to the contexts in which this claim is made shows that these agent-causalists don't understand 'event' in the broad sense I do. They're concerned, not to deny that actions are happenings or occurrences, but that they are happenings or occurrences *of certain kinds*. Specifically, they mean to deny that actions are the bodily events that

---

[23] For earlier discussions of this puzzle, see Davidson (1971) and Thomson (1971).

[24] The original has 'was performed' where I have put 'occurred'. Lowe is assuming his view that actions don't occur, but are performed (2002: 223). This view confuses doings with things done. To perform an action is to do it, and the things we do aren't doings. In any case, since the relevant issue for our purposes is whether token actions can be said to *occur* at particular places and times, I take my substitution to be harmless.

agents cause when they act (Hyman 2015: 61), or that actions are cau*ses* of these bodily events, rather than cau*sings* of them (Alvarez & Hyman 1998: 232), or that they are causings of bodily events by mental events, rather than causings of bodily events by agents (Alvarez & Hyman 1998: 232 n.29).

In what follows, I'll assume that doings are events, understood as happenings or occurrences. I'll discuss the metaphysics of events in more detail in Chapter 7.

1.3.2   Ontological Commitment to Doings

The claim that there are such things as doings is supported by a 'Neo-Davidsonian' approach to the analysis of action sentences, i.e. sentences which describe an agent as acting in a certain way or doing a certain thing. On this approach – which I'll discuss in more detail in Chapters 4–6 – action sentences are analyzed as first-order existential quantifications over events. For example, ignoring tense, (4) is analysed as (4*):

(4) Alice kissed Beth.
(4*) $\exists e(Agent(\text{Alice})(e)$ & $Patient(\text{Beth})(e)$ & $Kiss(e))$.

In English: there exists an event e such that Alice is the 'agent' of e, Beth is the 'patient' of e, and e is a kiss (where, roughly, the agent of e is the doer of whatever e is a doing of, and the patient of e is the person or object, if any, which has that thing done to it). In short, (4*) reports the occurrence of an event in which Alice kisses Beth. Since (4*) is true only if there really is such an event, acceptance of (4) commits us to believing that such an event exists.[25]

In Section 1.2.2, I noted that a perfect nominal, 'x's φ-ing', which is used to refer to an event in which x φ-s, is derived from the sentence 'x φ-s'. The Neo-Davidsonian approach to action sentences casts the relationship between perfect nominals and corresponding sentences in a different light. Given that 'x φ-s' is an existential quantification over events in which x φ-s, we can say, roughly, that the derived nominal 'x's φ-ing' denotes the event which witnesses 'x φ-s' – that is, 'x's φ-ing' denotes the event which serves

---

[25] Although the Neo-Davidsonian approach is often presented as an approach to the analysis of 'action sentences', 'action' isn't to be understood, here, in the robust sense relevant to the philosophy of action. As Davidson (1967a: 120–121) notes, the arguments for the analysis – to be examined in Sections 4.2.2 and 6.2.1 – apply to sentences like 'Alice fell asleep' and 'Alice tripped on the rug', which apparently don't impute agency in the robust sense, just as well as they apply to sentences like (4), which do.

as the value of the bound event-variable in the logical analysis of that sentence.

This claim is only *roughly* correct, however. For, as Davidson (1969: 167–168) himself notes, there isn't guaranteed to be just one event which witnesses 'x φ-s'. If the time with respect to which (4) is evaluated is sufficiently long, then Alice might kiss Beth *twice* within that time. In that case, there are two events which can serve as the value of 'e' in (4*), i.e. two kisses which witness (4). In that case, the denotation of 'Alice's kissing of Beth' is indeterminate.

In fact, the phenomenon of indeterminacy threatens to ramify quite widely. Consider a scenario in which, as we'd ordinarily say, Alice kisses Beth only once: by ordinary standards, at least, there occurs a single kiss, rather than two or more discrete kisses, and this kiss is singled out by its relatively determinate temporal boundaries, i.e. the times at which it begins and ends. Call the beginning- and end-points 't_1' and 't_n', respectively. Is it really true that exactly one kiss occurs within the interval t_1–t_n? It seems not. Consider the interval t_1–t_{n-1}: there *seems* to be an event which occupies this interval, and this event *seems* to have all it takes to be a kissing of Beth by Alice. If that's right, we must conclude that, despite initial appearances, there occurred *two* kisses, one which occupies the interval t_1–t_n and one which occupies the sub-interval t_1–t_{n-1}. But if *that* argument succeeds, then so does an analogous argument that a *third* kiss occupies the sub-interval t_1–t_{n-2}, and so on. It turns out that there are many kisses, not just one. And of course, this is only one example. The reasoning suggests that the referent of a perfect nominal is typically indeterminate, since we typically don't delineate the precise spatiotemporal boundaries of an event when we refer to it.

Of course, this line of reasoning is simply an application to events of Unger's (1980) 'problem of the many': quite generally, when we seem to refer to a single object – a table, a cloud, a cat, etc. – there are many seemingly distinct objects vying to be the referent of the relevant term – 'the table', 'that cloud', 'my cat', etc. – and no obvious way to privilege one over the others. I won't defend a general solution to this problem here. For our purposes, I'll indulge in the assumption that a perfect nominal denotes, if anything, a single event, at least in cases where our ordinary methods of distinguishing events (kisses, arm-raisings, explosions, etc.) suggest that this is so.[26]

---

[26] See Lewis (1992) for a classic discussion of the problem of the many, including a survey of various solutions. Steward (2012b: 378–379) applies the problem to events to argue that, since we

Returning to the main thrust of this section, the argument for events with which I began assumes a Quinean criterion of ontological commitment. On this criterion, you're ontologically committed to *F*s – equivalently, you're committed to accepting the existence of *F*s, or to thinking that there are *F*s – if, and only if, you're committed to accepting a sentence whose best regimentation into a first-order language is a sentence of the form '∃*xFx*'. In short, you're committed to *F*s just in case you're committed to quantifying over *F*s.[27]

Those who have developed the Neo-Davidsonian approach to action sentences have found it useful to distinguish a class of first-order variables that can take events as values ('*e*', '*e'*', etc.) from the more familiar class of first-order variables that can take other kinds of things as values ('*x*', '*y*', etc.). However, what's important for a Quinean isn't the type of first-order variable we use, but simply that we use a first-order variable at all. To engage in first-order quantification is to quantify into the position of a name or referring term. That is, to engage in first-order quantification is to require, for the truth of your sentence, that there's some object which can (in principle) be named or referred to and which satisfies the relevant description.[28] If action sentences are best regimented as quantifying over doings – construed as events – and we're committed to thinking that such sentences are (at least sometimes) true, then we're ontologically committed to doings *qua* events.

As I've presented it, the Quinean criterion imposes only a sufficient condition on ontological commitment to *F*s. Quine's own view is that first-order quantification over *F*s is not only sufficient for commitment to *F*s, but necessary. The point of imposing the necessary condition is to rule out the idea that higher-order quantification – i.e. quantification in predicate position – carries ontological commitment. Predicates seemingly don't function as names or referring terms, and so Quine thinks that, even if such quantification is legitimate – which he denies on independent grounds – to engage in higher-order quantification is *not* to require, for the truth of your sentence, that there's some object which can (in principle) be named or

---

apparently *can* determinately refer to individual actions, actions can't be events. I find this argument unpersuasive, since the problem is so general, and the solutions with which I'm familiar tell a thoroughly linguistic story about how reference to a particular *F* is achieved (or perhaps mimicked), a story which has little to nothing to say about the ontological category to which *F*s belong.

[27] See Quine (1948, 1969). For recent discussion and development of Quine's criterion, see Rayo (2002, 2007) and van Inwagen (1998, 2009).

[28] You might appeal to substitutional quantification to give an account of how '∃*xFx*' can be true even if no object satisfies '*F*'. However, I find van Inwagen's (1981) criticism of substitutional quantification compelling, and so won't discuss this alternative in detail. See also Azzouni (2004: 72).

referred to and which satisfies the relevant description.[29] In what follows, I'll remain neutral on whether higher-order quantification is ontologically committing.[30] Davidson's argument requires that first-order quantification is committing, not that no other kind of quantification is.

The Quinean criterion isn't without its critics. While a complete development and defense of the criterion is beyond the scope of this book, I'll briefly consider some arguments against it.

It's sometimes thought that if the Quinean criterion is correct, then ontological questions can be answered entirely by appeal to facts about our language(s), and ontology collapses into linguistics (specifically formal semantics). Rather than engaging in paradigmatically philosophical reasoning and argumentation to determine whether, e.g., numbers exist, we could simply 'read off' the existence of numbers from the fact that our language(s) contain sentences that are apparently best regimented as quantifying over them – e.g. 'There are primes greater than two'. This would do little justice to metaphysicians' conception of themselves as engaging in substantive inquiry about the nature of the world, rather than inquiry about the means we use to talk about it.[31]

This worry is based on a misunderstanding. The Quinean criterion is only designed to tell us what we're committed to thinking there is, *given that we accept certain sentences as true*. Recall from the Introduction that an appeal to the Quinean criterion takes the following form:

(α) 'S' is true $\equiv S$
(β) 'S' is true $\equiv \exists x Fx$
(γ) $\therefore S \equiv \exists x Fx$

The cash-value of (γ) is that *if* we accept that S, *then* we must accept that there are Fs. In order to conclude that there really are Fs, we must add an extra premise, (δ):

(δ) S
(ε) $\therefore \exists x Fx$

---

[29] '[T]he word "red" ... is true of each of sundry individual entities which are red houses, red roses, red sunsets; but there is not, in addition, any entity whatever, individual or otherwise, which is named by the word "redness"', (1948: 10). Quine's thought, here, is that if 'redness' succeeded in naming something, it would name whatever is named by 'red'. Since 'red' doesn't even function as a name, it doesn't name anything, and so 'redness' doesn't either.
[30] See Rieppel (2016: 682–684) and sources cited therein for further discussion.
[31] '[M]etaphysical questions appear to be about what there is, what it is like, and how existing entities are related. What do such questions have to do with language? ... [T]he supposition that ontological questions are quantificational questions would fail to accommodate the *prima facie* understanding of ontological questions as substantive, philosophical, and autonomous' (Wilson 2011a: 181). See also Cameron (2008: 4–5) and Dyke (2008: 35–36).

And unless '*S*' is a meta-linguistic sentence, the evidence for (8) will come, not from linguistics, but from substantive inquiry into whatever domain *S* concerns.

Thus, even for the Quinean, the mere fact that 'There are primes greater than two' quantifies over numbers isn't evidence that numbers exist, any more than the fact that 'There's a monster under my bed' quantifies over monsters is evidence that monsters exist. The evidence that numbers exist is just whatever evidence counts in favour of the truth of the sentence, 'There are primes greater than two', and that evidence is to be found by doing mathematics and metaphysics, not formal semantics. As Quine puts the point, the criterion 'explicates only the *ontological commitments* of a theory and not the *ontological truth* about the world' (1951: 12, emphasis in the original).

Wilson claims that '[o]nly if we were in possession of an ideal, nature-revealing language would [Quine's] dictum be a guide to what there is, as opposed to what a theory says there is' (2011a: 181). I take it that Wilson has in mind a language of the sort that Sider (2011) hopes for, in which all sub-sentential elements – predicates, quantifiers, logical operators, etc. – are perfectly 'structural': they 'carve nature at the joints', and so a true sentence framed in such a language not only reveals a fact about the world, but reveals (part of) the 'structure' of the world. But it's clear that, even for a Quinean, mere possession of such a language wouldn't allow us to know what the world was like. Suppose that the unrestricted first-order quantifier, '∃', and first-order predicate '*Number*' are both perfectly structural. Then (5) is perfectly structural:

(5) $\exists x(Number(x))$

Still, we can't 'read off' the existence of numbers from this fact about (5). In order to know whether there are numbers, we must know, not merely whether (5) is formulated in an 'ideal, nature-revealing language', but whether (5) is *true*, and this requires mathematical and metaphysical investigation.

Granting that the Quinean isn't making a simple mistake in reasoning, you might think that their conception of ontological commitment is still misguided. Some have argued that ontological questions (i.e. the questions ontologists debate, and which are naturally framed using the form, 'Do *F*s exist?') can't be assimilated to quantificational questions (i.e. questions naturally framed using the form, 'Are there *F*s?', or '∃*xFx*?'), on the ground that quantificational questions have trivial answers, while ontological questions don't (Fine 2009; Schaffer 2009). That ontological questions are non-trivial is presumably shown by the fact that there's little agreement about them – e.g. there's little agreement about whether numbers, construed as objects named or referred to by numerals, exist. That the corresponding quantificational questions are trivial is allegedly shown by the fact that arguments of the following sort seem to be not only valid, but sound:

(6) 3 is a prime number greater than 2.
(7) ∴ There is at least one prime number greater than 2.
(8) ∴ There is at least one prime number.
(9) ∴ There is at least one number.

Thus, Fine writes, 'given the evident fact that there is a prime number greater than 2, it trivially follows that there is a number' (2009: 158). Since the quantificational sentence 'There is at least one number' – or '∃x (Number(x))' – is trivially true, while the ontological sentence 'Numbers exist' isn't, the latter shouldn't be assimilated to the former.

The obvious Quinean rejoinder is that what Fine considers to be an evident fact is nothing of the sort. Prior to philosophical reflection, it *seems* evident that there are prime numbers greater than 2 – it seems that we can point to 3 as an example. But philosophical puzzles about numbers (Where, if anywhere, are such things to be located? Are they material, or immaterial? Can they cause anything? If not, how could we ever come to know about them?) can lead us to doubt it. Surely, a metaphysician shouldn't balk at the suggestion that philosophical reflection can lead us to doubt what previously seemed evident.

Even if you agree that philosophical reflection should *sometimes* lead us to doubt what previously seemed evident, you might have trouble allowing this in the case of sentences which appear to be about numbers. In this vein, Schaffer writes, '["There are prime numbers"] is a mathematical truism. It commands *Moorean certainty*, as being more credible than any philosopher's argument to the contrary. Any metaphysician who would deny it has *ipso facto* produced a *reductio* for her premises' (2009: 357, emphasis in the original).

There are two points to be made, here. First, the claim that there are prime numbers – construed as quantifying over numbers, and hence as requiring that there be such things – *isn't* a mathematical truism. For, it isn't a mathematical truism that numerals must be construed as names for such entities as numbers, and that the only way to express what mathematicians aim to express, when uttering 'There are prime numbers', is in terms of first-order quantification over those entities. That mathematical discourse must be so construed is a claim within the domain of the *philosophy* of mathematics, and not in the domain of mathematics proper.

Second, and relatedly, the Quinean who doubts the existence of numbers isn't worried that she's made an *arithmetical* mistake. She accepts the arithmetical demonstration that, as we would put it, '3 is a prime number greater than 2'. What she doubts is that there are such things as numbers for '3' and '2' to name, and over which we could quantify when saying, 'There are prime numbers greater than 2'. Thus, the Quinean who rejects the existence of numbers does not, *on that basis alone*, reject large swathes of mathematics. Rather, because she *accepts* the deliverances of mathematics, she takes on a burden to explain away apparent quantification over numbers, i.e. to show how to construe mathematical claims so that they can come out true even if there are no numbers. The ontological question, as she conceives of it, is intimately tied to the question of whether this burden can be discharged. And this question is far from trivial.[32]

Finally, Fine (2009: 165–166) argues that assimilating ontological questions to quantificational ones gets the logical form of ontological claims wrong. Suppose that Alice is a realist about positive integers (1, 2, etc.) but not negative ones (−1, −2, etc.), while Beth is a realist about both. Intuitively, Fine says, Beth holds the stronger position, since she believes in everything Alice does and more besides. But it seems that, if we accept the Quinean criterion, we must say that Beth holds the weaker position, for Alice believes only in positive integers, while Beth believes in integers *tout court*, and so Alice accepts (10) while Beth accepts (11):

(10) $\exists x(Integer(x) \ \& \ Positive(x))$
(11) $\exists x(Integer(x))$

(11) is logically weaker than (10), since '$\exists x(Fx \ \& \ Gx)$' entails '$\exists xFx$' but not vice-versa.

The problem lies not with the Quinean criterion, but with Fine's attempt to deploy it. Fine represents Alice and Beth as disagreeing about whether (11) is true or only (10) is. But this can't be right, since Alice and Beth both *accept* (11): they both agree that there are integers; they disagree about whether any of them are negative. We do better to represent Alice and Beth as disagreeing about whether (12) is true, since Alice rejects it while Beth accepts it.

(12) $\exists x(Integer(x) \ \& \ Positive(x)) \ \& \ \exists y(Integer(y) \ \& \ Negative(y))$

But now, we get the desired result that Beth holds the stronger view: (12) is logically stronger than (10), since '$p \ \& \ q$' entails 'p', but not vice-versa.

---

[32] See Burgess and Rosen (1999) for detailed discussion.

Here, I've defended the argument for the existence of doings, by defending the Quinean criterion of ontological commitment. But the position I've adopted is doubly conditional: *if* action sentences are best regimented as quantifying over doings *qua* events *and* we're committed to thinking that such sentences are at least sometimes true, *then* we're ontologically committed to doings *qua* events. I'll simply assume that action sentences are sometimes true. I'll consider the evidence in favour of the Neo-Davidsonian approach to action sentences in more detail in Chapters 4–6.

1.3.3   Things Done as Properties of Agents

Recall that, while doings are *prima facie* particulars, things done are *prima facie* universals. In Section 1.2.2 I noted that doing-types are also *prima facie* universals. According to some philosophers, these two categories are identical: the things we do *are* the types under which our doings fall (Hanser 2008: 272–273; Hornsby 1980: 4–5; 1999: 623–625; Steward 2012a: 152).

There's some motivation for this view. First, to every thing done there corresponds a type under which any doing of that thing falls – e.g. the type *betrayal* corresponds to *betray*. Parsimony suggests that we should identify each thing done with the corresponding doing-type, unless we have good reason to distinguish them.

Second, the view is suggested by the Neo-Davidsonian approach to action sentences sketched in Section 1.3.2. Recall that, on that approach, (4) is analysed as (4*):

(4)   Alice kissed Beth.
(4*) $\exists e(Agent(\text{Alice})(e) \;\&\; Patient(\text{Beth})(e) \;\&\; Kiss(e))$.

Here, what corresponds to the verb 'kissed' is a predicate of events, '*Kiss*'. The natural reading of '*Kiss(e)*' – suggested by Davidson (1967a: 118–119) and endorsed by Neo-Davidsonians – is '*e* is a kiss'. Since the property of being a kiss is plausibly identical to the doing-type, *kiss*, we have some reason to identify that doing-type with the thing done which 'kiss' denotes. Generalizing: things done are identical to the corresponding doing-types.

Sandis resists the identification, claiming that 'the things we do are not types of action, but actions that fall under types' (2017: 115). Sandis is surely right that things done fall under types – they can be, e.g. polite things to do, or impolite things to do. But it doesn't follow that they aren't types of action, since types can fall under further, higher-order types – e.g.

the species *canis simensis* (Abyssinian wolf) and *canus anthus* (African golden wolf) are plausibly thought of as types, but they are tokens of the type, *species*.

There is, however, a better argument against the identification. If things done are doing-types, then they're properties possessed, not by agents, but by their doings – e.g. when I raise my arm, the thing I do, *raise my arm*, is a property possessed, not by me, but by my raising of my arm. That seems wrong. If things done are properties, they're properties of agents, not of doings – to say that I raise my arm is to say that *I* possess a certain property, the property of raising my arm.

At least one metaphysical theory of properties and events allows us to say that things done are *both* properties of agents *and* doing-types. Suppose you believe in tropes, i.e. properties understood as particulars rather than universals. Suppose, further, that you think that all talk of 'general prop-erties' – i.e. shareable, repeatable properties – is to be replaced by talk of trope-types – e.g. the general property *redness* is a type under which all and only redness tropes fall, and to say that x and y are both red is to say that each possesses a trope of this type. Finally, suppose that you think events are tropes – more specifically, you think that any event in which an object φ-s is an instance of the general property φ. Given this combination of views, things done *qua* general properties are both properties of agents (when x φ-s, there is a φ trope that x possesses) and doing-types (the general property φ is a type under which all φ tropes fall, and φ tropes are particular doings of φ).[33]

I think this combination of views ought to be rejected (see Chapter 7, note 18). Thus, I'll assume that things done are to be distinguished from doing-types, and understood as properties of agents.

What, then, of the argument from Neo-Davidsonian analyses of action sentences? It's true that, on the Neo-Davidsonian approach, to say that an agent does a certain thing is to report the occurrence of an event of a certain type. But this doesn't force us to conclude that things done *are* doing-types. Compare: (13) is plausibly analysed as (13*).

(13) Alice owns a car.
(13*) $\exists x(Car(x) \ \& \ Owns(\text{Alice})(x))$.

To say that Alice owns a car is to say that there is an x such that x is a car and Alice owns x. It would be wrong to conclude that the property of owning a car is a property of the object quantified over in (13*) – that

---

[33] Ehring (2011) adopts this combination of views.

property is one that *Alice* possesses, not one that her car possesses. Thus, we shouldn't immediately conclude that the property of kissing Beth is a property of the event quantified over in (4*). More generally, we shouldn't conclude that things done are properties of events.

A better suggestion, and one which sits nicely with the Neo-Davidsonian approach to action sentences, is that things done are properties that we possess by virtue of being the agents of events of certain kinds. Where φ is a thing done, and Φ is the corresponding doing-type, φ is the property of being an *x* such that there is an *e* such that *e* is a Φ and *x* is the agent of *e*.

More concretely, the property of kissing Beth, which Alice possesses just in case (4) is true, is the property of being the agent of an event which is a kissing of Beth. We can generate a predicate that denotes this property by performing λ-abstraction on the occurrence of 'Alice' in (4*):

$$\lambda x.\exists e(\textit{Agent}(x)(e) \ \& \ \textit{Patient}(\text{Beth})(e) \ \& \ \textit{Kiss}(e))$$

An object satisfies this predicate just in case it is the agent of an event of which Beth is the patient, and which is a kiss, which, on the Neo-Davidsonian view, means that an object satisfies this predicate just in case it kisses Beth.

1.3.4   Ontological Commitment to Things Done

Davidson provides the best-known argument for ontological commitment to doings. He is, however, skeptical of things done.[34] To see why, consider the opening passage of 'The Logical Form of Action Sentences':

> Strange goings on! Jones did it slowly, deliberately, in the bathroom, with a knife, at midnight. What he did was butter a piece of toast. We are too familiar with the language of action to notice at first an anomaly: the 'it' of 'Jones did it slowly, deliberately, ...' seems to refer to some entity, presumably an action, that is then characterized in a number of ways. Asked for the logical form of this sentence, we might volunteer something like, 'There is an action *x* such that Jones did *x* in the bathroom, ...' and so on. But then we need an appropriate singular term to substitute for '*x*'. In fact we know Jones buttered a piece of toast. And, allowing a little slack, we can substitute for '*x*' and get 'Jones buttered a piece of toast slowly and Jones buttered a piece of toast deliberately and Jones buttered a piece of toast in the bathroom ...' and so on. The trouble is that we have nothing here that we would ordinarily recognize as a singular term. (Davidson 1967a: 105)

---

[34] See especially Davidson (1999).

Our inclination, Davidson thinks, is to take the English pronoun 'it' in 'Jones did it slowly, deliberately . . .' as the correlate of a first-order variable at the level of logical form. That is, he thinks that our inclination is to analyze this sentence as quantifying over *things that Jones did*. A first-order variable can only take names or referring terms as substitutions. But the only available substitution, here – 'buttered toast' – is a *verb*, whose correlate at the level of logical form should be a *predicate*. Davidson follows Quine in resisting higher-order quantification, and so he proposes an analysis of action sentences on which apparent quantification over things done at the level of grammatical form is replaced with quantification over doings at the level of logical form. Thus, he allows doings into his ontology, but sees no reason to believe in things done.

Of course, we want some way to replicate quantification over things done, if only to capture the truth-conditions of sentences like (14):

(14) Alice did something.

Ludwig (2016: 20–23) suggests that we can regiment (14), without relying on higher-order resources or quantification over things done, as (14*):

(14*) $\exists e(Agent(\text{Alice})(e))$

But this leaves us without a satisfying regimentation of (15):

(15) Alice did something, and Beth did it, too.

Here, 'it' functions as an anaphoric pronoun, referring back to whatever gets quantified over by 'something'. Since, on Ludwig's account, we have only quantification over events to work with, the best we can do to regiment this sentence is:

(15*) $\exists e(Agent(\text{Alice})(e) \ \& \ Agent(\text{Beth})(e))$

But this gets the truth-conditions of the sentence wrong: if each of Alice and Beth went for a walk independently of the other, then they did the same thing – go for a walk – but there is no event of which they are both agents.[35]

Davidson's own suggestion is that, while quantification over things done can't be eliminated *solely* in favour of quantification over doings, it can be eliminated in favour of quantification over doings *and* the descriptions under which they fall, i.e. the derived sortals discussed in Section 1.2.2 (1999: 636–638). Consider again the case where I raise my arm, and thereby cast a vote. I've said that my act of voting just *is* my act of raising of my arm, and so a single event is a doing of two things. This quantification

---

[35] For discussion of predicate anaphora more generally, see Liebesman (2015: 531–533).

over things done can apparently be eliminated in favour of quantification over descriptions: instead of saying that my action is a doing of two things, we can say that it falls under two descriptions.

Hornsby argues that this replacement strategy should be resisted, but her argument isn't convincing. She suggests that Davidson's way of speaking brings with it the temptation to say that the things we do, as opposed to our doings of them, can fall under multiple descriptions. This is a temptation she thinks we ought to resist. '[T]hings that people do', she says, 'are *not* redescribable things, they are repeatable things; when spoken of as if they were redescribable, they get confused with [doings] (which *are* redescribable particulars)' (1999: 625, emphasis in the original).[36] Thus, Hornsby suggests, '[t]he "description" way of talking can ... reintroduce the confusion it was intended to eliminate' (ibid.).

It's not clear why Hornsby thinks that things done aren't redescribable. First, as Davidson (1999: 637) points out, *any* entity can be described in more than one way. Second, 'redescribable' and 'repeatable' are not, as Hornsby seems to suggest, contradictories – e.g. I can describe the colour that two blue flowers share as 'the colour of those flowers' or as 'my favourite colour'.

Hornsby is right that Davidson and others have been liable to confuse doings and things done, when talking about actions falling under multiple descriptions. Consider the following, famous passage:

> I flip the switch, turn on the light, and illuminate the room. Unbeknownst to me I also alert a prowler to the fact that I am home. Here I need not have done four things, but only one, of which four descriptions have been given. (Davidson 1963: 4)

Davidson almost certainly has in mind an equally famous passage from Anscombe's *Intention*. In Anscombe's example, a man moves his arm up and down, thereby operating a water pump, thereby replenishing the water supply of a nearby house from a tainted source, thereby poisoning the inhabitants. Here, she says, we have a single action that falls under many descriptions.

> For moving his arm up and down with his fingers round the pump handle *is*, in these circumstances, operating the pump; and in these circumstances, it *is* replenishing the house water-supply; and, in these circumstances, it *is* poisoning the household. (Anscombe 1963: §26)

---

[36] In the original, Hornsby uses the term 'action', rather than 'doing', explicitly restricted so as to apply only to doings, not things done. To avoid confusion, I've replaced the occurrence of 'actions' in the quoted passage with 'doings'.

If we keep in mind the distinction between doings and things done, we can see that both Davidson's claim and Anscombe's are false. Allowing for the sake of argument that *By-Identity* is true, there is, in each case, a single doing that is a doing many things, and so this *doing* falls under many descriptions. But the *things done* don't fall under those descriptions. Even if there is a single event in which Davidson both flips the switch and turns on the light, 'flip the switch' and 'turn on the light' aren't descriptions of the same thing done. If they were, then these would be one thing done, not two, which is false, since it's possible to flip the switch without turning on the light. (Anscombe's more nuanced claim that the things done are the same 'in these circumstances' doesn't help, since identity is absolute, not relative to circumstance.)

So, Hornsby is right that those who talk of actions falling under descriptions often confuse doings with things done. But this confusion isn't a *result* of description talk. Description talk is perfectly acceptable, since both doings and things done – and doing-types, for that matter – are redescribable. Confusion about which things fall under which descriptions only arises if we *already* fail to distinguish doings from things done.

Nonetheless, there are reasons to be dissatisfied with Davidson's replacement strategy. For one thing, the descriptions needed to implement the strategy may not always be available. If language L_1 contains a verb for the thing that Alice and Beth both do, and a sortal derived from it, then we can truly say, within L_1, that there is a description under which Alice's doing and Beth's doing both fall. If language L_2 contains no such verb and no such sortal, then we apparently can't truly say, within L_2, that there is such a description. Nonetheless, it's still *true* – whatever language we happen to speak – that Alice and Beth do the same thing.

In any case, Davidson's skepticism about things done is insufficiently motivated. According to our Quinean criterion of ontological commitment, first-order quantification over *F*s is sufficient for ontological commitment to *F*s. Davidson presumably follows Quine in taking this to be *necessary* for ontological commitment to *F*s, as well, but that point won't concern us. The important point is that, *contra* Davidson, we are sometimes required to engage in first-order quantification over things done.

To see why, first consider properties that aren't also things done. We typically ascribe properties using predicates, not names or referring terms – e.g. (16) is analysed as (16*):[37]

---

[37] For the sake of simplicity, I ignore difficult issues about how demonstrative phrases like 'this rose' are to be analyzed.

(16) This rose is red.
(16*) *Red*(rose).

However, we sometimes need to use names or other referring terms to refer to the properties we ordinarily ascribe using predicates – e.g. we sometimes need to use 'redness' to refer to the property that we ascribe with 'red'. Specifically, we need to do this in order to say what predicates denote. For, while (17) is acceptable, (18) isn't.

(17) 'Red' denotes redness.
(18) 'Red' denotes red.

The verb 'denotes' requires a name for its object – or, to put the point at the level of logical form, the predicate '*Denotes*' is a first-order predicate, requiring two first-order arguments. Since 'red' is a verb, it can't be the object of 'denotes', and since '*Red*' is a predicate, it can't be an argument of '*Denotes*'. So, we can't use (18) to say what 'red' denotes, and must use something like (17), in which 'redness' functions as a name contributing a first-order argument.[38]

You might think that (17) can't be right. 'Redness' denotes redness, if anything does. If (17) is true, then 'red' and 'redness' are co-denoting. You might think this is impossible. 'Red' functions as a predicate while 'redness' functions as a name. But, it's often said, while predicates denote second-order objects (i.e. the kind of thing that can take other objects as arguments), names can only denote first-order objects (i.e. the kind of thing that can be an argument of a predicate but can't take any other object as argument). Since nothing can be both a second-order object and a first-order object, no predicate can be co-denoting with any name.

The view that predicates and names denote different kinds of things can be, and ought to be, rejected. It's precisely this view that lands Frege in his famous quandary about the concept *horse*. According to Frege, concepts are second-order objects, and so can never be referred to using names or descriptions, like 'the concept *horse*', which can only refer to first-order objects. As a result, (19) comes out true, when it ought to be false:

(19) The concept *horse* is not a concept.

On Frege's view, whatever 'the concept *horse*' refers to, it isn't a concept, and so the referent of this phrase satisfies the predicate, 'is not a concept'.

---

[38] See Rieppel (2016: 649–655), and sources cited therein, for discussion. I say we need 'something like' (17), since what's important is that 'denotes' needs a name for its object, not which name we use. Davidson (2005) argues that we needn't say that predicates denote anything at all, in order to give a satisfying semantics. For critical discussion of Davidson's view, see Liebesman (2015: 548–553).

Moreover, the view that predicates and names denote different kinds of things leaves us unable to say what it is that predicates denote since, as we've seen, 'denote' requires a name for its object.

Of course, there's an important difference between names and referring terms on one hand, and predicates on the other. But if we want to avoid the muddle in which Frege landed himself, we shouldn't say that the difference lies in *what* these things denote. The difference lies, rather, in *how* they denote: names and referring terms *refer to* their denotations; predicates *ascribe* their denotations. Thus, 'red' and 'redness' both denote the same thing, the property of being red. But while 'redness' refers to this property, 'red' ascribes it.[39]

Thus, we have good reason to think that reference to properties is ineliminable. But with reference comes the possibility of first-order quantification. Indeed, we must quantify over properties in order to capture the view described in the previous paragraph:

(20) There is some x such that 'red' ascribes x and 'redness' refers to x.

Therefore, we have good reason to think that first-order quantification over properties is ineliminable. Since first-order quantification over Fs suffices for ontological commitment to Fs, we're ontologically committed to properties.

The same argument applies, *mutatis mutandis*, to those properties that are things done. We typically ascribe these properties using verb phrases, not names or referring terms. However, we need to use names or referring terms to refer to these properties, in order to say what our verb phrases denote. For, while (21) is acceptable, (22) isn't.

(21) 'Kisses Beth' denotes the behaviour of kissing Beth.
(22) 'Kisses Beth' denotes kisses Beth.

With reference comes the possibility of first-order quantification and, indeed, we must quantify over things done in order to give a satisfying semantics:

(23) There is an x such that 'kisses Beth' ascribes x and 'the behaviour of kissing Beth' refers to x.

Therefore, we have good reason to think that first-order quantification over things done is ineliminable.[40] Since first-order quantification over Fs

---

[39] For detailed discussions of this view, and of problems for the Fregean alternative, see Hale (2013: ch. 1), Hale and Wright (2012), Liebesman (2015), and Rieppel (2016).

[40] To say that 'kisses Beth' ascribes the property of kissing Beth – i.e. the property $\lambda x.\exists e(Agent(x)(e) \ \& \ Patient(Beth)(e) \ \& \ Kiss(e))$ – isn't necessarily to say that that property is the contribution 'kisses Beth' makes to the compositional semantics. On some views, the contribution 'kisses Beth' makes

suffices for ontological commitment to *F*s, we're ontologically committed to things done.[41]

1.3.5 Sparse and Abundant Properties

I've argued that we need first-order quantification over the things we do, and hence that we're ontologically committed to them. You might nonetheless have worries about adding such properties to your ontology.

Properties – whether universals or tropes – are generally posited when they do some explanatory work. Specifically, they're posited to explain:

(a) Why certain predicates are true of certain objects. 'The rose is red' is (allegedly) true, in part, because there's a property, redness, which 'red' denotes and which the rose instantiates (Armstrong 2004: 41).

(b) Why two or more objects are genuinely similar when certain predicates apply to them. If two roses are red, they genuinely have something in common. This is (allegedly) because there's a property,

---

to 'Alice kisses Beth' is $\lambda e(Patient(\text{Beth})(e)\ \&\ Kiss_{\text{ND}}(e))$, a property of *events*. If those views are right, then the claim defended in the text is better construed as the claim that *a* denotation of 'kisses Beth' is the property of kissing Beth: we *can* use this verb phrase to talk about that property, although it plays no role in the compositional semantics of action sentences.

    Compare: in Montague Grammar, the contribution 'Alice' makes to the compositional semantics of English sentences is not Alice herself, but the higher-order property $\lambda F.F(\text{Alice})$, i.e. the property *being an F such that F is true of Alice*. This approach to compositional semantics is consistent with the view that we *can* use 'Alice' to refer to Alice (indeed, we use it that way when specifying the contribution of 'Alice' in our semantic theory).

[41] It's worth noting that, in my view, not *all* quantification over things done is first-order. Consider (14) and (15) again. We've already seen that, unless we adopt Davidson's replacement strategy, analyses of (14) and (15) will involve quantification over things done. Williamson (2013: 239) suggests that we analyse sentences like (14) and (15) using first-order quantification over things done – which he equates with doing-types – related to the agent by a predicate, '*Do*':

    (14**) $\exists x(Do(\text{Alice})(x))$

    (15**) $\exists x(Do(\text{Alice})(x)\ \&\ Do(\text{Beth})(x))$

    But this analysis has little motivation. Williamson seemingly takes it to be clear that the English quantifier phrase 'something', as it occurs in (14) and (15), is quantifying into name position. But the only acceptable substitutions for the pronoun 'it' in (15) are verb phrases. Since, in the Neo-Davidsonian view, the contribution of a verb phrase is a predicate of events, the more natural analyses of (14) and (15) are (14***) and (15***):

    (14***) $\exists F\exists e(Agent(\text{Alice})(e)\ \&\ F(e))$

    (15***) $\exists F\exists e\exists e'(Agent(\text{Alice})(e)\ \&\ F(e)\ \&\ Agent(\text{Beth})(e')\ \&\ F(e'))$

    Since, for all I've argued here, higher-order quantification isn't ontologically committing, not all quantification over things done need reveal an ontological commitment to a certain kind of property.

redness, which they both instantiate (Armstrong 1989: 82–84; Rodriguez-Pereyra 2002: 15–17).

(c)   Why objects possess certain causal powers. If a rose is red, it has certain causal powers, e.g. the power to produce certain visual sensations in certain circumstances. This is (allegedly) because there's a property, redness, which the rose instantiates, and which bestows these powers (Armstrong 1989: 82–84).

The things we do are ill-suited to play these roles.

The things we do are 'higher-level' properties, i.e. properties we possess by virtue of possessing other properties.[42] More specifically, they are, loosely speaking, 'existentially quantified' properties: the property of φ-ing is the property *being an x such that there exists some φ-ing event of which x is the agent*.[43] Existentially quantified properties are highly analogous to 'disjunctive' properties, i.e. properties denoted by predicates of the form '$\lambda x.(Fx \lor Gx)$', since '$\exists x Fx$' is roughly equivalent to '$Fa_1 \lor \ldots \lor Fa_n$', where a_1–a_n are all the possible exemplifiers of F. Thus, if the property of φ-ing is the property of being the agent of some φ-ing event or other – $\lambda x.\exists e(Agent(x)(e) \ \& \ \varphi(e))$ – then the predicate denoting that property is roughly equivalent to '$\lambda x.((Agent(x)(e_1) \ \& \ \varphi(e_1)) \lor \ldots \lor (Agent(x)(e_n) \ \& \ \varphi(e_n)))$', where e_1–e_n are all the possible φ-ing events of which x is the agent. But disjunctive properties are famously ill-suited to play the explanatory roles generally required of properties (Armstrong 1989: 82–84).

First, disjunctive properties aren't obviously needed to explain why disjunctive predicates are true of objects. If 'Fa' is true, '$Fa \lor Ga$' trivially follows, and so it trivially follows that '$\lambda x.(Fx \lor Gx)$' is true of a. Thus, if a exemplifies F, we needn't posit an extra property denoted by '$\lambda x.(Fx \lor Gx)$' to explain why that predicate is true of a.

Second, the fact that two or more objects satisfy a disjunctive predicate doesn't, on its own, make for genuine similarity. Consider: from the predicates '*Red*' and '*Square*' we can generate the predicate '$\lambda x.(Red(x) \lor Square(x))$'. Satisfaction of this predicate doesn't make for genuine similarity: it might be that a satisfies it by virtue of being a red triangle while b satisfies it by

---

[42]   MacDonald and MacDonald (2006: 550 n.23) distinguish 'higher-order' properties (or states) from 'higher-level' properties (or states). The former are properties (or states) of properties (or states). For example, the property being red has the property being a colour, and so being a colour is a higher-order property of being red. The latter are properties (or states) that one has (or is in) by virtue of having (or being in) some other property (or state). For example, x has the property being coloured by virtue of having some other, more specific, colour property (being red, being green, etc.), and so being coloured is a higher-level property.

[43]   This is loose talk because what's existentially quantified are the predicates denoting the properties, not the properties themselves. The same goes for other 'logically complex' properties: 'disjunctive' properties, 'conjunctive' properties, 'negative' properties, etc.

virtue of being a blue square; in this case, it doesn't seem that a and b genuinely have something in common, by virtue of being *either* red *or* square.

You might think that this reasoning doesn't generally apply to the things we do. Granting that the predicate '$\lambda x.\exists e(Agent(x)(e)$ & $\varphi(e))$' is roughly equivalent to the predicate '$\lambda x.((Agent(x)(e_1)$ & $\varphi(e_1))$ ∨ ... ∨ $(Agent(x)(e_n)$ & $\varphi(e_n)))$', you might think that satisfaction of either predicate *does* – or at least *can* – make for genuine similarity. Surely, if two people kiss Beth, they thereby have something in common?

This reply echoes recent discussion of determinates and determinables. Roughly, F is a determinable of G – equivalently, G is a determinate of F – just in case to exemplify G is to exemplify F in a specific way. Standard examples include colour properties – *scarlet* and *crimson* are both determinates of *red*, which in turn is a determinate of *coloured* – and shape properties – *scalene* and *isosceles* are both determinates of *triangular*, which in turn is a determinate of *shaped*. Now, predicates denoting determinables are roughly equivalent to disjunctive predicates, all of whose 'disjuncts' denote that property's various determinates – e.g. 'is red' is roughly equivalent to 'is scarlet or crimson or ...'. Nonetheless, satisfaction of these predicates *does* seem to make for genuine similarity: while two objects which satisfy 'is either red or square' needn't thereby have anything in common, two objects which satisfy 'is 'red' arguably do, even if they satisfy it by exemplifying distinct determinates of *red*.[44]

So, you might think, the things we do aren't *mere* disjunctive properties. Rather, they're *determinable* properties: the property $\lambda x.\exists e(Agent(x)(e)$ & $\varphi(e))$ is a determinable of which $\lambda x.(Agent(x)(a_1)$ & $\varphi(a_1))$, $\lambda x.(Agent(x)(a_2)$ & $\varphi(a_2))$, etc. are determinates; to be the agent of a particular φ-ing event is just to φ in a particular way.

There are two problems with this reply. First, the issue isn't just whether satisfaction of '$\lambda x.(Fx$ ∨ $Gx)$' implies genuine similarity, but whether we must posit a property denoted by this predicate in order to *explain* this similarity. And, it seems, we *don't* need to do this, even for determinable properties. If a is scarlet and b is crimson, we don't obviously need to posit the property *redness* in order to explain the resulting similarity between a and b. The nature of the properties *scarlet* and *crimson* seems to suffice.

Second, even if we wanted to posit determinable properties, the reply falters, because the things we do generally *aren't* determinable properties, at least not in the way the reply requires. More is required, for F and G to

---

[44] For discussion of determination, see Funkhouser (2006, 2014: chs. 1 and 2) and sources cited therein.

stand as determinable to determinate, than for F and G to stand roughly as disjunctive property to disjunct property (otherwise, *red* and *square* would be determinates of *red or square*). For one thing, same-level determinates of a single determinable – i.e. properties G and H which are both determinates of F, but neither of which is a determinate of the other – are incompatible: a red object can be scarlet or crimson, but not both; a triangle can be scalene or isosceles, but not both; etc. (Bernstein 2014a: 432). But, it seems, the properties $\lambda x.(Agent(x)(e_1)$ & $\varphi(e_1))$ and $\lambda x.(Agent(x)(e_2)$ & $\varphi(e_2))$ – which would, on the view under consideration, be same-level determinates of $\lambda x.\exists e(Agent(x)(e)$ & $\varphi(e))$ – needn't be incompatible. Consider the property of raising one's arm, or *being an x such that there exists an event which is a raising of x's arm by x*. I can exemplify this property in (at least) two ways: by being the agent of a particular raising of my left arm, e_1, and by being the agent of a particular raising of my right arm, e_2. But the properties *being the agent of e_1* and *being the agent of e_2* needn't be incompatible, since I might be able to raise both arms, in the ways that are distinctive of e_1 and e_2, at the same time.

Finally, disjunctive properties aren't needed to explain the causal powers objects possess. It seems that the property $\lambda x.(Fx \lor Gx)$ couldn't bestow on its possessor any powers not already bestowed by F or by G. For example, if an object is square, it thereby has the powers to exclude other objects from certain regions of space (namely, those of the same size and shape as the square), to cast a certain kind of shadow in certain lighting conditions, etc. It's difficult to see what additional powers could be bestowed on it by the disjunctive property *is either square or red*. (Of course, if the square is *also* red, it will thereby have certain powers not bestowed by *squareness*. But those powers are naturally thought of as being bestowed by *redness*, not the disjunctive property, since the object could exemplify the latter without exemplifying the former.)

Likewise, *mutatis mutandis*, for the things we do. If I raise my arm in a specific way, and am thereby the agent of a certain arm-raising event, e_1, I thereby have certain causal powers, e.g. the power to cast shadows of certain shapes, in certain lighting conditions, during the time that I raise my arm. It's difficult to see what additional powers could be bestowed on me by the disjunctive property *is the agent of either e_1 or e_2*, where e_2 is a distinct possible arm-raising.

Wilson (2009: 165 n.24) argues that the property $\lambda x.(Fx \lor Gx)$ *can* bestow causal powers not bestowed by either of its disjuncts. Some object, a, may exemplify $\lambda x.(Fx \lor Gx)$ by virtue of exemplifying F (but not G) or by virtue of exemplifying G (but not F). Now, suppose (i) that if a has F but not G, then a has the power to φ, and (ii) that if a has G but not F, then a has the power to ψ. Then, it might seems there's at least one power that $\lambda x.(Fx \lor Gx)$ can bestow on a but which F can't, namely, the power to ψ when not F; no property can bestow a power that can only be exercised by an object that lacks that very property.

The problem with this argument is that, while the conditional, 'If a exemplifies $\lambda x.(Fx \lor Gx)$, then, if a doesn't exemplify F, then a has the power to ψ' might be true, we needn't think that the power to ψ when not F is bestowed upon a by the disjunctive property $\lambda x.(Fx \lor Gx)$. There is, after all, another natural candidate for the property that bestows this power, namely G. For, as the case is described, any x which exemplifies G is such that, as long as it doesn't also exemplify F, it can ψ.

Thus, disjunctive properties are generally ill-suited to play the explanatory roles required of properties. *Mutatis mutandis*, existentially quantified properties, such as the things we do, are ill-suited to play these roles.

Lewis (1983: 10–19) distinguishes what are frequently called 'sparse' and 'abundant' properties. Abundant properties are posited merely to serve as the denotations of predicates, and to play a role in semantic theorizing. Because predicates can be as abundant as we like, so can their denotations – hence the label 'abundant properties'. Indeed, we may think of these properties as nothing more than functions of the sort appealed to in compositional semantics.

Sparse properties are different. Sparse properties are meant to be 'worldly' entities, to make real contributions to the natures of the objects that possess them, and to play various roles in metaphysical theorizing, namely, those roles with which I began this section. As such, general constraints on metaphysical theorizing, such as the demand for simplicity, apply. We can't posit sparse properties whenever and wherever we like: we must keep such posits to a minimum, and justify them by the role they play in our theories – hence the label 'sparse properties'.

The justification for believing in things we do isn't that they make real contributions to the natures of their possessors, bestow causal powers on them, etc. The justification is that the things we do play a certain role in *semantic* theorizing, namely, to be the meanings of verb phrases. Thus, we needn't think that the things we do are sparse properties. We may, and I will, take them to be abundant properties.

1.4   Conclusion

With these preliminaries in place, we can now turn to the phenomenon of negative action, and the problem it poses for metaphysical theories of action.

CHAPTER 2

The Problem of Negative Action

2.1 Introduction

In this chapter, I introduce the topics that will form the subject matter of the rest of the book, namely the phenomenon of 'negative' action and the problem that it poses for event-based theories of action and agency. In Section 2.2, I give a more detailed account of the nature of negative action than that given in the Introduction. I consider the differences between two paradigmatic kinds of negative behaviour – namely, omitting and refraining – and what distinguishes them from merely not doing something. I also consider what distinguishes negative actions proper from 'mere negative behaviours'. In Section 2.3, I give a detailed statement of the problem of negative action, drawing both on Section 2.2 and on the general discussion of action and ontology in Chapter 1.

2.2 Negative Actions

2.2.1 Doing and Not Doing

As noted in the Introduction, it seems that we can exercise our agency both by doing things and by not doing them. Suppose, once again, that I'm in a department meeting where a vote is to be held by a show of hands. It seems that I can exercise my agency in at least two ways: by raising my arm, thereby casting a vote; and by not raising my arm, thereby abstaining. If I choose to abstain, and I don't raise my arm, I thereby exercise my agency just as much as I would have if I had raised my arm. I'll call those behaviours which seem to consist – perhaps *inter alia* – in an agent not doing a certain thing 'negative behaviours'. When these behaviours are, or seem to be, ways in which an agent can exercise her agency, I'll call them 'negative actions'.[1] When a behaviour or action isn't negative, I'll call it 'positive'.

The paradigm negative behaviours, and the ones which are most frequently discussed in the literature, are omitting and refraining. I'll say more about what distinguishes omitting and refraining from merely not doing something, and what distinguishes them from each other, in Section 2.2.2. When I want to speak of negative behaviour more generally, without focusing on a specific type, I'll use the schematic verb, 'NEG', and speak of agents NEG-φ-ing.

I've said that a negative behaviour, NEG-φ, consists – perhaps *inter alia* – in an agent not φ-ing. To say this is to say more than that NEG-φ doesn't consist in φ-ing. Raising one's arm doesn't consist, even in part, of tapping one's foot; although I can raise my arm and tap my foot at the same time, the latter behaviour isn't part of the former. Nonetheless, raising one's arm isn't a negative correlate of tapping one's foot, as NEG-φ is a negative correlate of φ. A necessary condition on NEG-φ-ing is that one doesn't φ – I can't omit to do something, or refrain from doing it, at the very same time that I do that thing.

Incompatibility Condition
Necessarily, for any agent x and time t, if x NEG-φ-s at t, then x doesn't φ at t.

Since it's perfectly possible for me to raise my arm and tap my foot, the former behaviour isn't a negative correlate of the latter.

Just as with positive behaviours, we can draw a distinction, with respect to negative behaviours, between the things we do and our doings of those things. It might seem that omitting to φ, refraining from φ-ing, etc. can't be *things we do*, since to omit to φ, refrain from φ-ing, etc. is precisely *not* to do something. But this is a mistake. To omit to φ is, *inter alia*, not to φ, but it doesn't follow that it isn't also to do something *else*. Indeed, there's an obvious candidate for this 'something else': *to omit to φ*. Negative behaviours are things we do in the weak sense licensed by the use of a grammatically active verb phrase: since 'omit to φ', 'refrain from φ-ing', etc. are grammatically active verb phrases, omitting and refraining are things we do. Whether they're also ways of acting – i.e. things we 'do' in the restricted sense of interest to philosophers of action – is a question I'll address in Section 2.2.3 and in more detail in Chapter 3.

---

[1] To my knowledge, the first occurrence of this terminology is Bentham (1780); see Bennett (1995: ch. 6) for discussion. This terminology is also used by Bach (2010), Vermazen (1985), and Woollard (2015: ch. 3).

We can derive noun phrases from verb phrases for negative behaviours, and use those noun phrases to (attempt to) refer to token negative behaviours. I take it that 'omission' is the nominalization of 'omit', and that it can be used to generate perfect nominals. Just as we can derive the imperfect 'Quisling's betraying Norway' and the perfect 'Quisling's betrayal of Norway' from 'Quisling betrays Norway', we can derive the imperfect (2) and the perfect (3) from (1):

(1) Alice omits to pick up milk.
(2) Alice's omitting to pick up milk.
(3) Alice's omission to pick up milk.

(Note that 'omission to pick up milk' can be count-quantified, while 'omitting to pick up milk' can't, and that 'omission to pick up milk' can be modified adjectivally, while 'omitting to pick up milk' can only be modified adverbially.) Thus, we can use phrases like (3) to talk not just about omitting or cases of omitting, but particular omissions. Likewise, I take it that 'refrainment' is the nominalization of 'refrain', and that we can derive the imperfect (5) and the perfect (6) from (4):

(4) Alice refrains from picking up milk.
(5) Alice's refraining from picking up milk.
(6) Alice's refrainment from picking up milk.

Thus, we can use phrases like (6) to talk, not just about refraining or cases of refraining, but particular refrainments.[2]

2.2.2 *Omitting, Refraining, and Not Doing*

What distinguishes omitting to φ and refraining from φ-ing, on the one hand, from merely not φ-ing, on the other? And what distinguishes these negative behaviours from each other?[3]

Take omitting first. Some philosophers use the term 'omission' as I use the term 'negative behaviour', i.e. as a catch-all for token behaviours that

---

[2] Admittedly, 'refrainment' isn't often used in ordinary conversation. You might worry that ordinary English doesn't contain a perfect nominalization of 'refrain' at all, only the imperfect 'refraining'. This worry is easily quashed by reference to Merriam-Webster's dictionary. However, even if 'refrainment' didn't already exist, I would be free to introduce it, and to *stipulate* that it stands to 'refrain' as 'omission' stands to 'omit' (recall Section 1.2.2).

[3] In asking what distinguishes omitting and refraining from merely not doing, I'm not asking what distinguishes negative actions from 'mere negative behaviours', i.e. negative behaviours which aren't ways of exercising agency. Whatever distinguishes omitting from not doing distinguishes *unintentionally* omitting to φ from simply not φ-ing, but it's plausible that one doesn't exercise one's agency by unintentionally omitting to φ – see Section 2.2.3.

consist, at least in part, in an agent not doing a certain thing.[4] This isn't how the term is used in ordinary English. Not all cases in which an agent doesn't φ would ordinarily be described as cases in which the agent *omits* to φ – e.g. I'm not currently running a three-legged race, but it would be incorrect to say that I'm *omitting* to run a three-legged race. Of course, there's no problem, in principle, with using 'omission' as these philosophers do, as long as it's understood that the term is being given a semitechnical use. However, the idiosyncrasies of the ordinary meaning of 'omit' will be relevant at various points in my discussion, and so I prefer to stick to ordinary usage as closely as possible.

Bach suggests, quite plausibly, that one can only omit to φ if one is, 'in a conveniently broad and vague sense, "supposed to φ"' (2010: 54, slightly modified). Thus, the reason I'm not currently omitting to run a three-legged race is that there's no sense in which I'm supposed to be running a three-legged race. The claim that one is supposed to φ can be grounded in various ways. It might be grounded in a norm, and this norm might be a moral one (if I find a stranger's wallet, I'm morally obliged to try to return it, and so if I fail to do so, my failure is an omission) or a rational one (if I intend to invite my friend to my party, then I'm arguably under some kind of rational imperative to follow through on that intention; if I fail do so, my failure is an omission). The claim that one is supposed to φ might also be grounded, not in a norm, but in a mere expectation. If it's my habit to take my shoes off when I come home, then if I come home and fail to take my shoes off, this failure might reasonably be called an 'omission' (Bach 2010: 54).

Clarke writes that 'one *seldom if ever* counts as having omitted to do something unless there was some norm, standard, or ideal that called for one's so acting' (2014: 29, emphasis added). Why 'seldom if ever', rather than 'never'? Clarke (2014: 32) thinks that intentionally omitting to do something is the same as refraining from doing it. Since one can refrain from doing something even if there is no sense in which one is supposed to do it – I can, after all, refrain from acting on base or immoral impulses – he concludes that one can omit to do something one isn't supposed to do.

Clarke's identification of refraining with intentionally omitting might be justified if we were using 'omitting' as a semi-technical catch-all. But if we want to adhere the ordinary meaning of 'omit', the identification isn't justified. Borrowing Vermazen's (1985) example, suppose that Alice refrains from taking a second helping of hors d'oeuvres, in order to stick

---

[4] See, e.g. Clarke (2010a, 2014) and Sartorio (2009).

to her diet. It's incorrect to say that Alice has *omitted* from taking a second helping. The reason this is incorrect, I suggest, is that (unless the case is filled out in an unusual way), there's no norm or expectation in place which could ground the claim that Alice is *supposed* to take a second helping of hors d'oeuvres.[5]

I say that an utterance of '*x* omits to φ' is incorrect or inappropriate if *x* isn't in any way supposed to φ. I don't say that such an utterance is *false*. '*x* omits to φ' doesn't *assert* that *x* is supposed to φ, and so it isn't automatically rendered false if *x* isn't supposed to φ. Rather, '*x* omits to φ' *presupposes* that *x* is supposed to φ, in a way that is familiar from pragmatics: *S* presupposes *p* just in case an utterance of *S* is incorrect or inappropriate if *S* isn't part of the 'common ground' in the conversational context, i.e. if it isn't assumed, by all parties to the conversation, that *p* is assumed by each party to the conversation.

Compare: (7) presupposes, but doesn't assert, (8).

(7) Alice's son is on his way to the airport.
(8) Alice has a son.

An utterance of (7) doesn't serve to *assert* that or inform the parties to the conversation that Alice has a son; rather, it takes for granted that there is such a person and that he is available to be talked about in the conversational context. If one or more parties to the conversation rejects (8), the utterance of (7) won't – or perhaps shouldn't – be accepted as a legitimate move within the conversation: if you don't think Alice has a son, you won't – or perhaps shouldn't – allow someone to get away with talking about him.[6] Likewise, (9) presupposes, but doesn't assert, (10).

---

[5] Clarke might attempt an alternative explanation: since, in his view, refraining *just is* intentionally omitting, '*x* omits to φ' is logically weaker than '*x* refrains from φ-ing'. Thus, if we're in a position to assert that Alice *refrained* from taking a second helping of hors d'oeuvres, to assert that she *omitted* to do so is to violate Grice's Maxim of Quantity: 'Make your contribution as informative as is required (for the purposes of the exchange)' (1975: 26).

There are two problems with this explanation. First the maxim only requires that your utterance be as informative *as is required by the conversation*; indeed, Grice's Maxim of Quality enjoins that we not make our contributions any *more* informative than is required (ibid.). Thus, Clarke's view predicts that, if it's irrelevant whether Alice *intentionally* omitted to take a second helping, then 'Alice refrained from taking a second helping' should be inappropriate and 'Alice omitted to take a second helping' preferred, since the former simply adds irrelevant information. But this is wrong; as long as Alice isn't *supposed* to take a second helping, use of 'omits' is inappropriate. Second, the explanation overgenerates, since it predicts that '*x* refrains from φ-ing' is *always* preferable to '*x* omits to φ', which it isn't. (Thanks to David Liebesman for this point.)

[6] Stalnaker (1970). For helpful recent discussion, see Stalnaker (2014: ch. 3) and sources cited therein. For discussion of the notion of 'common ground' and its role in pragmatics, see Stalnaker (2014: ch. 2).

(9) Alice omitted to take a second helping of hors d'oeuvres.
(10) Alice was supposed to take a second helping of hors d'oeuvres.

If one or more parties to a conversation rejects (10), an utterance of (9) won't – or perhaps *shouldn't* – be accepted as a legitimate move: if you don't think Alice was *supposed* to take a second helping, you won't – or shouldn't – allow someone to get away with saying that she *omitted* to do so.

To see this, consider some standard tests for presupposition. First, the presuppositions of S typically 'project' into more complex sentences in which S is embedded. In particular, if S presupposes p, then so does 'Not-S'. If you reject (8), then you should object to (7~) just as strongly as to (7):

(7~) Alice's son isn't on his way to airport.

Like (7), (7~) takes it for granted that there is such a person as Alice's son, and attempts to say something about him; if you think that there is no such person, then (7~) is objectionable in the same way that (7) is. Likewise, if you reject (10), then you should object to (9~) just as strongly as to (10):

(9~) Alice didn't omit to take a second helping of hors d'oeuvres.

Intuitively, (9~) is true only if Alice *did* take a second helping of hors d'oeuvres.[7] But the fact that she took a second helping does not, on its own, license an assertion of (9~). If you reject (10), then an assertion of (9~) is objectionable, although an assertion of 'Alice takes a second helping ...' isn't. Explanation: (9) and (9~) both presuppose (10).

Second, there's what von Fintel (2004: 316–317) calls the 'Hey, Wait a Minute!' test.[8] If S presupposes p, and I don't already accept p, then I can object to your utterance by saying, 'Hey, wait a minute! I didn't know that p!', or some variant thereupon. The phrase 'Hey, wait a minute' effectively signals that I'm not objecting to the *content* of your utterance; I'm putting it on hold in order to address one of its presuppositions. Thus, if I object to an utterance of (7) by saying, 'Hey, wait a minute! I didn't know that Alice

---

Note that, for an utterance of (7) to be accepted, it isn't necessary that (8) *already* be in the common ground, prior to the utterance. The parties to the conversation, recognizing that (7) can only be true if (8) is, might *update* the common ground in order to allow the speaker to get away with asserting (7) – see Karttunen (1974: 191) and Stalnaker (2014: 56–58).

[7] The relationship between '~(x NEG-(φ))' and 'x φ' is actually more complex than this suggests. I return to this issue in Chapters 5 and 6.

[8] von Fintel traces this test at least as far back as Shanon (1976).

had a son!', I'm not objecting directly to the *content* of (7). More specifically, I'm not objecting to (7) on the ground that (7~) is, or might be, true. I'm putting that question on hold, in order to address (8); only once I accept (8) will I allow the question of the truth or falsity of (7) to arise. Likewise, if I object to an utterance of (9) by saying, 'Hey, wait a minute! I didn't know that Alice was supposed to take a second helping of hors d'oeuvres!', I'm not objecting to the *content* of (9). More specifically, I'm not objecting to (9) on the ground that (9~) is, or might be, true. I'm putting that question on hold, in order to address (10); only once I accept (10) will I allow the question of the truth or falsity of (9) to arise. Thus, (9) presupposes (10).

If S presupposes that p, then an utterance of S is inappropriate unless p is part of the common ground in the conversational context. To say that an utterance of S is inappropriate in these circumstances isn't necessarily to say that the content of S is untrue (although it might be). Presumably, if (8) is false, then both (7) and (7~) are untrue – we can't truly say either that Alice's son is on his way to the airport or that he isn't, if there is no such person. However, it may be that what hinges on p is not the *truth* of S, but its *assertibility*: it may be that, if p isn't part of the common ground, then parties to the conversation can recognize that the *content* of S is true, but the choice of S as a vehicle for that content becomes inappropriate. This, I think, is the case with omission sentences and their presuppositions. If it's not part of the common ground that x is supposed to φ, then it's not the *content* of 'x omits to φ' that is objectionable, but the use of the word 'omit'.

When we wish to object to a sentence, S, used to express a certain proposition, p, without objecting to p itself, we can engage in 'meta-linguistic negation': we can negate S in a way which signals that we aren't objecting to p – presumably on the ground that ~p is true – but to the choice of S as a vehicle for p. Consider (11):

(11) Alice is a secretary.

There are two ways to deny (11). The first way is to deny that Alice occupies the position that 'secretary' denotes, i.e. that she performs the tasks and duties appropriate to people occupying that position. This denial is naturally expressed as (11~):

(11~) Alice isn't a secretary.

The second way to deny (11) is not to deny that Alice occupies the position that 'secretary' denotes, but to object to the use of 'secretary' to

denote that position – presumably on the ground that that word carries
certain connotations that ought to be avoided. This denial is naturally
expressed as (11-_{ML}), in which the objectionable word is given special
emphasis, and a corrective is offered:

> (11-_{ML}) Alice isn't a *secretary*; she's an *administrative assistant*.

Now, recall that (9-) is intuitively true only if Alice took a second
helping of hors d'oeuvres. Thus, to object to (9) by uttering (9-) is
apparently to assert that Alice took a second helping, and so to object to
the *content* of (9) on the ground that the negation of that content is true.
But this isn't the most natural way to object to (9), if the problem is that
(10) isn't part of the common ground. If you and I both observe that Alice
doesn't take a second helping, and you utter (9), I can still object to your
utterance on the ground that (10) is false. The most natural way to express
my denial of (9), in this case, is to use the device of meta-linguistic
negation:

> (9-_{ML}) Alice didn't *omit* to take a second helping of hors d'oeuvres; she
> wasn't supposed to!

What's objectionable isn't your claim that Alice didn't take a second
helping, but your description of her behaviour as an 'omission'.[9]

Turning now to refraining, the major difference between refraining
from doing something and merely not doing it is that one only counts as
refraining from doing something if one *intentionally* doesn't do it (Bach
2010: 52; Clarke 2014: 92). Suppose that Alice doesn't deliberately avoid
the hors d'oeuvres in order to stick to her diet; instead, she is completely
unaware that there are any hors d'oeuvres left, and the thought of having a
second helping doesn't even cross her mind. In this case, it would be
wrong to say that Alice *refrained* from taking a second helping.

This also distinguishes refraining from omitting. I can unintentionally
omit to do something, because omitting only requires that I'm supposed to
do the relevant thing, not that I intentionally fail to live up to this
expectation. But I can't unintentionally refrain from doing something.

While 'x omits to φ' presupposes, but doesn't assert, that x is supposed
to φ, 'x refrains from φ-ing' asserts, and doesn't presuppose, that x
intentionally doesn't φ. If 'x refrains from φ-ing' presupposes that x
intentionally doesn't φ, then 'x doesn't refrain from φ-ing' should too.

---

[9] The example of (11), (11-), and (11-_{ML}) is due to Almotahari (2014a: 498–499). The classic
discussion of meta-linguistic negation is found in Horn (1989).

But it doesn't: I can assert, 'Alice didn't refrain from taking a second helping of hors d'oeuvres' on the ground that Alice did, in fact, take a second helping; but such an assertion can hardly presuppose that she intentionally *didn't* take a second helping. Moreover, if 'x refrained from φ-ing' presupposes that x intentionally didn't φ, then it should be appropriate to object to that presupposition by saying, 'Hey, wait a minute! I didn't know that x intentionally didn't φ!' But it isn't: that x intentionally didn't φ isn't something that an utterance of 'x refrained from φ-ing' takes for granted, in order to assert something *else*; it is part of what's being asserted.

2.2.3   *Negative Action and Mere Negative Behaviour*

It's generally assumed that the difference between negative actions and mere negative behaviours – here understood as things done, rather than doings – is that the former are intentionally performed while the latter aren't: that is, x only exercises her agency by NEG-φ-ing if x intentionally doesn't φ. Sometimes, this assumption is merely implicit. The typical examples of negative action in the literature are cases in which an agent *intentionally* omits to do something, or *refrains* from doing it. (Recall, one only counts as refraining from φ-ing if one intentionally doesn't φ.) Sometimes, the assumption is made explicit, and philosophers claim outright that, if x *un*intentionally doesn't φ – as in the case where Alice gives no thought to having a second helping of hors d'oeuvres – then x doesn't exercise her agency by NEG-φ-ing; she performs no negative *action*, but a 'mere negative behaviour' (Bach 2010: 55; Clarke 2014: 16; Davidson 1985a: 218; Vermazen 1985: 96–97).

It would be tempting to explain the assumption that negative actions are intentional negative behaviours as arising from the assumption of an 'intentionalist' theory of action, i.e. a theory of action according to which *what it is* for an agent to act is for her to do something intentionally. (The Event-Causal Theory of Action sketched in Chapter 1 is one such theory, and not only has it dominated the literature on action in general, but at least three philosophers who explicitly claim that negative actions must be intentionally performed – namely, Clarke, Davidson, and Vermazen – defend some version of it.) But this explanation is incorrect. Even philosophers who reject the Event-Causal Theory of Action in particular, and intentionalist theories of action more generally, tend, in their discussions of negative action, to restrict their attention to cases of intentional negative behaviour – see, e.g., Alvarez (2013: 105) and Hornsby (2004: 5). The general denial of the possibility of non-intentional negative action stems, I suggest, not from implicit or explicit adherence to intentionalist theories of action, but simply from a failure to see how one's non-intentionally not doing something could be an exercise of one's agency.[10]

We must distinguish between intentionally not φ-ing, on the one hand, and intentionally *bringing it about* that one doesn't φ, on the other. Sometimes, an agent intentionally does one thing in order to bring it about that she doesn't do another thing. For example, Bach (2010: 54) imagines a case in which I throw away a tempting container of ice cream, in order to make sure that I don't eat it, and that I stick to my diet. It seems incorrect to say that I *intentionally* don't eat the ice cream, at some later time when I've already thrown it away. Rather, the right thing to say is that, at the earlier time, I intentionally *bring it about* that I won't eat ice cream at the later time. Thus, cases like this are *not* cases of negative action, as I understand the phenomenon. (Compare: if I take a sleeping pill, I intentionally *bring it about* that I'll fall asleep, although falling asleep isn't something I do intentionally, and my falling asleep isn't an action.)

The reason I don't intentionally fail to eat the ice cream in this case *isn't* that actions can't be stretched out through space and time: in Section 1.2.3, I gave some reasons for thinking that actions can extend beyond the body, and in Section 8.2.2, I'll argue that negative actions can occupy large stretches of time.[11] Even if negative actions can be stretched out in these ways, there's still a distinction to be drawn between intentionally doing something and intentionally *bringing it about* that one doesn't do it. I'll discuss this distinction again in Section 3.3.2, and a related distinction in Section 5.3.1.

If we distinguish negative actions from mere behaviours – in the sense of *things done* – by saying that the former are intentionally performed while the latter aren't, how should we distinguish negative actions from mere

---

[10] Some philosophers argue for the existence of 'sub-intentional' actions, i.e. actions that agents perform without having formed any intention with relevant content, and without even being aware that they're acting in these ways. If there are such things as sub-intentional actions at all, it's not clear why there shouldn't be *negative* ones. However, the question whether there are such things as sub-intentional actions is fraught with dispute, and I won't aim to settle it here. In what follows, I'll focus on intentional negative actions as the paradigm cases of negative action; whether there are, in addition, sub-intentional actions won't affect my argument.

For defenses of sub-intentional action, see O'Shaughnessy (1980: ch. 10) – although compare O'Shaughnessy (2008: ch. 10) – and Steward (2009). On the connection between awareness and intentionality, see Anscombe (1963: §6ff.), Davidson (1971: 50–52), Paul (2009: 548–554), and Setiya (2008: 43–48; 2009: 62–66).

[11] Thanks to an anonymous referee for pressing me on this.

negative behaviours, in the sense of *doings*? The natural thing to say is that token negative actions are intentional, while token mere negative behaviours aren't. But here we must recall a point made about intentions and intentionality in Section 1.2.4. On a plausible view of act-individuation, a single event may be an intentional doing of one thing and an unintentional doing of another: x's φ-ing might *be x's* ψ-ing, even if x φ-s intentionally but ψ-s unintentionally. Thus, the claim that actions *tout court* are intentional is best understood as the claim that x's φ-ing is an action only if it's an intentional doing of *something*, though not necessarily φ – as Davidson puts it, an action is an event that is intentional 'under some description'. But if we understand the claim that negative actions are intentional in this way, we seem to overgenerate negative actions. Suppose that I unintentionally omit to wave to my friend across the street, that I intentionally scratch my nose, and that my omission is identical to my scratching of my nose. Since my omission is intentional 'under some description', it counts as a negative action by the criterion just given. But surely, unintentional omissions aren't negative actions in any interesting sense, even if they're identical to positive actions. Likewise, in Bach's case, it may be that I'm engaged in some positive action at the time when I don't eat the ice cream, but it seems wrong to describe my failure to eat the ice cream at that time as a negative action.

We must, it seems, distinguish two things we might mean to talk about when we talk about 'negative actions'. We might mean to talk about thingsthat are actions, and which are doings of negative things (or fall under negative descriptions), without implying that the relevant agents exercise their agency *by* doing those negative things. In this broad sense, my omission to wave to my friend counts (and my failure to eat the ice cream *might* count) as a negative action, since it's both an action and a doing of something negative. Or, we might mean to talk about doings of negative things (or fall under negative descriptions), and which are such that the relevant agents exercise their agency *by* doing those negative things. In this narrower sense, neither my omission to wave to my friend nor my failure to eat the ice cream counts as a negative action: although they may be actions, they are so because I exercise my agency by doing something positive, and not because I exercise by agency by doing something negative. In what follows, I'll intend this narrower sense of 'negative action' unless I specify otherwise; I classify negative behaviours which count as negative actions only in the broad sense as mere negative behaviours.

2.3 The Problem

In the Introduction, I presented the problem of negative actions as an inconsistent triad. Each of (PNA 1)–(PNA 3) is highly intuitive and/or widely accepted, but they can't all be true.

(PNA 1)   Negative actions – in the sense of things done – are genuine actions; necessarily, if NEG-φ is a negative action for x at t, then if x NEG-φ-s at t, then x acts by NEG-φ-ing at t.

(PNA 2)   Necessarily, if x acts by φ-ing at t, then there exists an event that is x's token φ-ing at t.

(PNA 3)   Possibly, x NEG-φ-s at t, and there exists no event that is x's token NEG-φ-ing at t.

We're now in a position to assess the credentials of (PNA 1)–(PNA 3), to see why each is compelling, and to feel the real force of the problem.

2.3.1   *Negative Actions as* Actions

The support for (PNA 1) is largely intuitive. As I've noted before, it certainly *seems* as though we can exercise our agency both by doing things and by not doing things. Cases of intentional omission and refrainment are clear examples. Thus, it *seems* that intentionally omitting to do something and refraining from doing it are actions, or ways of acting.

To make the point more vivid, recall that, when sketching the task of a theory of action, I claimed that the task isn't primarily to give an extensional account of the distinction between cases in which an agent acts and cases in which this isn't so. Rather, we begin with a good sense of which cases are which, and the task of a theory of action is to explain *why*each case belongs in the category it does. We already know that a case in which I intentionally raise my arm in order to hail a cab is a case of action, while a case in which my arm rises as the result of an involuntary spasm isn't, and we want to know *why* that is, what the crucial difference between the two cases is. Now, our sense of which cases are which certainly classifies cases of intentional omission and refrainment as cases of action, rather than as cases of mere behaviour. The case in which I refrain from raising my arm, and thereby abstain from voting, belongs in the same category as the one in which I raise my arm in order to hail a cab. It doesn't belong in the same category as the one in which my arm rises as the result of a spasm.

We can bolster the point even further by noting that negative actions share many of those features which philosophers have thought to be especially relevant when considering the difference between actions and mere behaviours. Thus, Clarke writes:

> Just as one can deliberate about whether to act in a certain way, one can deliberate about whether to refrain from acting in a certain way, for example, about whether to abstain or boycott. There are reasons for omitting or refraining as well as for acting, and they are reasons of the same general kind: practical reasons, considerations bearing on what to do, on whether to act in one way or another. One can omit or refrain for such reasons, just as one can act for them. Omitting or refraining can be commanded ('Don't move!') or otherwise required, and such a command or requirement can be obeyed or fulfilled, or, alternatively, disobeyed or flouted. Omitting or refraining can be something one chooses or intends, and one can intentionally omit to do, or refrain from doing, a certain thing ... (Clarke 2014: 11)

The list goes on.[12] It's highly natural to classify both positive and negative actions as genuine actions.

I noted in Section 1.2.1 that our intuitions about whether a given case involves action or mere behaviour aren't sacrosanct, any more than pre-theoretical intuitions in any other area of philosophy are. Even firm intuitions may need to be given up, if that's the price of an otherwise satisfying theory. The point of this discussion hasn't been to establish that negative actions are genuine actions, but to create a presumption that this is so. *Prima facie*, negative actions are precisely the sort of thing that a theory of action is supposed to be a theory *of*.

2.3.2 *Negative Actions, Events, and Absences*

We encountered the motivation behind (PNA 2) in Sections 1.3.1 and 1.3.2: on the Neo-Davidsonian approach to the analysis of action sentences, such sentences are existential quantifications over token actions, and token actions are plausibly thought of as events. However, while the view that *positive* actions are events is widespread, many philosophers of action deny that all *negative* actions are events, and some go so far as to claim that *none* are. That is, many philosophers of action endorse (PNA 3).

---

[12] I won't consider all the parallels Clarke notes, but those listed here will be especially important in Section 3.3.

Clarke gives a pithy statement of the view:

> Often when someone omits to do a certain thing, there's no action that is
> the omission, and the agent performs no action in order to prevent herself
> from doing that thing. When I forget to stop and buy milk on my way
> home from work, my omission seems to be, in the first place, an absence,
> the absence of an action by me of buying milk. (Clarke 2014: 35)

Although Clarke's chosen example is an unintentional omission, he applies
this line of thought to intentional omissions and refrainments, as well:
'there need be no action that is one's intentionally not doing a certain
thing on a certain occasion when, in fact, one intentionally doesn't do that
thing' (2014: 60). The exceptions, for Clarke, are cases of non-basic
negative action, i.e. cases where an agent performs some positive behaviour
ψ *in order not to* ϕ. If x intentionally ψ-s in order to prevent herself from
ϕ-ing – as in Brand's (1971: 45–46) example of a police officer who holds
her arm at her side to prevent herself from shooting a fleeing suspect – and
ψ-ing is a positive action, then x's omission (or refrainment, or . . .) can be
identified with x's ϕ-ing by the principle of *By-Action Identity*. However, in
cases of basic negative action, there is no positive action with which x's
negative action might be identified. In such cases, Clarke thinks, there is
no such event as x's omission (or refrainment, or . . .). Basic negative
actions aren't events, but absences thereof.

Clarke is far from being alone in his skepticism about negative actions
qua events. As early as 1914, Stroud writes that '[a]n omission is not like
an act, a real event, but merely an artificial conception consisting in the
negation of a particular act' (1914: 4). Stroud's thought appears to be that,
when x omits to ϕ, what happens isn't that some particular event occurs,
but simply that no event of x ϕ-ing occurs. A token omission is an 'artificial
conception' birthed by the creation of a derived nominal – 'x's omission to
ϕ' – which doesn't refer to any event.[13]

Vermazen (1985) discusses the ontological status of negative actions,
and his view seems to have influenced Clarke. Vermazen claims that, if x
performs some positive action ψ which 'generates' or 'results in' x not

---

[13] Bennett complains that Stroud's phrase 'artificial conception' is 'a rather hapless way of referring to
something that is quite straightforward, namely a negative fact about conduct' (1995: 87). But
Stroud's point is surely that, over and above the fact that x omits ϕ, there is no event that is x's
omission. This is a point with which Bennett should be sympathetic, since he's skeptical of negative
actions *qua* events – see especially (1995: 32, 85–88). However, since he's also resistant to
approaches on which talk about *positive* actions is cashed out in terms of quantification over
events – see (1988: ch. 11; 1995: 29–33) – Bennett doesn't fit nicely among the philosophers
I'm interested in, who claim that all positive actions are events, even if not all negative ones are.

φ-ing, and *x* ψ-s in order not to φ, then *x*'s omission to φ (refrainment from φ-ing, etc.) can be identified with *x*'s ψ-ing (1985: 95–96). However, in cases of basic negative action, there is no such event as *x*'s omission to φ (refrainment from φ-ing, etc.).

> '[N]ot φ-ing' need not pick out an event of any sort. Positive acts are bodily movements;[14] negative acts, when they are resistings or identical with positive acts, are also bodily movements; but simple negative acts, mere refrainings, need not be bodily movements at all. (Vermazen 1985: 103)

In his reply to Vermazen, Davidson evidently agrees: '[I]n some cases a relevant belief and desire rationalize an agent's not doing something, and the belief and desire cause it ("in the right way") to be the case that he does not do it ... [T]here need be no action at all' (1985a: 220).

More recently, Hornsby criticizes event-based theories of action on the ground that they can't accommodate negative actions:

> [S]omeone can do something intentionally without there being any *action* that is their doing the thing. Consider A who decides she shouldn't take a chocolate, and refrains from moving her arm towards the box; or B who doesn't want to be disturbed by answering calls, and lets the telephone carry on ringing; or C who, being irritated by someone, pays that person no attention ... Notice that one cannot put the point by saying that there are 'negative actions' on the parts of A, B and C. Of course not: where 'action' is taken in the standard story's sense, there could not be any such thing as a negative action. It is true that philosophers who are interested in categories such as *omitting, refraining, letting happen* sometimes speak of these as categories of 'negative actions'. But then they don't use the word 'action' as having application to events. (Hornsby 2004: 5–6; emphasis in the original)

If 'action' is used to mean 'token action', and token actions are taken to be events, then, Hornsby thinks, there are – and can be – no such things as negative actions. At least, there are no such things as *basic* negative actions. Like Vermazen, Davidson, and Clarke, Hornsby is willing to allow that non-basic negative actions can be identified with events, via *By-Action Identity*. 'If D's temptation to take a chocolate was so powerful that she had to tense her muscles in order to hold herself back, then arguably "her refraining from taking a chocolate" would apply to an event even though

---

[14] Vermazen explicitly follows Davidson in allowing the term 'bodily movement' to apply to token behaviours which consist in an agent keeping some part(s) of her body still – what Vermazen (1985: 94) calls 'null movements'.

her body did not move: it would apply to D's tensing her muscles, perhaps' (2004: 5).

One more example: Moore writes that 'an omission is literally nothing at all. An omission to kill is not some ghostly kind of killing. It is like an absent elephant, which is no elephant at all. An omission to kill is an absent event of killing . . .' (2009: 53). Although Moore's phrasing is suggestive, it isn't quite right. The view we've seen defended so far is that negative actions are absences of events: x's omission to φ (refrainment from φ-ing, etc.) is an absence of events in which x φ-s. But an absence of Fs isn't an absent F. Thus, Moore shouldn't say that an omission to kill is an absent event of killing. He should say, instead, that an omission to kill is an absence of events of killing.[15] Note that Moore is less sanguine about identifying negative actions with events than the other philosophers I've quoted – he seems happy to claim that *no* negative action is an event.

Like (PNA 2), (PNA 3) is motivated (though often only implicitly) by considerations from the philosophy of language. Recall that the distinction between positive and negative behaviours is the distinction between behaviours which consist in an agent doing something and those which consist in an agent not doing something. The thought behind (PNA 3) is that, if an agent's doing something is a matter of the occurrence of an event, then her *not* doing something must be a matter of the *absence* of an event. Putting the thought in a more linguistic mode: if positive action sentences are analyzed as expressing existential quantifications over events, then negative action sentences – i.e. sentences describing agents as intentionally omitting, refraining, etc. – should be analyzed as negative-existentials; these sentences report not the occurrence of an event of a certain type, but the *absence* of events of a certain type. For instance, if (12) is analysed as (12*), then (13) should be analysed as (13*):

(12) Alex kisses Beth.
(12*) $\exists e(Agent(\text{Alice})(e)\ \&\ Patient(\text{Beth})(e)\ \&\ Kiss(e))$

(13) Alex omits to kiss Beth.
(13*) $\neg\exists e(Agent(\text{Alice})(e)\ \&\ Patient(\text{Beth})(e)\ \&\ Kiss(e))$

In English: there occurs no event e such that Alice is the agent of e, Beth is the patient of e, and e is a kiss.[16]

---

[15] Although he continues to treat 'absence of Fs' and 'absent F' as though they are equivalent, Moore does seem to recognize the problem, here, since he goes on to deny that an omission is 'an absent act-token' (2009: 53).

[16] A proponent of this view isn't committed to thinking that *all* there is to the meaning of a negative action sentence is a negative existential. 'x omits to φ' carries the presupposition that x is supposed to φ, and 'x refrains from φ-ing' asserts, in part, that x intentionally doesn't φ. The point is simply that, whatever else we say about the meanings of various negative action sentences, they express negative existentials and don't quantify over negative actions *qua* events.

Call this view 'Deflationism'. The Neo-Davidsonian approach, if applied to positive action sentences, inflates our ontological commitments, revealing that those sentences carry with them commitment to events of certain kinds. The Deflationist approach to negative action sentences deflates our ontological commitments, revealing that those sentences carry no such commitment.

Moore is explicit in his commitment to Deflationism:

> [T]here are no 'negative events'. There are negative propositions about events, such as 'James omitted to kill Smith' meaning 'it is not the case that James killed Smith'. Such negative statements are negative existentially quantified ones: if there is an omission to kill, then what is true is that it is not the case that some instance of the type of event, killing, existed. (Moore 2009: 53)

Similarly, although Davidson expresses concern that *There is no e such that e is a φ-ing by x* doesn't capture the sense of sentences like '*x* omits to φ' or '*x* refrains from φ-ing', context makes clear that his concern is merely that such sentences can report that *x* *intentionally* doesn't φ, and hence that there is sometimes *more* to the meaning of a negative action sentence than a negative existential (1985a: 218–219). Vermazen explicitly express sympathy for Deflationism, but suggests that it only applies when the negative action described is basic (1985: 99–100 n.14). I'll consider this more nuanced view in Section 2.3.3.

Not everyone who inclines towards Deflationism is as explicit in their endorsement. Consider again Hornsby's denial that in the cases of her agents A, B, and C, there occurs any event that is the agent's intentionally doing something. Hornsby acknowledges that 'there will be plenty of events in the region of these agents at the times at which they do their things' (2004: 5) but insists that, in these cases, 'that which ensures that something is done intentionally is not a matter of the occurrence of an event at all' (ibid.). What justifies the claim that, e.g. A's refraining from taking a chocolate isn't a matter of the occurrence of an event? The obvious answer, given that Deflationism is in the air, is that the sentence, 'A refrains from taking a chocolate' is a negative-existential: this sentence merely reports the absence of events in which A takes a chocolate, and so the occurrence of any event that *does* occur in the imagined case is irrelevant to the truth of the sentence. And, indeed, this seems to be Hornsby's answer. In support of her claim that there are no negative actions, she cites Mellor (1995), who argues that, because sentences like 'Alice falls' quantify over events, sentences like 'Alice doesn't fall' are 'negative existential statements, made true by the *non-existence* of such particulars' (Mellor 1995: 132). Thus, it seems that Hornsby is extending what Mellor says about these sentences to negative action sentences, thereby endorsing Deflationism.[17]

After claiming that (at least some) negative actions are not events, but absences thereof, Clarke claims that negative action sentences require for their truth 'only that there be no things of certain kinds (at certain places and times)' (2014: 48), and hence that terms like 'x's omission to φ' are non-referential. This fits naturally with Deflationism: if 'Alice omits to kiss Beth' is a negative-existential then, plausibly, it requires for its truth only that there be no event of Alice kissing Beth.

We can now feel the full force of the problem of negative action. *Prima facie*, negative actions are genuine actions: they are precisely the sort of thing that a theory of action is supposed to be a theory *of*. It's generally assumed that actions are events. However, negative actions seem to be an exception: at least some negative actions are not events, but absences thereof.

2.3.3   Are Some Negative Actions Events?

(PNA 3) only says that it's *possible* for an agent to perform a negative action even if there is no such thing as her token negative action. (PNA 3) is thus weaker than (PNA 3*):

(PNA 3*)   Necessarily, if x NEG-φ-s at t, then there exists no event that is x's token NEG-φ-ing at t.

Moore seems to accept (PNA 3*). Clarke, Hornsby, and Vermazen seem sympathetic only to (PNA 3), allowing that non-basic negative actions might be identified with events.

In what follows, I'll continue to frame the problem of negative action using (PNA 3) rather than (PNA 3*), since the former is all that's needed to generate the inconsistency. However, it's worth noting that, if you're sympathetic to Deflationism – and Clarke, Hornsby, and Vermazen all seem to be – then it will be difficult to endorse (PNA 3) without endorsing the stronger (PNA 3*).

Recall from Section 1.3.2 that positive action sentences and the perfect nominals derived from them are related in an important way: 'x φ-s' says that there exists an e such that e is a φ-ing by x, and 'x's φ-ing' refers, if at all, to the value of 'e'. If 'x NEG-φ' doesn't quantify over NEG-φ-ing

---

[17] I'll consider Mellor's argument for his view in Section 4.4.3.

events, and instead expresses the negative existential *There exists no e such that e is a φ-ing by x*, then the derived nominal 'x's NEG-φ-ing' can't even purport to refer to the value of 'e' in that proposition. Thus, it's not clear that 'x's NEG-φ-ing' can refer to anything.[18]

This point makes trouble for the claim that non-basic negative actions can be identified with events. If 'x's NEG-φ-ing' has no referent, then no matter what we put in for 'ψ', 'x's NEG-φ-ing is identical to x's ψ-ing' can't be true, since there is simply nothing there to be identified with x's ψ-ing. Indeed, if there is no such thing as x's NEG-φ-ing, then this identity claim may be not only untrue, but senseless.

We've seen that Vermazen and others appeal to *By-Action Identity* in order to identify x's NEG-φ-ing with x's ψ-ing, where x ψ-s in order not to φ. However, if 'x NEG-φ-s' expresses a negative existential, then the mere fact that x NEG-φ-s *by* ψ-ing doesn't guarantee that 'x's NEG-φ-ing' has a referent, and so doesn't guarantee that the identity claim is true. Putting it another way, the statement of *By-Action Identity* given in Section 1.2.3 simply assumes that, if x φ-s, then there is a φ-ing by x. Making this assumption explicit:

By-Action Identity*

If x φ-s by ψ-ing, and there is some y such that y is a φ-ing by x, and there is some z such that z is a ψ-ing by x, then $y = z$.

The problem is that, substituting 'NEG-φ' for 'φ', Deflationism calls into question whether there can be such a thing as x's NEG-φ-ing. If there isn't, then *By-Action Identity** doesn't allow us to identify x's NEG-φ-ing with any event, since there is simply nothing to be identified.

As noted above, Vermazen suggests that Deflationism only applies to sentences which describe basic negative actions. On this view, if x's omission to φ is basic, then 'x omits to φ' expresses a negative existential, but if x omits to φ by ψ-ing, then 'x omits to φ' quantifies over ψ-ing events (1985: 99–100 n.14). But this looks miraculous. I can utter the sentence, 'Alice omits from taking a second helping of hors d'oeuvres', without having any idea whether omitting is, in this case, a basic negative action. On Vermazen's view, if omitting is basic in this case, then my sentence expresses a negative existential, but if omitting is non-basic, then, as if by magic, my sentence quantifies over events in which Alice ψ-s, where 'ψ' denotes whatever Alice does in order to prevent herself from eating more hors d'oeuvres. This view ought to be rejected.

---

[18] Clarke (2014: 48–49) seems to be aware of this issue but offers no solution to it.

If you accept Deflationism for sentences describing basic negative actions, you ought to accept it for all negative action sentences. If you accept Deflationism for all negative action sentences, then you ought to deny that 'x's NEG-φ-ing' ever has a referent. Thus, you ought to deny that identity claims of the form 'x's NEG-φ-ing is identical to x's ψ-ing' are ever true, and deny that *any* token negative action is an event. You ought to accept (PNA 3) only if, and because, you accept the stronger (PNA 3*).

2.3.4   Realism About Absences

I've expressed (PNA 3) as the claim that at least some negative actions are not events, but absences thereof. There are two ways to understand talk of absences. To understand it in an ontologically serious way is to think that there really are such things as absences, to be given a place in our ontology alongside ordinary objects, properties, etc. Thus, to claim that negative actions are absences isn't to deny that they exist, but merely to deny that they exist in the same ontological category as positive actions.

By contrast, to understand talk of absences in an ontologically deflationary way is to take it as a useful shorthand: we talk *as if* there are such things as absences, but there really are no such things; to say that there is an absence of *F*s is just to say that *F*s are absent, or that there are no *F*s. Thus, to claim that negative actions are absences isn't to place them in a special ontological category, but to deny that they exist at all. I recommend that the Deflationist take this ontologically deflationary route. Ontological commitment to absences is neither desirable nor necessary.

Taking the first point first, those who take absences ontologically seriously tend to think of them as concrete entities of a certain kind, namely facts or state of affairs: the absence of *F*s (from a certain place and time) is the fact, or state of affairs, of there being no *F*s (at that place and time).[19] Crucially, states of affairs aren't true propositions, but constituents of the world to which true propositions correspond and which serve to make those propositions true. The absence of *F*s is the truthmaker for the proposition *There are no Fs*.

Following Armstrong (1997, 2004), say that a positive state of affairs – i.e. a truthmaker for some positive proposition – consists in some object (or objects) instantiating (or possessing, or exemplifying) some property (or properties) – e.g. if a certain rose is red, then the state of affairs of its being red consists in that rose instantiating the property redness. Given

---

[19] See especially Barker and Jago (2012), Martin (1996), and Thompson (2003).

this view of positive states of affairs, what should we say about negative states of affairs? And what, more specifically, should we say about absences, the alleged truthmakers for negative existentials?

One answer is that, if *a* isn't *F*, then the state of affairs of *a*'s not being *F* consists in *a* instantiating the property *not-F*, or *being non-F* – thus, the rose's not being blue consists in its instantiating *not-blue*, or *being non-blue*. However, if such 'negative' properties are to be constituents of worldly states of affairs, they must be *sparse* properties, and negative properties fail the tests for sparseness discussed in Section 1.3.5. They aren't needed to explain why negative predicates are true of certain objects: we needn't posit a property of *not being blue* to explain why 'The rose isn't blue' is true; the fact that the rose lacks the property *blue* suffices (Armstrong 2004: 55). Nor are they needed to explain the genuine similarity between objects which satisfy the same negative predicate, since such objects needn't be genuinely similar: a red rose and a yellow canary seem to have nothing in common, simply by virtue of not being blue (Armstrong 1989: 83). Finally, they aren't needed to explain why certain objects have – or perhaps lack – certain causal powers. A red rose lacks the power to produce sensations of blueness in ordinary conditions, but we needn't explain this by positing a property *not-blue* which the rose instantiates; we need only say that the rose lacks the property *blue*.

The same point extends to absences. Presumably, if negative states of affairs are exemplifications of negative properties, then the absence of *F*s at spacetime region *r* consists in *r*'s exemplifying the property of containing no *F*s. But there's no obvious need to posit this property in order to explain, e.g. why 'There are no *F*s at *r*' is true. Indeed, even supposing that there is such a property, the purported explanation seems to get things backwards: *r* possesses the property of containing no *F*s *because* there are no *F*s located at *r*, not vice-versa.[20]

---

[20] Armstrong (2004: chs. 5 and 6) defends a slightly different view of negative states of affairs. The truthmaker for '*a* isn't *F*' doesn't contain the negative property of *not being F*. To generate the truthmaker, for '*a* isn't *F*', we first consider all the 'first-order' positive states of affairs of which *a* is the object (i.e. all the truthmakers for positive propositions of the form '*a* is *G*'); we then say that these states of affairs collectively exemplify the property of *totalling* the first-order positive states of affairs of which *a* is the object, where the *X*s total the *Y*s just in case the *X*s are all the *Y*s there are. This 'higher-order' state of affairs is the truthmaker for '*a* isn't *F*'. Likewise, the truthmaker for 'There are no *F*s at *r*' is the state of affairs of some first-order states of affairs *totalling* all the states of affairs of which *r* is the object, where none of these first-order states of affairs consists in an *F* being located at *r*.

Armstrong acknowledges that this solution doesn't avoid negative properties altogether: to say that the *X*s total the *Y*s is just to say that there are no *Y*s other than the *X*s, so *totalling* is a negative property. Thus, the arguments against positing sparse negative properties apply to the relational

On a competing conception of negative states of affairs, if *a* is not *F*, then *a*'s not being *F* consists, not in *a* instantiating the property *not being F* or *being non-F*, but rather in *a*'s not instantiating the property *F*. Departing slightly from Armstrong, Barker and Jago's (2012) claim that objects and properties can be bound together *either* by the relation of instantiation *or* by the relation of non-instantiation. Using their formalism, '[*Fa*]$^+$' denotes the positive state of affairs of *a* instantiating *F*, while '[*Fa*]$^-$' denotes the negative state of affairs of *a* not-instantiating *F*. Thus, we needn't posit such properties as *not-blue*. The rose's not being blue is the rose's not-instantiating blueness, or [*Blue*(rose)]$^-$.

Positing a relation of non-instantiation seems no less odd than positing negative properties. Intuitively, 'The rose isn't blue' is true, not because the rose *possesses* a property, but because it *lacks* one. Similarly, 'The rose is not blue' seems to be true, not because the rose stands in a special relation of non-instantiation to blueness, but because the rose *doesn't* stand in the relation of instantiation to blueness (Clarke 2014: 41).

Kukso (2006) proposes that we add absences to our ontology, but that we don't take them to be states of affairs. Unfortunately, it's not clear what absences *are* in his view. He writes, 'Absences, according to my view, are not objects, things, or states of affairs. An absence, by definition, is not an entity, it is an absence of entity' (2006: 29). To deny that absences are states of affairs is to deny that they belong in a certain ontological category. To deny that they are *things* or *entities* seems to be to deny that they exist at all, and hence to abandon realism about absences.

Kukso suggests that we can have absences in our ontology while denying that they belong in the category of 'thing' or 'entity' – the category which, in my view, encompasses absolutely everything. He writes, 'I propose to treat absence as a basic and irreducible category on par with existence or presence. It is not to be explained or analysed any more than existence is. It is a necessary and analytic truth that an entity is absent just in case it does not exist' (2006: 29). But this explication of the category of absence shows that Kukso has confused absences of things with the things which are said to be absent (recall the discussion of Moore in Section

---

property of *totalling* as well. Armstrong claims only that his solution achieves ontological economy: rather than positing distinct truthmakers for '*a* isn't *F*' and '*a* isn't *G*', containing distinct negative properties, we can posit a single truthmaker for both: the state of affairs of *these* states of affairs – none of which consists in *a* exemplifying either *F* or *G* – being all the first-order states of affairs involving *a* (2004: 58). But we achieve greater ontological economy if, as I argue at the end of this section, we can explain the truth of these sentences without appealing to higher-order states of affairs at all.

2.3.2). Although absent (i.e. non-existent) things don't belong in the category of 'thing' or 'entity', that's because they don't belong in our ontology – *they don't exist.* If absences belong in our ontology, they must be things, or entities.

Ontological commitment to absences is undesirable, because there is – to my knowledge, at least – no satisfying account of what they are like. It would be better not to add them to our ontology if we could get away with it. Fortunately, we *can* get away with it: ontological commitment to absences is unnecessary.

According to the Quinean criterion of ontological commitment defended in Section 1.3.2, it's a sufficient condition for being committed to *F*s that we be committed to engaging in first-order quantification over *F*s. First-order quantification over absences is easily avoided. To say that there is an absence of *F*s is to say that *F*s are absent, or that there are no *F*s. 'There is an absence of *F*s' is a useful shorthand for a *negative existential*: '$\sim\exists x Fx$'. Thus, apparently ontologically serious talk of absences is easily avoided. (I consider a potentially problematic case of absence-talk in Section 6.2.3.)

Believers in absences might appeal to a competing criterion of ontological commitment. According to the Quinean criterion, we're committed to the entities quantified over in (what we take to be) true sentences. According to 'truthmaker theory', by contrast, we're committed to whatever entities are needed to *make* (what we take to be) true sentences true, whether or not those entities are quantified over in those sentences. Thus, even if '$\sim\exists x Fx$' doesn't quantify over absences of *F*s, such things might be required in order to explain why that sentence is true. And, you might think, absences are sometimes needed to explain the truth of '$\sim\exists x Fx$'. For example, you might think that no ordinary object or state of affairs necessitates the truth of 'There are no penguins at the North Pole': it's possible for every object actually located at and around the North Pole to be just as it is, *and* for there to be at least one penguin there. What's needed is an object which exists only if there are no penguins at the North Pole, which is exactly what an absence of penguins from the North Pole is supposed to be.[21]

Truthmaker theory is insufficiently motivated. The fundamental thought behind it is that, if a sentence or proposition is true, there must

---

[21] Demos (1917) argues that for any true proposition of the form '$\sim\exists x Fx$', there exists some ordinary object or positive state of affairs whose existence is incompatible with the existence of *F*s. See Armstrong (2004: 60–63) for criticism, and Cheyne and Pigden (2006) for defense.

be something that *makes* it true (Armstrong 1997: 115). The truthmaker theorist understands 'something', here, as playing the role of a first-order quantifier: if p is true, then there's some *thing*, some *entity*, which makes it true. But we needn't understand it that way. Truthmaking is supposed to be an explanatory relation: truthmakers are said to be the 'ontological grounds' of truths (Armstrong 1997: 155), to 'account for' or be 'responsible for' the truth of sentences and propositions (Mulligan et al. 1984: 59; MacBride 2005: 118), or to be that 'in virtue of which' sentences and propositions are true (Armstrong 2004: 5; Rodriguez-Pereyra 2005: 17). But it's sentences or propositions which play the role of *explanans*, and so we should understand 'something', in 'Something makes sentence S true', as quantifying into the position of a *proposition*: for every true sentence, there must be some p which makes it true, i.e. some proposition which explains why the sentence is true. But now, we can explain why 'There are no penguins at the North Pole' is true, without positing absences: the reason that sentence is true is simply that there are no penguins at the North Pole. Likewise, a Deflationist can say, 'Alice omitted to kiss Beth' is true because there is no event of Alice kissing Beth.[22]

The claim that negative actions are absences of events is best construed in the ontologically deflationary way, rather than the ontologically serious way. Thus, if (PNA 3*) is true – and recall I've argued that you ought to accept (PNA 3) only if, and because, you accept (PNA 3*) – then 'x's NEG-φ-ing' has no referent: there are no such things as token negative actions.

This puts the problem of negative action in sharper relief. The problem isn't just that negative actions seem to belong in a different ontological category than the one which is required by event-based theories of agency. The problem, rather, is that there seem to be no such things at all. When an agent 'performs a negative action', there's no such thing as her token negative action (omission, refrainment, etc.).

2.4   Conclusion

At least one of (PNA 1)–(PNA 3) has to go. Given that the motivations behind (PNA 2) and (PNA 3) are tightly connected, it's perhaps

---

[22] Hornsby (2005) and Melia (2005) develop versions of this approach to truthmaking. Williamson (2013: 391–403) puts the point in terms of quantification into the position of a proposition. For further critical discussion of truthmaker theory, see Lewis (1998, 2001) – although compare Lewis (2003) – and Merricks (2007).

unsurprising that many philosophers reject (PNA 1), denying that cases of negative action are cases of genuine action at all. Of course, if so-called negative actions aren't really actions, their ontological status can hardly pose a problem for event-based theories of action. In Chapter 3, I'll consider the prospects of this position, and whether we might reject (PNA 1) while preserving the intuitions I've used to motivate it.

Mere Manifestations of Agency?

3.1 Introduction

In Chapter 2, I introduced the problem of negative action: in brief, token negative actions seem to be not events, but absences thereof; thus, they seem to be counterexamples to well-developed, event-based theories of action, of the sort sketched in Section 1.2.4. Some defenders of those theories seem to think that the problem can be solved rather simply: they just deny that so-called negative actions aren't really *actions* at all. If that's right, then negative actions can't be counterexamples to event-based theories of action, since they aren't in the purview of those theories to begin with.[1]

Given the similarities between positive and negative actions, sketched in Section 2.3.1, and the seemingly obvious fact that we can exercise our agency by omitting to do things (refraining from doing them, etc.), this looks like a tough bullet to bite. But those who make this move have a way of making it more palatable. 'True', they say, 'we can manifest our agency by omitting to do things, refraining from doing them, etc. But manifesting one's agency isn't the same as *acting* – in these cases, we manifest our agency precisely by *not* acting'. On this view, so-called negative actions aren't actions, but 'mere manifestations of agency' (hereafter, 'MMAs').

However, this claim has its own problems. Those who claim that intentional omissions can be manifestations of agency without being actions typically do so in a few sentences, without elaborating on the difference between actions and MMAs.[2] But some elaboration is required.

Recall, the major task for a theory of action is to explain the difference between cases in which agents act and cases in which they don't. We have a pre-theoretical grasp of which cases fall into which category – e.g. I act

---

[1] See especially Clarke (2010a: 172; 2010b: 161; 2014: 85–86). See also Alvarez (2013: 105–106) and Moore (2010: 34).

[2] See sources cited in note 1.

when I raise my arm in order to hail a cab, but not when my arm rises due to a spasm. These judgments seem to track a distinction between cases in which agents exercise their agency and cases in which they don't: I exercise my agency when I raise my arm, so that is a case of action; I don't exercise my agency when my arm rises due to a spasm, so that isn't a case of action. Pre-theoretically, then, there's no clear difference between acting and manifesting one's agency.

Of course, a defender of the distinction is free to explain what they mean by it, and why what I'm calling 'negative actions' belong in the category of MMAs. But it's worth noting that there's a risk of ad hocery, here. Suppose that a defender of event-based theories of action claims that MMAs are just those manifestations of agency which aren't events, and that since so-called negative actions aren't events, they belong in that category. All she will have done is to stipulate that actions must satisfy one of the criteria given by her metaphysical theory, and that since 'negative actions' don't satisfy that criterion, they aren't actions. That's a quick and easy way to eliminate counterexamples to your theory, but surely we should demand something more by way of independent characterization of the distinction.

In this chapter, I won't consider all the ways in which one might attempt to draw the action/MMA distinction independently of the event/non-event distinction. Rather, having noted the risk of ad hocery, I'll now present two arguments against the distinction, arguments which rely on plausible claims about the connection between token actions and other phenomena. In Section 3.2, I present an argument which concerns the relation between actions and agency, where agency is considered as a power or ability. In Section 3.3, I present an argument which concerns the relation between actions, on the one hand, and practical reasons and practical deliberation, on the other. I don't take either of these to be a knockdown argument. The point is that, if we want to draw the action/MMA distinction, we must apparently reject some *very* plausible claims about how actions relate to these other phenomena. The 'simple solution' to the problem of negative action isn't as simple as it appears.

3.2   Powers, Manifestations, and MMAS

3.2.1   Powers and Manifestations

What does it mean to say that x's NEG-φ-ing is a 'manifestation' of agency? The notion of a 'manifestation' is familiar from philosophical discussions of powers, or dispositional properties. Indeed, the distinction between powers and non-powers (or between dispositional and categorical properties) is plausibly drawn in terms of manifestations:

Power Criterion
F is a power, or dispositional property, iff there's a difference between manifesting F and merely possessing F.[3]

Every power is a power to do something (in certain circumstances); in Molnar's (2003: 60–61) terminology, every power is 'directed' towards a certain behaviour. Because of this, there's a difference between *manifesting* a power and *merely possessing* it: x manifests a power just in case it engages in that behaviour towards which the power is directed; x merely possesses a power just in case it retains the ability to engage in that behaviour, but doesn't actually engage in it. For example, water-solubility is the power to dissolve when placed in the right kind of contact with water. A sugar cube manifests this power only when it's placed in the right kind of contact and dissolves, and its dissolving is a manifestation of that power. A dry sugar cube sitting in a jar, on the other hand, possesses water-solubility without manifesting it.

Compare the property of being six feet tall. *Prima facie*, this property isn't the power to *do* anything (although it may bestow some powers on the things that possess it, e.g. the power to cast a shadow of a certain length in certain lighting conditions). Rather, to possess this property is simply to *be* a certain way. Thus, there's no distinction to be drawn between possessing this property and manifesting it: there's nothing for manifesting this property to consist in, over and above being six feet tall; that is, there's nothing for manifesting this property to be, over and above possessing it.[4]

Under what conditions does x's φ-ing count as the manifestation of a particular power? Letting '$P(c_1 . . . c_n, \psi)$' denote the power to ψ in circumstances $c_1–c_n$,[5] I propose the following:

Manifestation Principle
Necessarily, x's φ-ing is a manifestation of $P(c_1 . . . c_n, \psi)$ iff it is a ψ-ing by x in some c_i among $c_1–c_n$.

That is, a token behaviour is a manifestation of a power just in case it's an instance of the behaviour towards which that power is directed – e.g. the

---

[3] See, e.g. Mumford (1998: 5–6) and Mumford and Anjum (2011: 4–5).
[4] Some metaphysicians argue that *all* properties are powers. However, all we need for my purposes is the conceptual distinction between powers and non-powers; it's okay if the latter class is empty.
[5] This way of denoting powers is a variant on Bird's (2007: 19).

sugar cube's dissolving in water is a manifestation of its water-solubility because that power *just is* the power to dissolve in water.[6]

You might think that the *Manifestation Principle* can't be quite right. Consider the following case, borrowed from Molnar (2003: 195): two horses, 'Lefty' and 'Righty' are moving a barge through a canal by pulling on it from opposite sides at 45° angles; although there's no force being exerted on the barge at a 0° angle, the result of Lefty's and Righty's actions is that the barge moves forward in a straight line. In this case, Lefty exerts a force which, had it not been counteracted by Righty, would have caused the barge to drift to the left side of the canal. But it's plausible that Lefty exerts the exact same force, and hence manifests the exact same causal power, both in the actual case and in the counterfactual scenario where Righty is absent. So, you might think, Lefty manifests the power to move the barge to the left side of the canal in *both* scenarios, even though the barge only moves that way in the counterfactual scenario.

However, we needn't reject the *Manifestation Principle* in order to accommodate the thought that there's a power which Lefty manifests in both scenarios. We may say that the power Lefty exercises in both scenarios is to exert a certain force in a certain direction. The power to move the barge to the left side of the canal is *only* manifested in the counterfactual scenario, since the barge only moves to the left side of the canal in that scenario, while it moves in a straight line in the actual case.[7]

3.2.2 The Simple Argument

We can now argue against the possibility of MMAs as follows:

The Simple Argument Against MMAs
(1) Agency is the power to act.

---

[6] Lowe (2010b: 10) and Molnar (2003: 60) take the *Manifestation Principle* to be definitive of the notion of a 'manifestation'. Note that, while the principle might be more naturally framed in terms of events – i.e. in terms of the conditions under which an *event* is a manifestation of a power – I'm attempting to remain neutral on whether intentional omissions, refrainments, etc. are events.

[7] Alternatively, we might say that the power Lefty exercises in both scenarios is the power to exert a certain force in a certain direction, and deny that there's such a power as 'the power to move the barge to the left side of the canal' to be manifested in the counterfactual scenario. Recall from Section 1.3.5, that realists about properties typically don't take there to be a worldly, 'sparse' property corresponding to every meaningful predicate. Thus, a realist about powers may deny that there's a worldly power corresponding to the predicate, 'able to move the barge to the left side of the canal', and insist that if this predicate is true of Lefty, this is explained entirely in terms of Lefty's possession of *other* powers. (Thanks to an anonymous referee for reminding me of this.)

(2) If agency is the power to act then, necessarily, x's φ-ing is a manifestation of agency only if it's an action.

(3) ∴ Necessarily, x's φ-ing is a manifestation of agency only if it's an action.

The argument is obviously valid. Premise (2) follows from the *Manifestation Principle*. But premise (1) requires some comment.

The *Power Criterion* suggests that agency is a power, since there seems to be a difference between *manifesting* one's agency and merely *possessing* agency: if I'm fast asleep, I don't cease to be an agent, but nothing I do (snore, roll over, kick my wife, etc.) counts as a manifestation of my agency. But why think that agency is the power to *act*?

Agency is that power which distinguishes agents from non-agents; it's that power which all and only agents possess. But then, it must be a power to do something (in some circumstances) that all and only agents can do.[8] The natural candidate for this 'something' is to *act*: *acting* is something that all and only agents can do.

Of course, there might be more than one thing that all and only agents can do. Perhaps the ability to form intentions is both necessary and sufficient for agency, even if forming an intention isn't itself a way of acting. But we can bolster the argument for (2). I've said that agency is that power which distinguishes agents from non-agents. This is so, not just in the sense that it's a power all and only agents possess, but in the sense that agency is that power which we attribute to something in calling it an 'agent'. And it's plausible that to call something an 'agent' is to attribute to it the power to *act*, not any other power. Even if the ability to form intentions is both necessary and sufficient for agency, that isn't an *obvious* fact: you don't betray any misunderstanding of the nature of agency if you suspect that some non-human animals are capable of acting despite lacking such sophisticated mental states as intentions. By contrast, you *do* betray such a misunderstanding if you suspect that some agents are incapable of acting,[9] or that some things which are capable of acting aren't agents.

---

[8] Suppose for *reductio* that agency is the power $P(c_1...c_n, \varphi)$, for some $c_1...c_n$ and φ, and yet it's not the case that all and only agents can φ in $c_1...c_n$. There are two ways for the latter supposition to hold: it might be that some agent lacks the ability to φ in some c_i among $c_1...c_n$; or it might be that some non-agent possesses $P(c_1...c_n, \varphi)$. But both of these cases contradict the assumption that agency just *is* $P(c_1...c_n, \varphi)$.

[9] Of course, an agent might be incapable of acting, in some sense of 'incapable', in some very specific situations – e.g. a person in a deep sleep is incapable of acting in *some* sense. But I take it this isn't the sense which is relevant to the argument.

You might think that (1) is in tension with my discussion of the case of Lefty and Righty. I claimed that while Lefty manifests the power to exert a certain force in a certain direction in both the actual case and the counterfactual scenario in which Righty is absent, he only manifests the power to move the barge to the left side of the canal in the counterfactual scenario. Molnar makes the same claim, and argues on that basis that 'we must distinguish sharply between *effects* and *manifestations*' (Molnar 2003: 195). Molnar accepts the *Manifestation Principle*, and so he thinks that each power is paired with a single manifestation type. However, a power can have many different effects, since what happens is typically the result of many powers working in tandem. Applied to the case at hand, Lefty and Righty each manifests a power to exert a certain force in a certain direction, and the event of their pulling the barge in a straight line is an *effect* of those powers, though it's a manifestation of neither.

Why is this a problem for (1)? Our actions are happenings or occurrences, and so they're no exceptions to the rule that what happens is typically the result of many powers working in tandem. If I walk across the room, this action is the result not just of my agency (in particular, my power to move my legs in a certain way) but of the floor's power to exert a frictional force on me, of Earth's power to exert a gravitational force on me, etc. If we understand the manifestation/effect distinction so that no event is both an effect of some power $P(c_1, \ldots c_n, \varphi)$ and a manifestation of it, then my action can't be the manifestation of any of these powers, and so it can't be a manifestation of my agency.

Fortunately, we needn't understand the distinction in this way. Indeed, we have good reason not to. Since what happens is typically a result of many powers working in tandem, the distinction so understood implies that powers are never, or almost never, manifested. Relatedly, although the distinction is intended to preserve the *Manifestation Principle*, it ends up running counter to it: the sugar cube's dissolving in water is no longer a manifestation of its water-solubility, since it's a result of that power working in tandem with the powers of the water.[10]

Properly understood, the effect/manifestation distinction is simply this: for any power $P(c_1, \ldots c_n, \varphi)$, only φ-ings can be *manifestations* of it; but things which aren't φ-ings can nonetheless be *effects* of that power (together, perhaps, with others). It doesn't follow that φ-ings can't *also* be effects of that power, and so it doesn't follow that no event can be both a manifestation and an effect of one and the same power. Thus, we can

---

[10] For discussion of these and other problems, see McKitrick (2010).

(and should) say that the sugar cube's dissolving in water is both a manifestation and an effect of its water-solubility, and we can (and should) say that my act of walking across the room is both a manifestation and an effect of my agency.

3.2.3   The Less Simple Argument

You might worry that *The Simple Argument* – and in particular, premise (1) – is based on an over-simplified conception of agency. Agents can exercise their agency in a variety of ways. Just considering human agents, we can exercise our agency in a variety of ways: by running, jumping, singing, dancing, etc. The point is even clearer if we consider non-human agents, which can exercise their agency in ways that no human can: by flapping their wings, twitching their tails, squirting ink from their ink-sacks, etc. Thus, you might think, there's no *one* thing that agency is the power to do, and so agency can't be the power to act.

Fortunately, the natural way to accommodate this point affords us an only slightly more complicated version of the argument against MMAs. Call those powers by which human and non-human agents manifest their agency 'agential powers'. Since we have every reason to think that an agent can possess some of these powers without possessing all of them, it's natural to say that to be an agent is to possess some subset of these powers. In short, agency is the higher-level property of possessing some (though not necessarily all) agential powers. We can now argue against MMAs as follows:

The Less Simple Argument Against MMAs
(4) Agency is the higher-level property of possessing at least one agential power.

(5) If (4), then every agential power is the power to act in a certain way.

(6) If (5) then, necessarily, x's φ-ing is a manifestation of an agential power only if it's an action.

(7) ∴ Necessarily, x's φ-ing is a manifestation of an agential power only if it's an action.[11]

Premise (6) follows from the *Manifestation Principle*, so everything hinges on (5). Why think that if being an agent consists in possessing at

---

[11] (7) isn't quite the claim that there are no mere manifestations of *agency*. On the view that agency is a higher-level property, agency isn't a power, and so it has no manifestations. But the notion of a 'mere manifestation of agency' is naturally reconstructed as the notion of a mere manifestation of an agential power. (7) is the claim that such things are impossible.

least one agential power, then every agential power must be the power to act in a certain way? Because, if being an agent consists in possessing at least one agential power, and some agential power, $P(c_1 \ldots c_n, \varphi)$, isn't the power to act in a certain way, then some x could be an agent by virtue of possessing that power, even if it possessed no other agential powers. But then, x would be an agent that was incapable of acting, which is impossible.

You might object to this argument on the ground that agential powers are powers of a special kind: namely, they're 'two-way' powers, where one-way and two-way powers are distinguished as follows:[12]

One-Way and Two-Way Powers

$P(c_1 \ldots c_n, \varphi)$ is a one-way power iff, necessarily, if x possesses $P(c_1 \ldots c_n, \varphi)$ and x is in $c_1 \ldots c_n$, then in the absence of interfering conditions, x φ-s.

$P(c_1 \ldots c_n, \varphi)$ is a two-way power iff, possibly, x possesses $P(c_1 \ldots c_n, \varphi)$ and x is in $c_1 \ldots c_n$, there are no interfering conditions, and yet x doesn't φ.

The idea is that, with perhaps some exceptions, my power to φ is only an *agential* power if the fact that I φ isn't completely determined by facts about my circumstances (including that nothing *prevents* me from φ-ing). It has to be *up to me* whether I φ.[13] Crucially, on this view, x only possesses the two-way power to φ in certain circumstances if x also possesses the two-way power *not* to φ in those circumstances.

How does this help the defender of MMAs? Suppose that the only agential powers whose manifestations aren't actions are powers to engage in negative behaviours, i.e. powers to not-φ, for some choice(s) of 'φ'. If agential powers are two-way, then x only possesses the *agential* power to not-φ if she also possesses the agential power to engage in the corresponding positive behaviour, φ. But then, my argument for (5) is apparently blocked. The only way for x to possess the agential power not to do something (raise one's arm, run, jump, sing, dance, etc.) is to possess the agential power to do that thing, and so, apparently, to possess the power to *act* in a certain way. Thus, we can deny that all agential powers are manifested in actions, without allowing for agents that are completely incapable of acting.

---

[12] Proponents of the distinction between one-way and two-way powers sometimes leave out the 'absence of interfering conditions' clause (Alvarez 2013: 109; Steward 2012a: 155–156). But the possibility of interfering conditions, famously raised by Martin (1994), suggests that *no* power P $(c_1 \ldots c_n \; \varphi)$ is such that, if x possesses that power, then, *necessarily*, x φ-s if placed in $c_1 \ldots c_n$.

[13] See especially Alvarez (2009, 2013). Steward (2012a: 182–184) argues that x is an agent iff x possesses some two-way powers, but denies that all agential powers must be two-way.

This response requires that the two-way power not to φ is an *agential* power. However, as the two-way power view is typically developed, this doesn't seem to be true. Consider the following case. Alice is deciding whether to raise her arm at *t*. Beth has implanted a device in Alice's brain that allows her to monitor Alice's thoughts and, if necessary, interfere with them in order to produce certain events in Alice's body. Beth wants Alice's arm to rise at *t*, so if it looks as though Alice is going to decide not to raise her arm, or as though she simply won't make up her mind in time, Beth will activate the device and cause Alice's arm to rise.[14] In this case, Alice has only one course of action available to her at *t*: the only way she can act at that time is by raising her arm. You might think that, because of this, Alice lacks the two-way power to raise her arm at *t*. But Alice actually *retains* that power. What's required for Alice to possess this power isn't that she be able to *act* in some other way than by raising her arm; all that's required is that she be able to not raise her arm. And Alice retains that ability: if she decides not to raise her arm, or fails to make up her mind, then Beth will interfere to cause Alice's arm to rise; but the event Beth causes will be a *mere* arm-rising, not an arm-raising. Moreover, since it was still up to Alice whether she would *raise* her arm (although not whether her arm would rise), her power not to raise her arm counts as a two-way power (Alvarez 2009: 65).

Now, suppose that Alice simply doesn't make up her mind whether to raise her arm or not, and that Beth activates her device, causing Alice's arm to rise. Alice has manifested her two-way power not to raise her arm since, although her arm *rises*, she doesn't *raise* it. Has she thereby manifested her agency? It seems to me that she hasn't: what's happened is simply that she's failed to make a decision, and Beth has interfered so as to cause a bodily movement that is completely involuntary on Alice's part. She hasn't manifested her agency, any more than she would have if, having failed to make up her mind, her arm had simply risen as the result of an involuntary spasm.

The two-way power not to φ doesn't count as an agential power, simply by virtue of the fact that it comes along with the two-way power to φ and is part of the explanation of why *that* power is agential. To think otherwise is to fail to draw the distinction between those NEG-φ-ings which are exercises of agency and those which are mere negative behaviours. Putting the point more generally, we can't claim that $P(c_1, \ldots, c_n, \varphi)$

---

[14] This is, of course, a variant on the famous case from Frankfurt (1969).

is an agential power simply on the grounds that it comes along with $P(c_1,\ldots,c_n, \psi)$ and is part of the explanation of why *that* power is agential. Thus, the two-way powers view of agency doesn't undermine the original argument for (5).

Summing up this section: if we adopt the *Manifestation Principle*, then neither the simple view of agency as the power to act nor the more complex view of agency as a higher-level property allows clear conceptual space for manifestations of agency that aren't also actions.

3.3   'Mere Intentional Behaviours'

3.3.1   The Very Idea, and an Argument Against

Recall from Section 2.2.3 that, leaving aside the possibility of sub-intentional actions in general, it seems plausible that we only exercise our agency through our negative behaviours when we *intentionally* don't do the relevant thing. I argued there that this seems plausible whether or not we adopt an 'intentionalist' theory of action (e.g. the Event-Causal Theory of Action, or CTA), according to which *what it is* for an agent to act is for her to do something intentionally. However, some proponents of non-intentionalist theories (e.g. the Agent-Causal Theory, or ACT) have suggested that, if we don't equate acting with doing something intentionally, we can allow that so-called negative actions are manifestations of agency without counting them as genuine *actions*. For, it seems, we might be able to intentionally do things, and thereby manifest our agency, without thereby *acting*. So-called negative actions are 'mere intentional behaviours' (Alvarez 2013: 105; Hornsby 2004: 5).

You might think that to deny the equivalence between acting and doing something intentionally (as, e.g. the agent-causalist does) is already to open up conceptual space for mere intentional behaviours and hence MMAs. But this isn't so. Even if we grant that acting and doing something intentionally aren't the very same phenomenon, it might still be that an agent can *only* φ intentionally if she *acts* in φ-ing, i.e. that all token intentional behaviours are actions.

Indeed, we can argue that all token intentional behaviours are actions as follows:

The Argument
(8) x's φ-ing at t is intentional under that description only if the fact that x φ-s at t is subject to rationalizing explanation.

(9) The fact that x φ-s at t is subject to rationalizing explanation only if it's subject to explanation in terms of reasons that (could have) figured in practical deliberation about whether to φ.[15]

(10) The fact that x φ-s at t is subject to explanation in terms of reasons that (could have) figured in practical deliberation about whether to φ only if φ-ing is, for x at t, a way of acting.

(11) ∴ x's φ-ing at t is intentional under that description only if φ-ing is, for x at t, a way of acting.

Premises (8) and (9) are widely accepted claims in the philosophy of action, and are often taken as starting points in theorizing about intentional action (Anscombe 1963: §5; Davidson 1963: 3), but some clarification of the notion of 'rationalizing explanation' is in order. In Section 1.2.4, I characterized it simply as the kind of explanation that an agent herself might give of her intentional behaviours, but there are (at least) two views about how such explanations work. On one view, the reasons that figure in a rationalizing explanation are, at least from the agent's perspective, *normative* reasons: they 'count in favour' of φ-ing, in the sense that x takes them to show φ-ing to be good, rational, or reasonable (Davidson 1963). On a competing view, the reasons that figure in a rationalizing explanation need only be *motivating* reasons; they need only 'count in favour' of φ-ing in the sense that they influence x to φ (Setiya 2007). In what follows, I assume only the latter, weaker view.[16]

The justification for (10) is that practical deliberation is deliberation about how to act. To engage in such deliberation is to deliberate about whether to φ, and what makes x's φ-ing intentional is that x φ-s in response to such deliberation. But it seems that x can only φ on the basis of such deliberation if φ-ing is a course of *action* that's available to her: to do something on the basis of practical deliberation is to *act*. Thus, practical deliberation is about how to act.

The argument for (11) appears sound. But if (11) is true, then all token intentional behaviours are actions. There can be no 'mere intentional behaviours'.

---

[15] The parenthetical 'could have figured' is required to accommodate cases where x apparently φ-s for reasons, but without engaging in explicit deliberation about whether to φ.

[16] You might wonder if 'rationalizing explanation' is an apt label, if this view is correct, since an explanation of x's behaviour in terms of the reasons which motivated her apparently needn't *rationalize* her behaviour in any intuitive sense (Setiya 2010: 100–101). I leave this terminological issue aside.

3.3.2 Negative Action and Rationalizing Explanation

You might object to (9) on the grounds that intentional negative behaviours are *not* subject to rationalizing explanation as ordinary intentional behaviours are. Elaborating on an argument due to Sartorio (2009), you might claim that intentional negative behaviours aren't explained by reasons which (could have) figured in practical deliberation, but by the *absence* of such reasons.

Sartorio argues, in the context of a discussion of CTA, that intentional omissions to φ aren't caused by intentions not to φ, as CTA requires. Consider the following case: a child is drowning in a nearby pond; I could jump in and save him but, after deliberating about it, I decide not to; I remain on the shore, eating ice cream instead. My omission seems intentional. But, Sartorio says, it isn't caused by my intention not to jump in:

> I failed to jump in because of what I omitted to intend to do, not because of what I intended to do. It seems, in fact, irrelevant that I actually formed the opposite intention: all that seems relevant is that I omitted to form the intention to jump in. (2009: 514)

Although she doesn't frame the argument in these terms, it's naturally understood using counterfactuals. It's irrelevant that I intended not to jump into the pond and save the child, because I might still have omitted to do so, even if I hadn't formed that intention: I might have simply failed to make up my mind. But it *is* relevant that I didn't intend to jump into the pond and save the child, because if I *had* formed that intention, I would have jumped in.

While Sartorio is concerned with intentions and causal explanation, her argument can be extended to rationalizing explanation (whether or not we think, with the event-causalist, that rationalizing explanation is a species of causal explanation). Whatever reasons I have for not jumping into the pond (that I want to finish my ice cream, that I don't want to get wet, etc.) are apparently irrelevant to whether I jump in, and hence unable to figure in a rationalizing explanation of my omission. It's irrelevant that I had those reasons, because I might still have omitted to jump into the pond, even if I hadn't had them: if those reasons had been absent, I might simply have failed to make up my mind.

If reasons not to jump into the pond don't explain my omission, what does? You might think that, just as my omission is explained by the *absence* of a certain intention, it's explained by the *absence* of certain reasons,

namely reasons which sufficiently motivate me to jump in. After all, if
I *had* had such reasons, I would have jumped in.[17] Thus, (9) is false: we
can provide a rationalizing explanation of x's φ-ing *either* by pointing to x's
reasons (whether normative or merely motivating) for φ-ing *or* by pointing
to the absence of reasons x had *not* to φ.

This argument fails. I grant that we can explain my omission in
Sartorio's case by pointing to the fact that (as I saw things) I had no
sufficient reason to jump into the pond and save the child. But this fact can
itself serve as a *reason* that (could have) figured in my practical deliberation.

When I deliberate about whether to φ, I'm not restricted to 'lower-level'
reasons, i.e. facts or propositions which count directly for or against φ-ing.
I can also consider 'higher-level' reasons, i.e. reasons which are about my
lower-level reasons. The obvious examples are facts or propositions about
the relative weights of my lower-level reasons. When I deliberate about
whether to φ, I needn't restrict myself to counting up the reasons for and
against φ-ing and taking the course of action that has more reasons in its
favour. I can also compare the relative weights of those reasons – indeed,
this is a good thing to do, since a single sufficiently weighty reason not to φ
can outweigh many less-weighty reasons to φ. Thus, the correct rationalizing explanation of my φ-ing might appeal, not only to my lower-level
reasons for φ-ing, but also to the fact that (as I saw things) the reasons to φ
outweighed the reasons not to φ.[18]

Given this, my rationalizing explanation of my omission in Sartorio's
case can be interpreted as appealing to a higher-level reason for which
I omitted to jump into the pond, namely, that the reasons *not* to jump in
weren't outweighed. If this interpretation is correct, then my omission is
no counterexample to (9).

To see that this interpretation *is* correct, suppose that there's a lifeguard
on duty but that he doesn't notice the child, and so he also omits to jump
into the pond.[19] The lifeguard's omission is unintentional. Yet, if asked,
'Why didn't you jump into the pond?', he can reply 'Because I had no
(sufficient) reason to'. Question: Why is it that, although the lifeguard and

---

[17] This isn't quite Sartorio's own view of why my omission is intentional. See Sartorio (2009: 522–523) for her account, and Clarke (2010a: 167–170; 2010b, 2014: 73–82) and Shepherd (2014b: 17–18) for criticism.

[18] Sartorio (2015: 109–110) argues that an absence of overriding reasons not to φ must always figure in a *causal* explanation of one's intentionally φ-ing. She leaves open whether it must also figure in a *rationalizing* explanation.

[19] Clarke (2010a: 168–169) considers this modification of the case, but doesn't use it to make the point I do.

I can give the same reply, my omission is intentional while his isn't?
Answer: Because the lifeguard's explanation isn't a rationalizing explanation. He's merely pointing to the absence of sufficient reason to jump into
the pond, not providing a reason *for* omitting to jump into the pond.[20] By
contrast, my explanation of my omission *is* a rationalizing explanation: I'm
providing a reason *for* omitting to jump into the pond.

You might suggest that what really explains my omission is not the
presence of a higher-level reason – i.e. the belief that nothing outweighs
my lower-level reasons not to jump into the pond – but the *absence* of
one – i.e. the absence of the belief that something *does* outweigh my lower-
level reasons not to jump into the pond. Certainly, my omission counterfactually depends on this absence; if I'd believed that I had overriding
reason to jump into the pond, I would have. But the same is true of the
lifeguard's omission, and it's unintentional. The difference between the
lifeguard and me is that I omit for a higher-level reason, while he doesn't.

Contrary to what Sartorio's case seems to suggest, intentional omissions,
like ordinary intentional behaviours, are explained by practical reasons, not
by their absence.[21] They aren't counterexamples to (9).

3.3.3   Are Any Non-Actions Responses to Practical Deliberation?

You might object to (10) on the grounds that there are clear cases in which
agents do things for reasons, and hence do them intentionally, without
thereby *acting*. Consider the following case: I'm told that if I sneeze within
the next ten seconds, I'll receive ten dollars; I pick up a nearby pepper
shaker and sniff from it, causing myself to sneeze. Sneezing isn't a way of
acting, but you might think that it's something I did for a reason, namely,
the reason that it'll get me ten dollars.

To see what's wrong with this, notice that my sneeze isn't subject to
rationalizing explanation. The correct answer to the question, 'Why did
you sneeze?' isn't 'Because I wanted the ten dollars', but 'Because I sniffed

---

[20] The lifeguard's response is like the one I would give if asked why I didn't book a flight to Peru this
morning: 'I had no reason to'. This response doesn't show that my omission was intentional.

[21] You might find it psychologically implausible to posit higher-level reasons, of the sort to which I've
appealed, in all cases: 'Do I *always* form judgments about the relative weights of my reasons?' But
my argument doesn't require that agents *always* form such judgments. It only requires that they *can*
do so, and that the presence of such a judgment explains why some omissions are intentional and
others aren't. Moreover, it doesn't require that beliefs about the relative weights of our reasons are
always 'occurrent' beliefs, i.e. beliefs of which we're aware and which are 'present before the mind'
(Audi 1994). Indeed, it's implausible to suppose that the beliefs, desires, and intentions which
explain our behaviour are generally 'occurrent' in this way (Ruben 2003: 115–119).

some pepper', or perhaps 'Because I had pepper in my nose'. These aren't rationalizing explanations. That I sniffed some pepper, or that I had pepper in my nose, aren't considerations that counted in favour of sneezing, even in the non-normative sense; they are facts that figure in a purely *causal* explanation of my sneeze. Neither can I answer the question, 'Why did you sneeze?' by saying, 'Because I wanted the ten dollars'. To give that answer would be to suggest that I sneezed *at will*, which is false: I had to do something else to make myself sneeze.[22] Indeed, on reflection, no rationalizing explanation of my sneeze seems possible. The reason is simple: sneezing isn't something I did *for* any reason at all.

Of course, there's *something* I did for reasons in this case, namely take a whiff of pepper: that I want the ten dollars, and that I'll get them if I sneeze, are reasons to bring it about that I sneeze. This is confirmed by the fact that, although my sneezing isn't subject to rationalizing explanation, my act of taking a whiff of pepper is: I can answer the question, 'Why did you take a whiff of pepper' by saying, 'I wanted to get the ten dollars for sneezing, and I knew that taking a whiff of pepper would cause me to sneeze', thereby giving my reasons for doing what I did.

What's the difference between sneezing and bringing it about that I sneeze? Why can I do the latter for reasons, but not the former? The answer, I suggest, is that the latter is a way of *acting*, while the former isn't. If φ-ing isn't a way of acting, then there's an important sense in which I can't deliberate about whether to φ. I can deliberate about whether to *bring it about* that I φ, but that's different.[23]

Alvarez (2013: 105) provides another potential example of a token behaviour which is a response to reasons, and hence intentional, but not an action. Suppose I'm about to undergo a medical procedure, and the

[22] Relatedly, recall that Clarke (2014: 11) notes that both positive and negative actions can be fulfillments of a command (Section 2.3.1). By contrast, since I can't sneeze at will, or in response to practical reasons, it seems that I can't reasonably be commanded to sneeze, or fulfill such a command by sneezing. I can only reasonably be commanded to *bring it about* that I sneeze, and fulfill such a command by doing *other* things.

[23] This case (and others like it; recall Section 2.2.3) makes trouble for Clarke's account of how omissions can be intentional if they aren't actions. According to Clarke, even if an intention not to φ, or a mental state corresponding to a reason not to φ, can't *cause* an omission to φ – since omissions aren't events – the latter can be a consequence, or result, of the former. For example, if I intend not to raise my arm, that intention can causally affect my subsequent thought and behaviour by closing off the question 'Shall I raise my arm?' from further deliberation. Since my omission results from my subsequent thought and behaviour, Clarke (2010a: 167–172; 2014: 73–85) claims, the omission is rendered intentional. But the case of my sneeze shows that a behaviour of mine can result from an intention (or other mental state), and from subsequent thought and behaviour, without being intentional.

attending nurse administers anaesthetic. To have anaesthetic administered to me is, it seems, not to *act* in any way, but rather to be acted upon. Nonetheless, it seems that I can deliberate about whether to be anaesthetized, and request the anaesthetic in response to this deliberation. So, it seems, I can intentionally have anaesthetic administered, even though having it administered isn't an action. Indeed, we can generalize: it seems that among the things I can do intentionally is *to have such-and-such done to me*, where having something done to me isn't a way of acting.

While I grant that there's a sense in which I can intentionally have something done to me, even when having the relevant thing done isn't a way of acting, this doesn't show that there are intentional behaviours which aren't actions. To see why not, note that sentences of the form '*x* had φ done to *x*' – e.g. the sentences (12)–(14) – are ambiguous.

(12) I had anaesthetic administered.
(13) I had a pizza delivered.
(14) I had my car stolen.

On one reading (call it the 'passive' reading), these sentences merely report the occurrence of an event in which someone, or something, did the relevant thing to me. On the passive reading, (12)–(14) report, respectively: the occurrence of an event in which the doctor or nurse administered anaesthetic; the occurrence of an event in which someone delivered a pizza; and the occurrence of an event in which someone stole my car. On the other reading (call it the 'active' reading), these sentences report that I took steps to ensure that such an event would occur. On the active reading, (12)–(14) report, respectively, that I took steps to ensure that I would be anaesthetized (perhaps by explicitly requesting it); that I took steps to ensure that a pizza would be delivered (most likely by ordering one); and that I took steps to ensure that my car would be stolen (perhaps by hiring someone to do the job).

Given this ambiguity, (15)–(17) are *also* potentially ambiguous between passive and active readings.

(15) I intentionally had anaesthetic administered.
(16) I intentionally had a pizza delivered.
(17) I intentionally had my car stolen.

On the passive reading, '*x* intentionally had φ done to *x*' reports that the event in which someone, or something, did φ to *x* was itself a token intentional behaviour on *x*'s part; on the active reading, it reports, rather, that *x*'s taking steps to ensure that *x* would be φ-ed was intentional. Only if the passive reading is true do we have a clear example of a mere intentional behaviour. But the passive readings of (15)–(17), and of similar sentences, seem to be either false or completely unavailable.

Consider (17). If we interpret the embedded phrase 'I had my car stolen' passively, it would be inappropriate to ask for my reasons for having my car stolen, since the event in which my car is stolen isn't one in which I do anything for any reason. That is, on the passive reading of 'I had my car stolen', my having my car stolen isn't subject to explanation in terms of my reasons for having my car stolen, and so isn't subject to rationalizing explanation in the way that's required for it to be a token intentional behaviour on my part. The passive reading of (17) is either false or unavailable. The idea that my having my car stolen, in this sense, *was* a token intentional behaviour on my part is of questionable coherence.

To get a true reading of (17), we must interpret 'I had my car stolen' actively. On that reading, my having my car stolen (i.e. my taking steps to ensure that it would be stolen) *can* be subject to rationalizing explanation, and so (17) can come out true. But then, we don't have a clear case of a mere intentional behaviour, since the steps I took to ensure that my car would be stolen (e.g. hiring someone to do the job) plausibly *are* actions.

Likewise, returning to Alvarez's example, if we interpret the occurrence of 'I had anaesthetic administered' in (15) passively, my having anaesthetic administered can't be a token intention on my part, since it isn't an event in which I do anything for any reason, and so can't be intentional on my part. The passive reading of (15) is either false or unavailable. To get a true reading of (15), we must interpret 'I had anaesthetic administered' actively. But then, we don't have a clear case of a mere intentional behaviour, since the steps I took to ensure that I would be anaesthetized (e.g. explicitly requesting it) plausibly *are* actions.

I know of no other compelling cases of agents doing things for reasons without acting. Without taking myself to have anticipated all possible objections to *The Argument*, I tentatively conclude that all token intentional behaviours are actions, and so we can't draw the action/MMA distinction by way of the action/mere intentional behaviour distinction.

3.4   Conclusion

If you find it plausible that agency is the power to act (or perhaps the higher-level property of possessing various powers to act in various ways), and that reasons which figure in practical deliberation and rationalizing explanation are reasons to act, then you ought to be skeptical of the action/

MMA distinction, and hence of attempts to solve the problem that negative actions pose by relegating them to the latter category. Again, I don't take myself to have shown that no such solution can be made to work. But in the remainder of this book, I'll develop an alternative, more satisfying solution.

CHAPTER 4

The Logical Form of Negative Action Sentences I
The Case for Deflationism

4.1 Introduction

In the Introduction and in Section 2.3.2, I presented the problem of negative actions as an inconsistent triad:

(PNA 1)   Negative actions – in the sense of things done – are genuine actions; necessarily, if NEG-φ is a negative action for x at t, then if x NEG-φ-s at t, then x acts by NEG-φ-ing at t.

(PNA 2)   Necessarily, if x acts by φ-ing at t, then there exists an event that is x's token φ-ing at t.

(PNA 3)   Possibly, x NEG-φ-s at t, and there exists no event that is x's token NEG-φ-ing at t.

I've just argued that we should be skeptical of solutions which attempt to reject (PNA 1), doing justice to the appearances by claiming that, while so-called negative actions aren't really *actions*, they are 'mere manifestations of agency'. If we don't want to reject (PNA 1), we must reject either (PNA 2) or (PNA 3). My own view is that we should retain (PNA 2) and reject (PNA 3): all token actions are events, including token negative actions.

As we saw in Chapters 1 and 2, both (PNA 2) and (PNA 3) are motivated by considerations from the philosophy of language. Ordinary action sentences are typically analyzed as existential quantifications over events, and this lends some strong support to (PNA 2). However, as I showed in Section 2.3.2, it's commonly assumed that this approach can't be extended to negative action sentences. According to the view I called 'Deflationism', negative action sentences are expressed as negative existentials. This view, if correct, provides strong evidence in favour of (PNA 3). In this chapter, I begin a more detailed assessment of Deflationism's credentials.

I begin in Section 4.2 by providing a more detailed account of the Neo-Davidsonian approach to action sentences and of some popular arguments in its favour. In Section 4.3 I sketch a simple extension of this approach to negative action sentences and compare it to the Deflationist alternative. In Section 4.4 I develop a three-pronged linguistic argument in favour of Deflationism. In Section 4.5 I consider how a proponent of the simple Neo-Davidsonian approach might respond, and argue that the response fails. Thus, a satisfactory Neo-Davidsonian approach to negative action sentences, which will allow us to reject (PNA 3) and retain (PNA 2), must depart from the simple one discussed here. The development of such an approach will be the task of Chapters 5 and 6.

There are two things to note before we continue. First, in this chapter and those that follow, I'll be concerned with *analysis*, not *compositional semantics*. To give an analysis of a sentence is to give an account of its semantic content which assigns to that sentence the correct truth-conditions and explains its inferential relations with other sentences.[1] To give a compositional semantics for a sentence is to explain why it has the content it does by showing how that content is composed out of the denotations of the sentence's constituents. I won't undertake the latter task here. However, nothing I say requires that we depart from standard approaches.[2]

Second, where appropriate, I make use of a denotation function '$[\![\,]\!]_{<w,\,t>}$' which maps a linguistic entity (i.e. a word, phrase, or sentence) to its denotation, which, in the case of a sentence, is its semantic content. Here, '$<\ldots>$' denotes an index, understood as an *n*-tuple of elements or features of concrete conversational contexts which can serve as the referents of certain kinds of terms (most notably 'indexicals' like 'I', 'here', and 'now'), can be shifted by various operators (most notably modal and temporal operators), and with respect to which sentences are evaluated

---

[1] Traditionally, the semantic content of a sentence is identified with what a speaker says when she utters that sentence, or with what that sentence 'literally means', as opposed to, e.g. what that sentence merely implies. While I distinguish the content of a sentence from its presuppositions – where the latter are the propositions which must be part of the conversational common ground, in order for an utterance of the sentence to be appropriate – I don't assume that semantic content is to be identified with what a speaker says. The arguments of this chapter are consistent with views on which the semantic content of a sentence constrains, but doesn't exhaust, what a speaker says when she utters that sentence (Borg 2004, 2012; Recanati 2004, 2010).

[2] See Heim and Kratzer (1998) for an introduction to compositional semantics in the tradition of Frege, and Bayer (1997) for a detailed discussion of compositional semantics in the context of Neo-Davidsonian analyses.

for truth or falsity.[3] It's a controversial matter just what features of a conversational context can be built into an index. Typically, an index is thought to include a designated possible world, a designated time (the referent of 'now'), a designated speaker (the referent of 'I'), and a designated spatial location (the referent of 'here'), although it may include more.[4] For the purposes of this chapter, I'll assume indexes that contain only worlds and times.

For the sake of thoroughness, I use this denotation function, $\llbracket \rrbracket_{<w,\ t>}$, when providing general schemata for the analysis of action sentences: schematic analyses make reference to worlds and times with respect to which sentences are evaluated. However, for the sake of readability, I drop such references when providing analyses of specific sentences, leaving the fact that sentences are evaluated with respect to worlds and times implicit.

4.2   The Neo-Davidsonian Approach to Action Sentences

4.2.1   The Traditional Approach and the Neo-Davidsonian Approach

Consider the following sentences:

(1) Alice ran.
(2) Alice kissed Beth.

You might think that (1) and (2) have subject-predicate and relational form, respectively. That is, you might analyze (1) as having the form 'Fa' and (2) as having the form 'Fab':

(1_T) Run(Alice)
(2_T) $Kiss$(Alice)(Beth)

Call this 'the traditional approach' to action sentences (hence the subscripted 'T's).

Davidson (1967a) argues that these simple analyses are incorrect. According to him, each of (1) and (2) contains a variable that isn't evident from its surface form, a variable that takes events as arguments and which

---

[3] Indexes, in this sense, are like Kaplan's (1989) 'contexts'. For further discussion, see Lewis (1980), MacFarlane (2014: ch. 3), and Stalnaker (2014: ch. 1). Readers familiar with this literature will notice that, in this chapter and the next two, I don't distinguish the *content* of a sentence from its *character*, a distinction which is naturally drawn once indexes are brought into the picture. For the purpose of these chapters, this is a harmless simplification. However, the distinction will be important in Section 8.5.

[4] See Section 8.5.

is bound by an existential quantifier. Thus, 'Alice ran' doesn't simply apply a predicate to Alice; rather, it reports the occurrence of an event, an event which is a run by Alice. Likewise, 'Alice kissed Beth' doesn't simply apply a relational predicate to Alice and Beth; rather, it reports the occurrence of an event, an event which is a kiss of Beth by Alice.[5]

Davidson's original proposal is that the postulated event variables should simply be treated as extra arguments of the predicates '*Run*' and '*Kiss*'. Thus, instead of (1_T) and (2_T), we have (1_D) and (2_D):

(1_D) $\exists e(Run_D(\text{Alice})(e))$
(2_D) $\exists e(Kiss_D(\text{Alice})(\text{Beth})(e))$

In English: there is some e such that e is a run by Alice; and there is some e such that e is a kiss of Beth by Alice. The subscripted 'D's, here, are for 'Davidsonian'. That the predicates 'Run_D' and '$Kiss_D$' are themselves subscripted marks that these predicates are understood differently than on the traditional approach.

Castañeda (1967) argues that our analyses of (1) and (2) should depart even further from (1_T) and (2_T). '*Run*' shouldn't take *both* Alice *and* an event as arguments; rather, it should take *only* an event as argument. That Alice is the one doing the running should be represented using a distinct predicate that explicitly encodes this information. Likewise, '*Kiss*' shouldn't take Alice and Beth as arguments, in addition to an event; rather, it should take *only* an event as argument. That Alice is the one doing the kissing, and that Beth is the one being kissed, should be represented using distinct predicates that explicitly encode this information.

This is the root idea behind the 'Neo-Davidsonian' approach.[6] Roughly, the idea is that there is a finite number of ways in which objects can participate in events – dubbed 'thematic roles' – each of which is encoded by a predicate at the level of logical form. For instance, one way to participate in an event is to be the doer of whatever thing that event is a doing of. To participate in an event in this way is to be the 'agent' of that event – the agent of a run is the runner, the agent of a kiss is the kisser, etc. That x is the agent of e is represented by the string, '$Agent(x)(e)$'. Another way to participate in an event is to be not the doer of the relevant thing,

---

[5] Davidson seems to have been anticipated by Ramsey, who writes, "'That Caesar died" is really an existential proposition, asserting the existence of an event of a certain sort' (1927: 156). However, Davidson (1967a) contains the canonical argument for, and development of, the approach.

[6] For detailed development see, e.g. Landman (2000) and Parsons (1990). For criticism, see Bayer (1997).

but the entity which has that thing done to it. To participate in an event in this way is to be the 'patient' of that event – e.g. the patient of a kiss is the thing kissed. That x is the patient of e is represented by the string, '*Patient* $(x)(e)$'.

On the Neo-Davidsonian approach, (1) and (2) are analyzed as follows:

(1_{ND}) $\exists e(Agent(\text{Alice})(e)\ \&\ Run_{\mathrm{ND}}(e))$
(2_{ND}) $\exists e(Agent(\text{Alice})(e)\ \&\ Patient(\text{Beth})(e)\ \&\ Kiss_{\mathrm{ND}}(e))$

The subscripted 'ND's are for – you guessed it – 'Neo-Davidsonian'. The predicates 'Run_{ND}' and '$Kiss_{\mathrm{ND}}$' roughly correspond to what I called 'event sortals' in Section 1.2.2: '$Run_{\mathrm{ND}}(e)$' says that e is a run in w at t, while '$Kiss_{\mathrm{ND}}(e)(w)(t)$' says that e is a kiss in w at t. This approach has become standard, among those who accept that action sentences contain implicit event variables. In what follows, I'll assume the Neo-Davidsonian approach, rather than the original Davidsonian one.[7]

4.2.2   Adverbs

The most well-known arguments for adopting the Neo-Davidsonian approach to action sentences appeal to the behaviour of adverbs. Davidson's own argument appeals to adverb-dropping inferences, i.e. inferences of the form

x φ-s F-ly; so, x φ-s

In some cases – although perhaps not all – such inferences are valid, and an account of the logical forms of the sentences involved ought to explain this. Davidson argues that we can give such an explanation if we treat both 'x φ-s' and 'x φ-s F-ly' as existential quantifications over events, and treat the adverb 'F-ly' as contributing a predicate that applies to the event-variable: the move from 'x φ-s F-ly' to 'x φ-s' is then validated by the rule $\exists x(Fx\ \&\ Gx) \vdash \exists xFx$. Others – e.g. Parsons (1990: 12–15) and Landman (2000: 2–15) – have expanded Davidson's argument by considering adverb-*adding* inferences, i.e. inferences of the form:

x φ-s; so, x φ-s F-ly

In some cases – although perhaps not all – such inferences are *in*valid, and an account of the logical forms of the sentences involved ought to explain this. If we treat both 'x φ-s' and 'x φ-s F-ly' as existential quantifications

---

[7] I owe my usage of the subscripts 'D' and 'ND' to Bayer (1997).

over events, and treat the adverb 'F-ly' as contributing a predicate that applies to the event-variable, we can give such an explanation: the move from 'x φ-s F-ly' to 'x φ-s' is then invalidated by the fact that $\exists x Fx \nvDash \exists x(Fx \,\&\, Gx)$.

These arguments don't straightforwardly apply to adverbs of all kinds.[8] Taylor (1985: 20–23) distinguishes what he calls 'sentence adverbs', 'phrase adverbs', and 'mode adverbs'. Only mode adverbs truly apply to, or modify, verbs. Sentence adverbs modify whole sentences – as in 'Fortunately, Alice kissed Beth', which says it is fortunate that Alice kissed Beth – while phrase adverbs modify the subjects of verbs – as in 'Alice bravely kissed Beth', which says that it was brave of Alice to kiss Beth. Ludwig (2010: 40) subdivides mode adverbs into the following categories (although there may be more): manner adverbs ('quickly', 'slowly', 'carefully'); locative adverbs ('in the dining room', 'under the table', 'here'); temporal adverbs ('at midnight', 'this morning', 'now'); frequency adverbs ('often', 'rarely', 'once', 'twice'); and degree adverbs ('very', 'hard'). I'll focus on the first two categories, and won't discuss the others in detail.

Consider the following sentences:[9]

(3) Alice kissed Beth quickly in the kitchen.
(4) Alice kissed Beth quickly.
(5) Alice kissed Beth in the kitchen.
(6) Alice kissed Beth.

(3) entails both (4) and (5): if Alice kissed Beth *both* quickly *and* in the kitchen, then it follows that she kissed Beth quickly, and it follows that she kissed Beth in the kitchen. Likewise, each of (4) and (5) entails (6) – and so, by transitivity, (3) entails (6), too: if Alice kissed Beth quickly, or if she kissed Beth in the kitchen, then it follows that she kissed Beth. To infer (4) or (5) from (3), or to infer (6) from any of (3)–(5), is to draw an adverb-dropping inference. Thus, with respect to these sentences, adverb-dropping inferences are valid. But the inverse, adverb-adding inferences are invalid. Neither (4) nor (5), on its own, entails (3), although they do entail it together: Alice might have kissed Beth quickly in the dining room but not in the kitchen, in which case (4) is true but (3) is false; and Alice might have kissed Beth in the kitchen, but done so slowly rather than quickly, in which case (5) is true but (3) is false. Likewise, (6) entails none

---

[8] Here, I'm indebted to Ruben's (2013) presentation of the Neo-Davidsonian approach.
[9] (6) is (2), renumbered here to improve readability.

of (3)–(5): Alice might have kissed Beth without kissing her quickly or kissing her in the kitchen.

The Neo-Davidsonian approach to action sentences explains these facts. On this approach, (3)–(6) are analyzed as follows:

(3_{ND}) $\exists e(Agent(Alice)(e)$ & $Patient(Beth)(e)$ & $Kiss_{ND}(e)$ & $Quick(e)$ & $At_L(e)(kitchen))$

(4_{ND}) $\exists e(Agent(Alice)(e)$ & $Patient(Beth)(e)$ & $Kiss_{ND}(e)$ & $Quick(e))$

(5_{ND}) $\exists e(Agent(Alice)(e)$ & $Patient(Beth)(e)$ & $Kiss_{ND}(e)$ & $At_L(e)$ $(kitchen))$

(6_{ND}) $\exists e(Agent(Alice)(e)$ & $Patient(Beth)(e)$ & $Kiss_{ND}(e))$

Here, '$Quick$' is a predicate of events, and '$Quick(e)$' says that e is quick. 'At_L' is a relational predicate of events and regions, and '$At_L(e)(r)$' says that e is located at, or occurs at, r.[10] On these analyses, the adverb-dropping inferences are validated by the rule, $\exists x(Fx$ & $Gx) \vdash \exists xFx$, while the adverb-adding inferences are blocked by the fact that $\exists xFx \nvdash \exists x(Fx$ & $Gx)$, as desired.

I should note that the treatment of 'quickly' assumed here is too simple, since it suggests that an event can be classified as 'quick' independently of any particular standard of quickness, which is false. 'Quickly' is a scalar adverb: to say that x φ-s quickly is to say that x's φ-ing meets a certain threshold for quickness. And there's no single threshold which is operative in all conversational contexts. I sketch a more sophisticated approach to 'quickly' and other scalar adverbs in Section 8.5, but the details don't affect the present point about adverb-dropping and adverb-adding inferences.

The validity of adverb-dropping inferences and the invalidity of corresponding adverb-adding inferences provide strong evidence that ordinary action sentences are to be analyzed as expressing existential quantifications over events, and that at least some adverbs are to be treated as contributing predicates of events. Schematically:

Neo-Davidsonian Schemata (Positive Action Sentences)

$[\![x \; \varphi]\!]_{<w, \, t>}$ $= \exists e(Agent(x)(e)(w)(t)$ & $\varphi_{ND}(e)(w)(t))$

$[\![x \; \varphi \; F\text{-ly}]\!]_{<w, \, t>} = \exists e(Agent(x)(e)(w)(t)$ & $\varphi_{ND}(e)(w)(t)$ & $F(e)(w)(t))$

Note that, although the sentences to which these schemata apply are often referred to in the literature as 'action sentences', these sentences needn't

---

[10] To say that an event e occurs at a certain region r isn't to say that it's *exactly* located there, in the sense that all of e is located in r and none of e is located outside r. 'Alice kissed Beth in the kitchen' can be true even if there are subregions of the kitchen in which the kiss isn't located. More likely, '$At_L(e)(r)$' corresponds to Parsons' (2007) notion of 'weak location': e is located at r just in case r isn't entirely free of e.

describe 'actions' in the restricted sense I attempted to articulate in Section
1.2. Sentences which report mere behaviour (e.g. 'Alice's arm rose') have
been argued to have the same logical form, and for the same reasons (e.g.
'Alice's arm rose quickly' entails 'Alice's arm rose', but not vice-versa).

4.3   Negative Action Sentences: Deflationism and the Simple Neo-Davidsonian Approach

So far, I've only been concerned with positive action sentences, i.e.
sentences which report that agents perform positive actions. How might
we extend the Neo-Davidsonian approach to negative action sentences?
The simplest suggestion is that a negative verb phrase 'NEG-φ' contributes
a predicate of events, '*NEG*-φ_{ND}', and that negative action sentences
express existential quantifications over events satisfying this predicate.
Schematically, bare negative action sentences – i.e. those which aren't
adverbially modified – have the following form:

$$\exists e(Agent(x)(e)(w)(t) \ \& \ NEG\text{-}\varphi_{ND}(e)(w)(t))$$

Notice that, on this approach, there is a single predicate, '*NEG*-φ_{ND}',
which is contributed by all ordinary English negative verb phrases ('omit to
φ', 'refrain from φ-ing', etc.). You might wonder why we shouldn't
suppose instead that each negative verb phrase contributes a distinct
predicate. I assume the approach I do because we can account for the
differences in meaning between, e.g. omission sentences and refrainment
sentences without introducing distinct predicates, '*Omit*-φ_{ND}' and
'*Refrain*-φ_{ND}' (see Sections 4.5.2 and 4.5.3).

Standing in opposition to the simple Neo-Davidsonian approach is the
Deflationist one sketched in Section 2.3.2. On that approach, negative
action sentences don't express existential quantifications over events.
Rather, they express negative existentials. Schematically, bare negative
action sentences have the following form:

$$\sim\exists e(Agent(x)(e)(w)(t) \ \& \ \varphi_{ND}(e)(w)(t))$$

Before presenting the simple Neo-Davidsonian and Deflationist schemata
for negative action sentences in full, I should note a potential ambiguity in
the interpretation of adverbially modified negative action sentences.
A complex negative verb phrase – 'omit to φ', 'refrain from φ-ing', etc. –
is a compound of a negative verb – 'omit', 'refrain', etc. – and another verb
phrase, not necessarily negative – 'φ'. Thus, when an adverb appears in a
negative action sentence, we can potentially interpret it *either* as modifying

the entire complex negative verb phrase *or* as modifying only the embedded verb phrase, 'φ'. On the former reading, the adverb modifies what the agent *does* – omit to φ, refrain from φ-ing, etc. That is, the sentence says that what x does F-ly is omit to φ (refrain from φ-ing, etc.). Call this the 'narrow-scope' reading. On this reading, 'NEG' takes scope only over 'φ', not over 'φ F-ly'. On the latter reading, the adverb modifies what the agent *doesn't* do – φ. That is, the sentence says that what x omits to do (refrains from doing, etc.) is to φ F-ly. Call this the 'wide-scope' reading. On this reading, 'NEG' takes scope over 'φ F-ly', not just 'φ'.

With this distinction in mind, consider how adverbially-modified negative action sentences like (7)–(9) must look, on the simple Neo-Davidsonian approach.

(7) Alice omitted to kiss Beth quickly in the kitchen.
(8) Alice omitted to kiss Beth quickly.
(9) Alice omitted to kiss Beth in the kitchen.

On this approach, a negative verb 'NEG' and a verb phrase 'φ' work together to contribute a single event variable, which is the argument of the predicate '$NEG\text{-}φ_{ND}$'. In the analysis of 'x NEG-φ F-ly', then, the event variable that serves as the argument of 'F' is a variable for NEG-φ-ing events – omissions to φ, refrainments from φ-ing, etc. Now, from a general Neo-Davidsonian perspective, a mode adverb 'F-ly' modifies a verb 'φ' by contributing a predicate which applies to a variable for φ-ing events. Thus, if, in 'x NEG-φ F-ly', 'F-ly' contributes a predicate which applies to a variable for NEG-φ-ing events, rather than to a variable for φ-ing events, then it seems that 'F-ly' modifies what x does, not what she doesn't do. In other words, this approach apparently captures the narrow-scope reading of 'x NEG-φ F-ly' but not the wide-scope reading:

Simple Neo-Davidsonian Schemata (Negative Action Sentences)

$[\![x\ \text{NEG-}φ]\!]_{<w,\ t>}$ $= \exists e(Agent(x)(e)(w)(t)\ \&\ NEG\text{-}φ_{ND}(e)(w)(t))$

$[\![x\ \text{NEG-}(φ)\ \text{F-ly}]\!]_{<w,\ t>} = \exists e(Agent(x)(e)(w)(t)\ \&\ NEG\text{-}φ_{ND}(e)(w)(t)\ \&\ F(e)(w)(t))$

$[\![x\ \text{NEG-}(φ\ \text{F-ly})]\!]_{<w,\ t>} = \ ???$

Here, the brackets in the sentence form being analyzed indicate the scope of 'NEG': 'x NEG-(φ) F-ly' is the narrow-scope reading, on which 'NEG' takes scope only over 'φ', and 'F-ly' takes scope over 'NEG'; 'x NEG-(φ F-ly)' is the wide-scope reading, on which 'NEG' takes scope over 'F-ly'.

Compare the Deflationist approach. On that approach, a negative action sentence, whether adverbially modified or not, contains no variable for negative actions. The only event variable to occur in the analysis of a bare negative action sentence, 'x NEG-φ', is a variable for φ-ing events, the kind of event that is said *not* to occur. This suggests that, on the Deflationist approach to 'x NEG-φ F-ly', 'F-ly' modifies what x doesn't do. In other words, this approach captures the wide-scope reading of 'x NEG-φ F-ly' (although apparently not the narrow-scope reading):

Deflationist Schemata (Negative Action Sentences)

$[\![x\ \text{NEG-}\varphi]\!]_{<w,\ t>}$ $= \neg\exists e(Agent(x)(e)(w)(t)\ \&\ \varphi_{ND}(e)(w)(t))$

$[\![x\ \text{NEG-}(\varphi)\ \text{F-ly}]\!]_{<w,\ t>} = ???$

$[\![x\ \text{NEG-}(\varphi\ \text{F-ly})]\!]_{<w,\ t>} = \neg\exists e(Agent(x)(e)(w)(t)\ \&\ \varphi_{ND}(e)(w)(t)\ \&\ F(e)(w)(t))$

This difference already raises a worry about the simple Neo-Davidsonian approach. In many cases, the most natural readings of adverbially-modified negative action sentences are the wide-scope readings that the approach apparently fails to capture. Consider (9). To my mind, the most natural reading of (9) is the wide-scope one on which the adverb 'in the kitchen' modifies what Alice *doesn't* do, not what she does. In Section 2.2.2, I argued that omission sentences presuppose that the agent is supposed to do the relevant thing. On the narrow-scope reading of (9), on which 'omitted' takes scope only over the unmodified 'kiss Beth', (9) only presupposes that Alice was supposed to kiss Beth (at the relevant time); it doesn't presuppose that she was supposed to do it any particular location. By contrast, on the wide-scope reading, on which 'omitted' takes scope over 'kiss Beth quickly in the kitchen', (9) presupposes that Alice was supposed to kiss Beth *in the kitchen* (at the relevant time). The latter reading seems more natural: if Alice kissed Beth, but not in the kitchen, then she fails to live up to the demands that (9) presupposes, and so (9) comes out true. But the simple Neo-Davidsonian can't capture this reading.

Of course, the Deflationist faces a similar worry, since her approach apparently fails to capture the narrow-scope reading of 'x NEG-φ F-ly'. However, the Deflationist seems to have room to manoeuvre here. In many cases – and especially in cases where the relevant adverb is a manner adverb – the narrow-scope reading seems, not only unnatural, but entirely unavailable. Consider (8). As noted in Section 4.2.2, 'quickly' is a scalar adverb: to say that x φ-s quickly is to say that x's φ-ing meets a certain threshold for quickness. Leaving aside the question of how such thresholds get put in place in a conversational context, it's not clear that such thresholds even *exist* where negative verb phrases are concerned. 'Alice kissed Beth quickly' is easy to interpret, since we have at least a rough idea of how quick a kiss needs to be, to count as quick. 'Alice omitted to kiss Beth quickly' is far more difficult to interpret, if we attempt a narrow-scope reading – what does it even mean for an *omission* to kiss someone to be quick? The same holds for other manner adverbs, like 'slowly' and 'carefully'.

This argument doesn't easily extend to other kinds of adverbs. Consider (9) again. I argued that the most natural reading of (9) is the wide-scope one, but the narrow-scope reading does at least seem to be available. That is, there seems to be a reading on which (9) says that what Alice did in the kitchen was omit to kiss Beth. However, the Deflationist might account for this by denying that 'in the kitchen', as it occurs in (9), is a *mode* adverb at all. She might insist that, as it occurs in (9), 'in the kitchen' functions as a *phrase* adverb: like 'bravely', it modifies, not Alice's behaviour, but Alice herself.[11]

Thus, the Deflationist might deny that narrow-scope readings for certain adverbially-modified negative action sentences even exist. And where they do exist, she might attempt to account for them in ways which don't require them to modify negative actions, considered as token events. I'll return to the issue of how the Deflationist might account for, or deny the existence of, the narrow-scope reading of 'x NEG-φ F-ly' in Section 6.3.

We've seen that, because it can only treat 'F-ly' as contributing a predicate of token negative actions in adverbially-modified negative action sentences, the simple Neo-Davidsonian approach arguably fails to capture the wide-scope readings of those sentences. Its treatment of adverbs also generates further problems. The most well-known arguments for adopting the Neo-Davidsonian approach to positive action sentences – surveyed in Section 4.2.2 – draw on facts about the inferential behaviour of adverbs in those sentences. But, as we'll now see, the inferential behaviour of adverbs in negative action sentences (on their natural, wide-scope readings) counts against the simple Neo-Davidsonian schemata, and in favour of the Deflationist alternatives.

---

[11] There's a precedent for this move. 'Intentionally' seems capable of taking scope over a complex negative action phrase: 'Alice intentionally omitted to kiss Beth' says that what Alice did intentionally is omit to kiss Beth. Davidson (1985a: 219) accounts for this by denying that 'intentionally' functions in this sentence as a mode adverb contributing a predicate which applies to a variable for negative actions. On his account, 'intentionally' functions in this sentence as a phrase adverb: the sentence says that it is 'intentional of Alice', or that it is 'intentional on her part', that she omitted to kiss Beth. I discuss this view in Section 6.3.2.

4.4   Three Problems with Adverbs

4.4.1   The Problem of Adverb-Dropping Inferences

Consider the following sets of sentences:

(7) Alice omitted to kiss Beth quickly in the kitchen.
(8) Alice omitted to kiss Beth quickly.
(9) Alice omitted to kiss Beth in the kitchen.
(10) Alice omitted to kiss Beth.

(11) Alice refrained from kissing Beth quickly in the kitchen.
(12) Alice refrained from kissing Beth quickly.
(13) Alice refrained from kissing Beth in the kitchen.
(14) Alice refrained from kissing Beth.

To infer either (8) or (9) from (7), or to infer (10) from any of these, is to draw an adverb-dropping inference. Likewise, *mutatis mutandis*, for (11)–(14). Davidson's argument for thinking that positive action sentences express existential quantifications over events is that this approach explains why, with respect to those sentences, certain adverb-dropping inferences are valid. But, on the natural readings of (7)–(14), the corresponding adverb-dropping inferences appear to be *in*valid.

Suppose that (7) is true, that is, that Alice omitted to kiss Beth quickly in the kitchen. It doesn't follow that (8) is true, since Alice might have kissed Beth quickly, even if she didn't do it in the kitchen. Nor does it follow that (9) is true, since Alice might have kissed Beth in the kitchen, even if she didn't do it quickly. Nor, finally, does it follow that (10) is true, since Alice might have kissed Beth, even if she did it neither quickly nor in the kitchen. So, (7) entails none of (8)–(10). For similar reasons, neither (8) nor (9) entails (10). The same argument applies, *mutatis mutandis*, to (11)–(14): (11) entails neither (12) nor (13), and none of these entails (14).

This is bad news for the simple Neo-Davidsonian schemata given in Section 4.3. According to those schemata, a bare negative action sentence – i.e. one which isn't adverbially modified – contains a single event variable, to which '*NEG*-φ_{ND}' is applied, and which is bound by '∃'. Since adverbs contribute predicates of events, adverbially modified negative action sentences are analyzed so that the contributed predicates are applied to this lone event variable. Thus, just as with positive action sentences, adverb-dropping inferences are validated by the rule, $\exists x(Fx \mathrel{\&} Gx) \vdash \exists x Fx$.

More concretely, if we follow the simple Neo-Davidsonian schemata, then (7)–(10) can only be analyzed as (7_{ND})–(10_{ND}):

(7_{ND}) $\exists e(Agent(\text{Alice})(e)$ & $Patient(\text{Beth})(e)$ & $NEG\text{-}Kiss_{ND}(e)$ & $Quick$ (e) & $At_L(e)(\text{kitchen}))$

(8_{ND}) $\exists e(Agent(\text{Alice})(e)$ & $Patient(\text{Beth})(e)$ & $NEG\text{-}Kiss_{ND}(e)$ & $Quick$ $(e))$

(9_{ND}) $\exists e(Agent(\text{Alice})(e)$ & $Patient(\text{Beth})(e)$ & $NEG\text{-}Kiss_{ND}(e)$ & $At_L(e)$ $(\text{kitchen}))$

(10_{ND}) $\exists e(Agent(\text{Alice})(e)$ & $Patient(\text{Beth})(e)$ & $NEG\text{-}Kiss_{ND}(e))$

These analyses validate our intuitively invalid adverb-dropping inferences: (7_{ND}) entails each of (8_{ND}) and (9_{ND}), and each of (7_{ND})–(9_{ND}) entails (10_{ND}). The same argument applies, *mutatis mutandis*, to (11)–(14).

Compare Deflationism. According to the Deflationist schemata from Section 4.3, a bare negative action sentence – i.e. one which isn't adverbially modified – contains a single event variable, to which 'φ_{ND}' is applied. This variable is bound by an occurrence of '$\exists$' which is itself in the scope of an occurrence of '$\sim$'. Since adverbs contribute predicates of events, adverbially modified negative action sentences are analyzed so that the contributed predicates are applied to this lone event variable. Thus, adverb-dropping inferences are invalidated by the fact that $\sim\exists x(Fx$ & $Gx) \nVdash \sim\exists x Fx$.

More concretely, if we follow the Deflationist schemata, then (7)–(10) are analyzed as (7_{DEF})–(10_{DEF}):

(7_{DEF}) $\sim\exists e(Agent(\text{Alice})(e)$ & $Patient(\text{Beth})(e)$ & $Kiss_{ND}(e)$ & $Quick(e)$ & $At_L(e)(\text{kitchen}))$

(8_{DEF}) $\sim\exists e(Agent(\text{Alice})(e)$ & $Patient(\text{Beth})(e)$ & $Kiss_{ND}(e)$ & $Quick(e))$

(9_{DEF}) $\sim\exists e(Agent(\text{Alice})(e)$ & $Patient(\text{Beth})(e)$ & $Kiss_{ND}(e)$ & $At_L(e)$ $(\text{kitchen}))$

(10_{DEF}) $\sim\exists e(Agent(\text{Alice})(e)$ & $Patient(\text{Beth})(e)$ & $Kiss_{ND}(e))$

These analyses block our intuitively invalid adverb-dropping inferences: (7_{ND}) entails neither (8_{ND}) nor (9_{ND}), and none of (7_{ND})–(9_{ND}) entails (10_{ND}). The same argument applies, *mutatis mutandis*, to (11)–(14).

Deflationism doesn't merely allow us to block these intuitively bad inferences. It also seems to capture our intuitive sense of *why* they're bad. Recall, from the fact that Alice omitted to kiss Beth quickly in the kitchen, it doesn't follow that she omitted to kiss Beth quickly, since she might have kissed Beth quickly even if she didn't do it in the kitchen. Cast in event terms: from the fact that there is no event of Alice kissing Beth *both* quickly *and* in the kitchen, it doesn't follow that there is no event of

Alice kissing Beth *quickly*, since there might be such an event even if it doesn't occur in the kitchen. This is just an application of '$\sim\exists x(Fx \,\&\, Gx)$ $\nvdash \sim\exists xFx$'.

The root of the problem of adverb-dropping inferences, of course, is the different treatments given to adverbs in the simple Neo-Davidsonian and Deflationist schemata. I said that, on the most natural readings of (7)–(14), adverb-dropping inferences are invalid. That's because the most natural readings are the wide-scope readings, on which the adverbs modify what Alice *doesn't* do, not what she *does*, and, in general, that x doesn't do something in a particular way doesn't entail that x doesn't do that thing *simpliciter*. The Deflationist schemata capture these readings nicely and, as we've just seen, do so in a way which reflects the fact that, on these readings of adverbially modified negative actions sentences, adverb dropping inferences are invalid. By contrast, the Neo-Davidsonian schemata arguably only capture the narrow-scope readings of (7)–(14), on which the adverbs modify what Alice *does*, not what she *doesn't* do. But, in general, that x does something in a particular way entails that x does that thing *simpliciter*.[12]

Thus, while adverb-dropping inferences provide strong evidence in favour of a Neo-Davidsonian approach to ordinary action sentences, they seem to provide strong evidence in favour of a Deflationist approach to negative action sentences.

4.4.2 The Problem of Adverb-Adding Inferences

In Section 4.2.2, we saw that taking a Neo-Davidsonian approach to ordinary action sentences allows us to explain why, with respect to those sentences, certain adverb-adding inferences are invalid. On the natural, wide-scope readings of negative action sentences like (7)–(14), however, the corresponding adverb-adding inferences appear to be *valid*.

Suppose that (10) is true, that is, that Alice omitted to kiss Beth *simpliciter*. It seems to follow that (8) is true, since if Alice didn't kiss

---

[12] There are two further problems with the proposal that (7)–(10) be analyzed as (7_{ND})–(10_{ND}), which I won't consider in detail here. First, each of (7_{ND})–(10_{ND}) requires that there exists some event of which Alice is the agent and Beth is the patient. That is, each requires that Alice did something to Beth $((7_{ND})$ and $(9_{ND}))$ or that she did it in the kitchen. This seems like an implausible requirement. It seems that Alice can omit to do one thing to Beth without doing something *else* to her. I'll consider this issue again in Section 6.4.1, in connection with Schaffer's (2012) approach to negative action sentences. Second, (7_{ND}) and (8_{ND}) report that Alice's omission itself is quick. As noted in Section 4.3, this seems, not just wrong, but *nonsensical*. I'll consider this and related issues in more detail in Section 8.5.

Beth at all, she can hardly have done it quickly. Likewise, it seems to follow that (9) is true, since if Alice didn't kiss Beth at all, she can hardly have done it in the kitchen. Finally, it seems to follow that (7) is true, since if Alice didn't kiss Beth at all, she can hardly have done it *both* quickly *and* in the kitchen. For similar reasons, both (8) and (9) entail (7). A same argument applies, *mutatis mutandis*, to (11)–(14): (14) entails both (12) and (13), and each of these entails (11). Thus, on the natural readings of negative action sentences, adverb-adding inferences appear to be valid.

This is bad news for the simple Neo-Davidsonian schemata given in Section 4.3. According to those schemata, 'x omits to φ' can only stand to 'x omits to φ F-ly' as '$\exists x Fx$' stands to '$\exists x (Fx \,\&\, Gx)$'. Thus, adverb-adding inferences are blocked by the fact that $\exists x Fx \nvdash \exists x (Fx \,\&\, Gx)$. More concretely, if we follow the simple Neo-Davidsonian schemata, then (7)–(10) are analyzed as (7_{ND})–(10_{ND}). But (10_{ND}) entails neither (8_{ND}) nor (9_{ND}), and none of these entails (7_{ND}). The same argument applies, *mutatis mutandis*, to (11)–(14).

Compare Deflationism. According to the Deflationist schemata, 'x omits to φ' stands to 'x omits to φ F-ly' as '$\neg\exists x Fx$' stands to '$\neg\exists x (Fx \,\&\, Gx)$'. Thus, adverb-adding inferences are validated by the rule, $\neg\exists x Fx \vdash \neg\exists x (Fx \,\&\, Gx)$. More concretely, if we follow the Deflationist schemata, then (7)–(10) are analyzed as (7_{DEF})–(10_{DEF}). (10_{DEF}) entails both (8_{DEF}) and (9_{DEF}), and each of these entails (7_{DEF}). The same argument applies, *mutatis mutandis*, to (11)–(14).

Deflationism doesn't merely allow us to validate these seemingly good inferences. It also seems to capture our intuitive sense of *why* they're good. Recall, from the fact that Alice omitted to kiss Beth *simpliciter*, it seems to follow that she omitted to kiss Beth quickly, since if Alice didn't kiss Beth at all, she can hardly have done it quickly. Cast in event terms: from the fact that there is no event which is a kissing of Beth by Alice, it follows that there is no event which is *both* a kissing of Beth by Alice *and* which is quick. This is just an application of the rule, $\neg\exists x Fx \vdash \neg\exists x (Fx \,\&\, Gx)$.

The root of this problem, as with the previous one, is the different treatments given to adverbs in the simple Neo-Davidsonian and Deflationist schemata. The simple Neo-Davidsonian schemata only capture the readings of (7)–(14) on which the adverbs modify what Alice *does*, and the fact that x does something *simpliciter* doesn't entail that x does it in any particular way. By contrast, the Deflationist schemata capture the more natural readings of (7)–(14) on which the adverbs modify what Alice *doesn't* do, and the fact that x doesn't do something *simpliciter* entails that x doesn't do it in any particular way.

Thus, while adverb-adding inferences provide strong evidence in favour of a Neo-Davidsonian approach to ordinary action sentences, they seem to provide strong evidence in favour of a Deflationist approach to negative action sentences.

4.4.3 The Problem of Adverb-Conjoining Inferences

The third problem for the simple Neo-Davidsonian schemata is suggested by Mellor (1995: 132–134; 2004: 314–315), although not in exactly the form I give it here. It seems that (9) and (15) can both be true, on their wide-scope readings, with respect to the same world and time:

(9) Alice omitted to kiss Beth in the kitchen.
(15) Alice omitted to kiss Beth in the hallway.

According to the simple Neo-Davidsonian schemata, both (9) and (15) are analyzed as existential quantifications over events, and so there are such events as Alice's omission to kiss Beth in the kitchen and her omission to kiss Beth in the hallway.

(9_{ND}) $\exists e(Agent(\text{Alice})(e)$ & $Patient(\text{Beth})(e)$ & $NEG\text{-}Kiss_{\text{ND}}(e)$ & $At_{\text{L}}(e)$ (kitchen))

(15_{ND}) $\exists e(Agent(\text{Alice})(e)$ & $Patient(\text{Beth})(e)$ & $NEG\text{-}Kiss_{\text{ND}}(e)$ & $At_{\text{L}}(e)$ (hallway))

Let 'o_1' and 'o_2' denote these omissions, respectively. Substituting 'o_1' for 'e' in (9_{ND}) yields (16), which entails (17):

(16) $Agent(\text{Alice})(o_1)$ & $Patient(\text{Beth})(o_1)$ & $NEG\text{-}Kiss_{\text{ND}}(o_1)$ & $At_{\text{L}}(o_1)$ (kitchen)
(17) $At_{\text{L}}(o_1)$(kitchen)

Likewise, substituting 'o_2' for 'e' in (15_{ND}) yields (18), which entails (19):

(18) $Agent(\text{Alice})(o_2)$ & $Patient(\text{Beth})(o_2)$ & $NEG\text{-}Kiss_{\text{ND}}(o_2)$ & $At_{\text{L}}(o_2)$ (hallway)
(19) $At_{\text{L}}(o_2)$(hallway)

In English: we've inferred that Alice's omission to kiss Beth in the kitchen occurs in the kitchen and that her omission to kiss Beth in the hallway occurs in the hallway. But now suppose, as seems plausible, that these omissions are identical: although *omit to kiss Beth in the kitchen* and *omit to kiss Beth in the hallway* are distinct things Alice does, a single doing is a doing of them both. Then we have (20), which, together with (17) and (19), entails (21):

(20) $o_1 = o_2$
(21) $At_{\text{L}}(o_1)$(kitchen) & $At_{\text{L}}(o_1)$(hallway)

In English: Alice's omission occurs in both the kitchen and the hallway. While (21) isn't logically inconsistent,[13] it doesn't seem like it should follow from (9) and (15), on their natural readings. Indeed, from the fact that Alice omitted to kiss Beth either in the kitchen or in the hallway, it doesn't seem to follow that *any* token behaviour of hers occurs in both places.[14]

Of course, a simple Neo-Davidsonian might reject (20), and insist that we have two omissions in this case, not one. But in order for this response to be sufficiently general, she'll have to deny that there are *any* cases in which x's omission to φ F-ly is identical to x's omission to φ G-ly. This is implausible, and requires the simple Neo-Davidsonian to greatly inflate her ontology.

Once again, the root of the problem is the simple Neo-Davidsonian's treatment of adverbs. The only available schema for 'x NEG-φ F-ly' has 'F-ly' contributing a predicate of a NEG-φ event, and so, leaving aside concerns of referential indeterminacy, 'x NEG-φ F-ly' entails that x's NEG-φ-ing satisfies the predicate, 'F'. Thus, if 'x NEG-φ F-ly' and 'x NEG-φ G-ly' are both true, and these two NEG-φ-ings are identical, then a single event satisfies both predicates, 'F' and 'G'.

Compare Deflationism. According to the Deflationist, (9) and (15) are analyzed as follows:

(9$_{\text{DEF}}$) $\sim\exists e(Agent(\text{Alice})(e)$ & $Patient(\text{Beth})(e)$ & $Kiss_{\text{ND}}(e)$ & $At_{\text{L}}(e)$ (kitchen))

(15$_{\text{DEF}}$) $\sim\exists e(Agent(\text{Alice})(e)$ & $Patient(\text{Beth})(e)$ & $Kiss_{\text{ND}}(e)$ & $At_{\text{L}}(e)$ (hallway))

Neither (9$_{\text{DEF}}$) nor (15$_{\text{DEF}}$) quantifies over omission events, and neither '$At_{\text{L}}(e)$(kitchen)' nor '$At_{\text{L}}(e)$(hallway)' is predicated of such an event. Thus,

---

[13] Recall that '$At_{\text{L}}(e)(r)$' plausibly expresses Parsons's notion of 'weak location' (see note 10). There's nothing logically inconsistent about the claim that a single event is weakly located at two regions, even if those regions are non-overlapping. If I'm sitting in my office, having a conversation with someone in the hallway outside, our conversation is weakly located in both my office and the non-overlapping hallway, since neither region is entirely free of that event.

[14] My presentation of the problem differs from Mellor's in two ways. First, he doesn't restrict his attention to negative action sentences. He is concerned more generally with sentences that appear to express negative existentials – e.g. 'Don does not die' and 'Don does not fall' – and the suggestion that these sentences can be rephrased as quantifying over 'negative events', i.e. 'events which exist by definition just in case some corresponding positive events ... do not exist' (1995: 133).

Second, Mellor uses the adverbs 'quickly' and 'slowly' to make his point: the simple Neo-Davidsonian approach implies that, if 'Alice omitted to kiss Beth quickly' and 'Alice omitted to kiss Beth slowly' are both true, then a single omission is both quick and slow, which appears outright contradictory. However, whether this result really *is* contradictory depends on complications surrounding the semantics of scalar adverbs which I left aside in Section 4.2.2. I'll return to those issues in Section 8.5.

we can't substitute 'o_1' and 'o_2' for the event variables in these propositions in order to derive (17) and (19). Moreover, as I argued in Section 2.3.4, the Deflationist should deny that there are such things as Alice's omission to kiss Beth in the kitchen and her omission to kiss Beth quickly, to which 'o_1' and 'o_2' could refer. Thus, she should reject the identity claim (20) on the ground that neither 'Alice's omission to kiss Beth quickly' nor 'Alice omission to kiss Beth slowly' has a referent.

4.5 An Unsatisfying Response

4.5.1 Divide and Conquer

I've presented the case for Deflationism as a case against the simple Neo-Davidsonian schemata for negative action sentences given in Section 4.3. These schemata don't account for the differences between omission sentences and refrainment sentences discussed in Section 2.2.2. In itself, this isn't a problem; they're *schemata*, after all. But you might hope that the Neo-Davidsonian can solve the problems raised in the previous section by appealing to more specific schemata which *do* account for the differences between omission sentences and refrainment sentences.

There's a problem of principle with this 'divide and conquer' strategy. 'Omit' and 'refrain' are only two negative action verbs. There are many more such verbs in English – e.g. 'abstain' – to say nothing of languages other than English. For *any* such verb, we can, in principle, produce sets of negative action sentences which use it, and which demonstrate the problems of adverb-dropping, adverb-adding, and adjective-conjoining inferences. There's no guarantee that attention to the meaning of each negative action verb will provide the resources to solve all these problems.

In any case, as I'll now show, the strategy fails. The complications which are needed to account for the differences between omission sentences and refrainment sentences don't allow us to give a satisfying response to the case for Deflationism.

4.5.2 Omission Sentences

Consider omission sentences first. In Section 2.2.2, I argued that these sentences carry the presupposition that the agent is supposed to do the relevant thing. The simple Neo-Davidsonian can provide schemata for omission sentences that reflect this:

Simple Neo-Davidsonian Schemata (Omission Sentences)

$[\![x \text{ omits to } \varphi]\!]_{<w,\ t>}$ $= \exists e(Agent(x)(e)(w)(t) \ \& \ NEG\text{-}\varphi_{ND}(e)(w)(t))$
π: x is supposed to φ at t.

$[\![x \text{ omits (to } \varphi) \text{ F-ly}]\!]_{<w,\ t>}$ $= \exists e(Agent(x)(e)(w)(t) \ \& \ NEG\text{-}\varphi_{ND}(e)(w)(t) \ \& \ F$
$(e)(w)(t))$
π: x is supposed to φ F-ly at t.

$[\![x \text{ omits (to } \varphi \text{ F-ly)}]\!]_{<w,\ t>}$ = ???

Here, what follows 'π' is a pragmatic presupposition, and not part of the semantic content of the sentence. Note that, according to these schemata, an agent can only omit to do something at a given time if she's supposed to do it *at that time*. This is highly plausible. Suppose that I agree to write a letter of recommendation, and that I have until the end of the month to complete the task. There's no specific time, within that one-month time-frame, such that I'm supposed to write the letter *then*. Thus, although there will be many times at which I'm not writing the letter, it won't be appropriate to say, at any of those times, that I'm *omitting* to write the letter then.

The simple Neo-Davidsonian might attempt to solve the problem of adverb-dropping inferences for omission sentences by appeal to these schemata. Given these schemata, (7)–(10) are properly analyzed as follows:[15]

(7_{ND_2}) $\exists e(Agent(Alice)(e) \ \& \ Patient(Beth)(e) \ \& \ NEG\text{-}Kiss_{ND}(e) \ \& \ Quick$
$(e) \ \& \ At_L(e)(kitchen))$
$π_{(7)}$: Alice is supposed to kiss Beth quickly in the kitchen.

(8_{ND_2}) $\exists e(Agent(Alice)(e) \ \& \ Patient(Beth)(e) \ \& \ NEG\text{-}Kiss_{ND}(e) \ \& \ Quick$
$(e))$
$π_{(8)}$: Alice is supposed to kiss Beth quickly.

(9_{ND_2}) $\exists e(Agent(Alice)(e) \ \& \ Patient(Beth)(e) \ \& \ NEG\text{-}Kiss_{ND}(e) \ \& \ At_L(e)$
$(kitchen))$
$π_{(9)}$: Alice is supposed to kiss Beth in the kitchen.

(10_{ND_2}) $\exists e(Agent(Alice)(e) \ \& \ Patient(Beth)(e) \ \& \ NEG\text{-}Kiss_{ND}(e))$
$π_{(10)}$: Alice is supposed to kiss Beth.

The simple Neo-Davidsonian might now try to explain away our intuition that, e.g. (7) doesn't entail (8). Consider: if $π_{(7)}$ is part of the common ground while $π_{(8)}$ isn't, then even if (7) and (8) are both *true*, (8) won't be properly *assertible*. In such a case, this Neo-Davidsonian might say, (7) only

---

[15] Recall, in my view, $π_{(7)}$–$π_{(10)}$ are presuppositions carried by the *sentences* (7)–(10), not by their *contents*.

seems not to entail (8), since (7) is assertible while (8) isn't. (Likewise, *mutatis mutandis*, for our other adverb-dropping inferences involving (7)–(10).)

This solution faces two problems of its own. First, this just seems to be the wrong account of why inferring (8) from (7) is bad. The reason Alice can omit to kiss Beth quickly in the kitchen without omitting to kiss her quickly is that Alice might kiss Beth quickly and simply not do it in the kitchen. The reason is *not* that Alice can be supposed to kiss Beth quickly in the kitchen without being supposed to kiss her quickly *simpliciter*.

Second, the explanation is unsatisfying, since it's difficult to imagine a conversational context in which $\pi_{(7)}$ is part of the common ground while $\pi_{(8)}$ isn't. In general, it's difficult to imagine a context in which it's part of the common ground that x is supposed to φ F-ly but *not* part of the common ground that x is supposed to φ.

The simple Neo-Davidsonian schemata for omission sentences do little to mitigate the problem of adverb-dropping inferences. With respect to the problem of adverb-adding inferences, however, the situation is *prima facie* better. The problem is supposed to be that, with respect to omission sentences like (7)–(10), such inferences are intuitively good ones, contrary to what the simple schemata from Section 4.3 would have us predict. However, once we account for the presuppositions carried by omission sentences, adverb-adding inferences lose some of their appeal.

Consider (9) and (10). It might seem that if (10) is assertible, then (9) is, too – that is, it might seem that if Alice omits to kiss Beth *simpliciter*, then she omits to kiss Beth in the kitchen. However, while (10) is assertible only if $\pi_{(10)}$ is part of the common ground, (9) is assertible only if $\pi_{(9)}$ is part of the common ground. And there's no reason to expect that, whenever $\pi_{(10)}$ is part of the common ground, $\pi_{(9)}$ is too. In general, it makes perfectly good sense to expect x to φ without expecting x to φ F-ly. Thus, there's no reason to expect that (9) is assertible whenever (10) is (and likewise, *mutatis mutandis*, for our other adverb-adding inferences involving (7)–(10)). Indeed, if Alice is simply supposed to kiss Beth, never mind where, then 'Alice omitted to kiss Beth in the kitchen', on its wide-scope reading, will sound wrong, even if 'Alice omitted to kiss Beth' is true.

The simple Neo-Davidsonian needs to be careful here. Given that a sentence can be true without being assertible – say, because that sentence carries a false presupposition – the fact that 'x omits to φ' can be assertible while 'x omits to φ F-ly' isn't doesn't show that adverb-adding inferences are invalid. The point of her appeal to pragmatics in this case should be, not to provide evidence that such inferences really are invalid, but merely to undermine our initial sense that they're valid. That is, she poses a challenge: 'Given that "x omits to φ" can be truly assertible while "x omits to φ F-ly" isn't, why do you think that the former can only be *true* if the latter is?' If no answer is forthcoming, she can bite the bullet and accept that adverb-adding inferences are invalid, as her analyses predict.

Unfortunately, we have good reason to think that at least *some* adverb-adding inferences involving omission sentences are good ones. Although $\pi_{(10)}$ can be presupposed while $\pi_{(9)}$ isn't, nothing prevents them from being presupposed simultaneously. (Indeed, in any ordinary context, $\pi_{(10)}$ is presupposed if $\pi_{(9)}$ is.) Now, suppose that $\pi_{(9)}$ and $\pi_{(10)}$ are both part of the common ground, and that Alice didn't kiss Beth. Then, (10) is truly assertible: Alice didn't simply fail to kiss Beth, she *omitted* to do so. It seems that (9) should be truly assertible too: since Alice was supposed to kiss Beth in the kitchen, and she failed to kiss Beth altogether, it follows that she didn't satisfy this expectation, and so she *omitted* to kiss Beth in the kitchen. The simple Neo-Davidsonian can't explain this, since the semantic content given by (10_{ND_2}) doesn't entail the semantic content given by (9_{ND_2}).

In short, the simple Neo-Davidsonian is right that the fact that 'x omits to φ' is truly assertible doesn't *always* render 'x omits to φ F-ly' truly assertible, since, in general, the presupposition carried by the former sentence can hold while that carried by the latter doesn't. But, as long as both presuppositions do, in fact, hold, the fact that 'x omits to φ' is truly assertible renders 'x omits to φ F-ly' truly assertible too. This is something the simple Neo-Davidsonian can't explain.[16]

Turning, finally, to the problem of adverb-conjoining inferences, recall that the problem begins from the assumption that (9) and (15) can both be true, with respect to the same world and time, and that they can report the occurrence of a single omission:

(9) Alice omitted to kiss Beth in the kitchen.
(15) Alice omitted to kiss Beth in the hallway.

The simple Neo-Davidsonian might appeal to her schemata for omission sentences to reject one of (9) and (15). (9) presupposes that Alice was supposed to kiss Beth in the kitchen, while (15) presupposes that she was supposed to do it in the hallway. You might think that, if no kiss can occur

---

[16] Compare Deflationism. Since (10_{DEF}) entails (9_{DEF}), the Deflationist can explain why, in a case where $\pi_{(9)}$ and $\pi_{(10)}$ are both presupposed, (9) is truly assertible if (10) is. By her lights, (9) is *true* if (10) is, and the only remaining obstacle to its assertibility is absent, since $\pi_{(9)}$ is part of the common ground.

in both places at once, then these presuppositions are incompatible, $\pi_{(9)}$ and $\pi_{(15)}$ can't both be part of the common ground, and (9) and (15) can't both be true.

There are two problems with this reply. First, it ignores the distinction between truth and assertibility. Even if (9) and (15) carry incompatible presuppositions, and so they can't both be truly assertible, their *contents* – as understood by the simple Neo-Davidsonian – are perfectly compatible, and so they can both be *true*.

Second, even if $\pi_{(9)}$ and $\pi_{(15)}$ are incompatible presuppositions in the sense that Alice can't do both things she would be expected to do if they both held, that doesn't show that they're incompatible in the sense that they can't both be part of the common ground of a single conversational context. Suppose that Alice makes a promise to Charlie that she'll kiss Beth in the kitchen, and makes a promise to David that she'll kiss Beth in the hallway. If Charlie and David discuss Alice's promises with one another, then it will become part of the common ground that Alice is supposed to kiss Beth in the kitchen *and* that she's supposed to kiss Beth in the hallway. Thus, even if Alice can't fulfill both promises, $\pi_{(9)}$ and $\pi_{(15)}$ can both be part of the common ground.

4.5.3 Refrainment Sentences

The situation is similar for refrainment sentences. In Section 2.2.2, I argued that part of the content of such sentences is that the agent intentionally doesn't do the relevant thing – or, as the simple Neo-Davidsonian should put it, part of the content of 'x refrains from φ-ing' is that x's NEG-φ-ing is intentional under that description. It's a contested issue how such a clause is to be represented in a Neo-Davidsonian framework, but for present purposes we can consider a simple proposal. We introduce a predicate of events, '*Intentional*', which takes as one of its arguments a predicate contributed by another verb phrase. '*Intentional*(e) ($\lambda e'.\varphi_{ND}(e')$)' says that e is intentional under the description '$\lambda e'.\varphi_{ND}(e')$' or that e is an event in which the agent of e intentionally φ-s.[17] With this predicate in place, we can give the following simple Neo-Davidsonian schemata for refrainment sentences:

Simple Neo-Davidsonian Schemata (Refrainment Sentences)

$[\![x \text{ refrains from } \varphi\text{-ing}]\!]_{<w,\, t>}$ $= \exists e(Agent(x)(e)(w)(t) \ \& \ NEG\text{-}\varphi_{ND}(e)(w)(t) \ \& $
$Intentional(e)(\lambda e'.[NEG\text{-}\varphi_{ND}(e')(w)(t)])(w)(t))$

---

[17] I defend this proposal in Section 6.3.2.

$[\![x \text{ refrains (from } \varphi\text{-ing) F-ly}]\!]_{<w,\ t>} = \exists e(Agent(x)(e)(w)(t)\ \&\ NEG\text{-}\varphi_{ND}(e)(w)(t)$
$\&\ F(e)(w)(t)\ \&$
$Intentional(e)(\lambda e'.[NEG\text{-}\varphi_{ND}(e')(w)(t)\ \&\ F(e')$
$(w)(t)])(w)(t))$
$[\![x \text{ refrains (from } \varphi\text{-ing F-ly)}]\!]_{<w,\ t>} = ???$

(Here, square brackets indicate the scope of 'λ'.)

The simple Neo-Davidsonian might attempt to solve the problem of adverb-dropping inferences for refrainment sentences by appeal to these schemata. Given these schemata, (11)–(14) are properly analyzed as follows:

(11$_{ND}$) $\exists e(Agent(\text{Alice})(e)\ \&\ Patient(\text{Beth})(e)\ \&\ NEG\text{-}Kiss_{ND}(e)\ \&\ Quick(e)$
$\&\ At_L(e)(\text{kitchen})\ \&\ Intentional(e)(\lambda e'.[NEG\text{-}Kiss_{ND}(e')\ \&\ Quick(e')$
$\&\ At_L(e')(\text{kitchen})]))$

(12$_{ND}$) $\exists e(Agent(\text{Alice})(e)\ \&\ Patient(\text{Beth})(e)\ \&\ NEG\text{-}Kiss_{ND}(e)\ \&\ Quick(e)$
$\&\ Intentional(e)(\lambda e'.[NEG\text{-}Kiss_{ND}(e')\ \&\ Quick(e')]))$

(13$_{ND}$) $\exists e(Agent(\text{Alice})(e)\ \&\ Patient(\text{Beth})(e)\ \&\ NEG\text{-}Kiss_{ND}(e)\ \&\ At_L(e)$
$(\text{kitchen})\ \&\ Intentional(e)(\lambda e'.[NEG\text{-}Kiss_{ND}(e')\ \&\ At_L(e')$
$(\text{kitchen})]))$

(14$_{ND}$) $\exists e(Agent(\text{Alice})(e)\ \&\ Patient(\text{Beth})(e)\ \&\ NEG\text{-}Kiss_{ND}(e)\ \&$
$Intentional(e)(\lambda e'.[NEG\text{-}Kiss_{ND}(e')]))$

But now, to make an adverb-dropping inference is not merely to drop a conjunct from within the scope of '$\exists e$', but also to drop the corresponding conjunct which is bound by '$\lambda e''$. For example, to infer (14$_{ND}$) from (13$_{ND}$) is to drop two occurrences of '$At_L(e)(\text{kitchen})(w)(t)$': one from within the scope of '$\exists e$'; and one from the second argument of '$Intentional$'. The latter sort of move might seem obviously bad. It is – in this approach – the formal correlate of the informal move from 'x intentionally doesn't φ F-ly' to 'x intentionally doesn't φ'. And the latter move seems like a bad one: 'Alice intentionally didn't kiss Beth in the kitchen' doesn't entail 'Alice intentionally didn't kiss Beth'; for she might have kissed Beth in another room.

Granting that the informal move from 'x intentionally doesn't φ F-ly' to 'x intentionally doesn't φ' is a bad one, the simple Neo-Davidsonian can't appeal to this fact to block the adverb-dropping inferences. As she sees things, to say that x intentionally doesn't φ is to say that x's NEG-φ-ing is intentional under a certain description, '$\lambda e'.NEG\text{-}\varphi_{ND}(e')$'. Thus, the move she's attempting to block is an instance of the following principle:

Intentionality Simplification
$Intentional(e)(\lambda e'.[\varphi_{ND}(e')\ \&\ F(e')]) \supset Intentional(e)(\lambda e'.[\varphi_{ND}(e')])$

That is, if e is intentional under the description '$\lambda e'.[\varphi_{ND}(e') \ \& \ Fe']$' then e is intentional under the description '$\lambda e'.[\varphi_{ND}(e')]$'. But a Neo-Davidsonian should accept *Intentionality Simplification*, for this principle is what licenses the *good* inference from (22) to (23):

(22) Alice intentionally kissed Beth quickly in the kitchen.
(23) Alice intentionally kissed Beth quickly.

The simple Neo-Davidsonian schemata for refrainment sentences do nothing to mitigate the problem of adverb-dropping inferences.

With respect to the problem of adverb-adding inferences, the situation is *prima facie* better. The problem is supposed to be that, with respect to refrainment sentences like (11)–(14), such inferences are intuitively good ones, contrary to what the simple schemata from Section 4.3 would have us predict. However, once we account for the information that refrainment sentences carry about the agent's intentions, adverb-adding inferences lose some of their appeal.

Consider (13) and (14). It might seem that if (14) is true, then (13) is, too – that is, it might seem that if Alice refrained from kissing Beth *simpliciter*, then she refrained from kissing Beth in the kitchen. However, (13) says, in part, that Alice *intentionally* didn't kiss Beth in the kitchen, and it seems that that can be false even if Alice refrained from kissing Beth in the kitchen. Alice might have formed the intention not to kiss Beth, or an intention with some other content which intuitively renders (14) true, without forming the intention not to kiss her in the kitchen, or an intention with some other content which intuitively renders (13) true. She may simply have decided not to kiss Beth, without thinking one way or the other about Beth's location. (Likewise, *mutatis mutandis*, for our other adverb-adding inferences involving (11)–(14).)

More formally, given the simple Neo-Davidsonian schemata, to infer (13$_{ND}$) from (14$_{ND}$) is to add two occurrences of '$At_L(e)$(kitchen)': one within the scope of '$\exists e$'; and one within the second argument of '$Intentional_{ND}$'. The latter move is an instance of the following principle:

Intentionality Complication
Intentional$(e)(\lambda e'.[\varphi_{ND}(e')]) \supset$ *Intentional*$(e)(\lambda e'.[\varphi_{ND}(e') \ \& \ F(e')])$

That is, if e is intentional under the description '$\lambda e'.[\varphi_{ND}(e')]$', then e is intentional under the description '$\lambda e'.[\varphi_{ND}(e') \ \& \ Fe']$'. But a Neo-Davidsonian should reject *Intentionality Complication*, for this principle licenses the bad inference from (24) to (25):

(24) Alice intentionally kissed Beth.
(25) Alice intentionally kissed Beth quickly.

Unfortunately, we have good reason to think that at least *some* adverb-adding inferences involving refrainment sentences are good ones. Suppose that Alice forms the following intentions: she intends not to kiss Beth quickly; she intends not to kiss Beth in the kitchen; and, doing a bit of practical reasoning, she combines these intentions to form an intention not to kiss Beth *both* quickly *and* in the kitchen. Suppose further that Alice follows through on these intentions by not kissing Beth at all. Then, (14) is true: Alice doesn't merely fail to kiss Beth; she *refrains* from doing so. But in this case, (13) seems to follow. That Alice doesn't kiss Beth at all entails that she doesn't kiss Beth *in the kitchen*, and since she gave some thought to whether to kiss Beth in the kitchen, decided not to, and followed through on that intention, it follows that she *refrains* from kissing Beth in the kitchen. The simple Neo-Davidsonian can't explain this, since the semantic content given by (14_{SND}) doesn't entail the semantic content given by (13_{SND}).

In short, the simple Neo-Davidsonian is right that we can't *always* infer 'x refrains from φ-ing F-ly' from 'x refrains from φ-ing', since the fact that x has the intentions required to make the latter true doesn't entail that x has the intentions required to make the former true. But, as long as x has the right sort of intention to refrain from φ-ing F-ly, we can infer 'x refrains from φ-ing F-ly' from 'x refrains from φ-ing'. This is something the simple Neo-Davidsonian can't explain.

Turning, finally, to the problem of adverb-conjoining inferences, it seems that (13) and (26) can both be true, with respect to the same world and time, and that they can report a single refrainment:

(13) Alice refrained from kissing Beth in the kitchen.
(26) Alice refrained from kissing Beth in the hallway.

But the simple Neo-Davidsonian might appeal to her schemata for refrainment sentences to reject one of (13) and (26), by claiming that Alice can't hold both of the intentions that (13) and (26) attribute to her. On the simple Neo-Davidsonian view, Alice's intention not to kiss Beth in the kitchen is satisfied only if some token behaviour of hers is intentional under the description, '$\lambda e.[\textit{NEG-Kiss}_{ND}(e)\ \&\ \textit{At}_L(e)(\text{kitchen})]$', and likewise, her intention not to kiss Beth in the hallway is satisfied only if some token behaviour of hers is intentional under the description, '$\lambda e.[\textit{NEG-Kiss}_{ND}(e)\ \&\ \textit{At}_L(e)(\text{hallway})]$'. Now, an event can only be intentional under a description that it actually satisfies: if x φ-s intentionally, it follows that x φ-s. If no event can satisfy both descriptions, no agent can hold both intentions, and so one of (13) and (26) must be false.

The problem with this response is that we *know* that Alice can hold both intentions, and so if the simple Neo-Davidsonian has an argument that this is impossible, she must have taken a wrong step. In fact, we know what that wrong step is. The simple Neo-Davidsonian claims that an event is intentional under the description, 'refrainment from kissing Beth in the kitchen' only if it's intentional under the description, '$\lambda e.[NEG\text{-}Kiss_{ND}(e)$ & $At_L(e)$(kitchen)]', and likewise that an event is intentional under the description, 'refrainment from kissing Beth in the hallway' only if it's intentional under the description, '$\lambda e.[NEG\text{-}Kiss_{ND}(e)$ & $Slow(e)$(hallway)]'. But on the most natural readings of (13) and (26), 'in the kitchen' and 'in the hallway' modify what Alice intends *not* to do, not what she does. The simple Neo-Davidsonian has simply imported her faulty treatment of adverbs in negative action sentences into her account of intentionality and intentional content.

Summing up: the simple schemata for omission sentences and refrainment sentences do nothing to mitigate the problems raised for the simple Neo-Davidsonian approach in Section 4.4.

4.6 Conclusion

The simple Neo-Davidsonian schemata for negative action sentences given in Section 4.3 must be rejected, and so the case for Deflationism seems strong. In Chapter 5, however, I'll show how we can answer the case for Deflationism by developing an alternative Neo-Davidsonian approach to negative action sentences.

The Logical Form of Negative Action Sentences II
A Neo-Davidsonian Approach

5.1 Introduction

In this chapter, I develop a Neo-Davidsonian approach to negative action sentences which has the resources to answer the case for Deflationism, and the acceptance of which will allow us to reject (PNA 3) and retain (PNA 1) and (PNA 2).

I begin, in Section 5.2, by sketching the main idea behind the approach. Negative action sentences quantify over events that play a certain role, which I call the 'ensuring' role: to say that x NEG-φ-s is to say that there occurs an event of which x is the agent and which ensures that x doesn't φ. I show how this approach solves the problems of adverb-dropping, adverb-adding, and adverb-conjoining inferences discussed in Chapter 4. In Section 5.3, I flesh out the approach, providing truth-conditions for claims of the form 'e ensures that p', and an account of how to identify a negative action with a particular ensuring event. In Section 5.4, I consider an objection regarding the relationship between negative action sentences and negated positive action sentences.

5.2 The Sophisticated Neo-Davidsonian Approach: A Sketch

5.2.1 Desiderata

A satisfying Neo-Davidsonian approach to negative action sentences must meet three *desiderata*. First, and most obviously, the proposition expressed by a negative action sentence must contain an event variable, 'e', which is bound by an occurrence of '$\exists$', and whose values can be taken to be token negative actions.

We've seen that, on the natural readings of 'x NEG-φ F-ly', the predicate contributed by 'F' can't plausibly be taken to apply to this variable. For, on that reading – what I called the 'wide-scope' reading –

'F-ly' modifies what the agent *doesn't* do, not what she does – that is, it modifies the embedded verb phrase 'φ', rather than the complex negative verb phrase 'NEG-φ'. Hence the second *desideratum*: the proposition expressed by a negative action sentence must contain a *second* event variable, '*e'*', which can take φ-ing events as values, and to which the predicates contributed by adverbs can be applied.

The simple Neo-Davidsonian schemata sketched in the Chapter 4 fail to meet this second *desideratum*. According to those schemata, the negative verb 'NEG' and the verb 'φ' work together to contribute a single event variable, which is the argument of the predicate 'NEG-$φ_{ND}$'. On reflection, this aspect of the simple Neo-Davidsonian schemata is suspect from the outset. On a general Neo-Davidsonian approach to action sentences, verb phrases contribute event variables and predicates thereof. It's odd to assume that 'NEG' and 'φ' work together to contribute a single event variable and a single predicate, 'NEG-φ'. The more natural assumption is that each of 'NEG' and 'φ' contributes a distinct event variable and a distinct predicate which applies to that variable.

Finally, this second event variable, '*e'*', must be bound by an occurrence of '∃' which is itself in the scope of an occurrence of '~'. Recall, Deflationism doesn't merely make the correct predictions about adverb-dropping and adverb-adding inferences, but seems to make them *for the right reason*: adverb-dropping inferences are invalid because the fact that there is no event of *x* φ-ing F-ly doesn't entail that there is no event of *x* φ-ing; and adverb-adding inferences are valid because the fact that there is no event of *x* φ-ing *does* entail that there is no event of *x* φ-ing F-ly. A satisfying Neo-Davidsonian approach must replicate the success of Deflationism in this regard.

Thus, we want a Neo-Davidsonian analysis of negative action sentences to take the following abstract form:

$$\exists e(Agent(x)(e)(w)(t) \ \& \ \dots \sim \exists e'(φ_{ND}(e')(w)(t)))$$

The question is, how is the placeholder '. . .' to be filled out? What predicate does a negative verb 'NEG' contribute?

5.2.2 *Ensuring*

It's a natural thought that whenever an agent omits to do something (refrains from doing it, etc.), she does something *else*, and that this behaviour ensures – in some sense of the word 'ensures' – that she doesn't do the relevant thing at that time. This is perhaps clearest in cases of non-basic negative action, i.e. cases in which an agent intentionally ψ-s *in order to* see to it that she doesn't φ. Vermazen's case of the tempting hors d'oeuvres is like this. As Vermazen imagines the case, I'm tempted to take a second helping of hors d'oeuvres, and I intentionally fiddle with the buttons on my jacket in order to keep my hands busy and prevent myself from taking a second helping (1985: 95–96). Brand (1971: 45–46) imagines a similar case, in which a police officer is tempted to shoot at a fleeing suspect, and exerts significant effort to keep his hand at his side, thereby preventing himself from shooting. In both cases, some behaviour – an act of fiddling buttons, or an act of holding one's arm at one's side – ensures that the agent doesn't do the relevant thing.

Smith (2010) claims, in effect, that all negative actions are like this. If that were the case, then the relevant sense of 'ensures' – i.e. the sense in which, in these cases, the agent's actual behaviour ensures that she doesn't do the relevant thing – could be unpacked in terms of intentions and practical knowledge: x ensures that she doesn't φ, in this sense, just in case there is some ψ such that x intentionally ψ-s and x relies on her practical knowledge of how to ψ in order to bring it about that she doesn't φ.

However, not all negative actions are like this. Some negative actions are *basic*: there is no positive behaviour ψ such that the agent intentionally ψ-s *in order* not to φ, relying on her practical knowledge of how to ψ in order to bring it about that she doesn't φ. Hornsby's case of the agent who refrains from taking a second chocolate, but who doesn't do anything to *prevent* herself from taking one, is a case of basic negative action. The case in which I intentionally abstain from voting is plausibly a case of basic negative action as well. If my hands are in my lap when the vote is called, and I decide to abstain, it seems that I don't need to intentionally do anything *in order* to bring it about that I don't raise my hand. Nonetheless, the natural thought with which I began applies in these cases, too: although these negative actions are basic, the agents' positive behaviour ensures, in some sense, that they don't do the relevant things – e.g. my behaviour of having my arms in my lap ensures that I don't raise my arm.[1]

---

[1] Clarke's (2010a: 167–172; 2014: 73–85) account of how a negative action is rendered intentional has a similar structure: even if there's no such event as my NEG-φ-ing which could be caused by an intention not to φ (or an intention with some other relevant content), that intention can help to cause some positive behaviour of mine which is incompatible with φ-ing, and so my negative behaviour can 'result' from that intention; whether that positive behaviour is intentional under a positive description is irrelevant to whether I NEG-φ intentionally (although it does make the difference between basic and non-basic negative actions). I'm skeptical of this account – see Section 3.3.3 and note 22 of that chapter – but the notion of x's ψ-ing 'ensuring' that x doesn't φ, which I'm

The natural thought even applies in cases of 'mere negative behaviour'. Consider a variant on the voting case, in which I'm not paying attention when the vote is called, and so I unintentionally omit to vote. My omission isn't a negative action, but nonetheless, my positive behaviour of having my arms in my lap ensures that I don't raise my arm.

Thus, there is a notion of 'ensuring that one doesn't φ' which can be applied in all cases of negative behaviour. Whenever x NEG-φ-s – whether her NEG-φ-ing is a non-basic negative action, a basic negative action, or a mere negative behaviour – x engages in some behaviour which ensures, in some sense, that x doesn't φ. I suggest that a negative action sentence reports not merely that there is no event of a certain kind, but that the relevant agent does something which *ensures* that there is no event of that kind.

More formally, the suggestion is that a negative action verb, 'NEG', contributes a predicate, '*Ensure*', which takes two arguments: an event, hereafter referred to as an 'ensuring event'; and a proposition. '*Ensure*$(e)(p)$ $(w)(t)$' is to be read as 'e ensures that p is true in w at t'. In the context of a negative action sentence, p is the proposition that there is no event of the relevant kind, i.e. no event in which the agent does the thing she omits to do (refrains from doing, etc.). Schematically:

Sophisticated Neo-Davidsonian Schemata (Negative Action Sentences)

$[\![x \text{ NEG-}\varphi]\!]_{<w,\ t>}$ $= \exists e(Agent(x)(e)(w)(t)\ \&\ Ensure(e)(\neg\exists e'(Agent(x)$
$(e')(w)(t)\ \&\ \varphi_{ND}(e')(w)(t)))(w)(t))$

$[\![x \text{ NEG-}(\varphi)\text{ F-ly}]\!]_{<w,\ t>} = \exists e(Agent(x)(e)(w)(t)\ \&\ F(e)(w)(t)\ \&\ Ensure(e)$
$(\neg\exists e'(Agent(x)(e')(w)(t)\ \&\ \varphi_{ND}(e')(w)(t)))(w)(t))$

$[\![x \text{ NEG-}(\varphi \text{ F-ly})]\!]_{<w,\ t>} = \exists e(Agent(x)(e)(w)(t)\ \&\ Ensure(e)(\neg\exists e'(Agent(x)$
$(e')(w)(t)\ \&\ \varphi_{ND}(e')(w)(t)\ \&\ F(e')(w)(t)))(w)(t))$

A bare negative action sentence, 'x NEG-φ' reports the occurrence of an event, e, of which x is the agent, and which ensures that no event e' is a φ-ing by x. On the narrow-scope reading, an adverbially modified negative action sentence, 'x NEG-(φ) F-ly', reports (a) the occurrence of an event, e, of which x is the agent, and which ensures that no event e' is a φ-ing by x, and (b) that e itself is F. On the wide-scope reading, 'x NEG-$(\varphi$ F-ly)', it

articulating here, seems to be what Clarke has in mind when he claims that ψ-ing and φ-ing are incompatible, and hence that x's ψ-ing 'results in' x NEG-φ-ing.

reports the occurrence of an event, e, of which x is the agent, and which ensures that no event e' (a) is a φ-ing by x and (b) is F.

It's worth pausing to emphasize that, because we now have two event variables – one for ensuring events and another for φ-ing events – we can capture both the narrow- and wide-scope readings of 'x NEG-φ F-ly'; this is something that neither Deflationism nor the simple Neo-Davidsonian approach could accomplish. The narrow-scope reading, 'x NEG-(φ) F-ly', is captured just as on the simple Neo-Davidsonian schemata: 'F-ly' modifies 'NEG-φ', and so the predicate it contributes is applied to 'e', the variable for NEG-φ-ing events, or ensuring events. The wide-scope reading, 'x NEG-(φ F-ly)', is captured just as on the Deflationist schemata: 'F-ly' modifies 'φ', and so the predicate contributed by 'F' is applied to 'e'', the variable for φ-ing events.

If these schemata are correct, then negative actions are 'ensuring events'. x's omission to φ (refrainment from φ-ing, etc.) is that event which ensures that x doesn't φ.

5.2.3   The Problems with Adverbs Solved

Because the sophisticated Neo-Davidsonian approach captures the wide-scope reading of 'x NEG-φ F-ly', it avoids the problems with adverbs which plagued the simple approach.

Taking the problem of adverb-dropping inferences first, recall our seemingly problematic sets of sentences from Chapter 4 (renumbered here):

(1) Alice omitted to kiss Beth quickly in the kitchen.
(2) Alice omitted to kiss Beth quickly.
(3) Alice omitted to kiss Beth in the kitchen.
(4) Alice omitted to kiss Beth.

(5) Alice refrained from kissing Beth quickly in the kitchen.
(6) Alice refrained from kissing Beth quickly.
(7) Alice refrained from kissing Beth in the kitchen.
(8) Alice refrained from kissing Beth.

To infer either (2) or (3) from (1), or to infer (4) from any of these, is to draw an intuitively invalid adverb-dropping inference. On the simple Neo-Davidsonian schemata, each of (1)–(4) is analyzed as containing a single event variable, and so the adverbs in these sentences are interpreted as contributing predicates applied to this variable. As a result, the intuitively invalid inferences are validated by the rule, $\exists x(Fx \ \& \ Gx) \vdash \exists x Fx$. Likewise, *mutatis mutandis*, for (5)–(8).

The sophisticated Neo-Davidsonian schemata face no such problem. The readings of (1)–(4) on which the adverb-dropping inferences are invalid are the wide-scope ones. On those readings, (1)–(4) are now analyzed as follows:

(1$_{\text{SND}}$) $\exists e(Agent(\text{Alice})(e)$ & $Ensure(e)(\sim\exists e'(Agent(\text{Alice})(e')$ & *Patient* $(\text{Beth})(e')$ & $Kiss_{\text{ND}}(e')$ & $Quick(e')$ & $At_{\text{L}}(e')(\text{kitchen}))))$

(2$_{\text{SND}}$) $\exists e(Agent(\text{Alice})(e)$ & $Ensure(e)(\sim\exists e'(Agent(\text{Alice})(e')$ & *Patient* $(\text{Beth})(e')$ & $Kiss_{\text{ND}}(e')$ & $Quick(e'))))$

(3$_{\text{SND}}$) $\exists e(Agent(\text{Alice})(e)$ & $Ensure(e)(\sim\exists e'(Agent(\text{Alice})(e')$ & *Patient* $(\text{Beth})(e')$ & $Kiss_{\text{ND}}(e')$ & $At_{\text{L}}(e')(\text{kitchen}))))$

(4$_{\text{SND}}$) $\exists e(Agent(\text{Alice})(e)$ & $Ensure(e)(\sim\exists e'(Agent(\text{Alice})(e')$ & *Patient* $(\text{Beth})(e')$ & $Kiss_{\text{ND}}(e')))$

On these analyses, the adverbs are interpreted as contributing predicates applied to the variable for kissing events – e.g. (1$_{\text{SND}}$) doesn't report that Alice's *omission* was quick, or that it occurred in the kitchen; rather, it reports that some token behaviour of Alice's ensured that no event was (a) a kissing of Beth by Alice, (b) quick, and (c) in the kitchen. Thus, the adverb-dropping inferences are no longer validated by the rule, $\exists x(Fx$ & $Gx) \vdash \exists xFx$. Likewise, *mutatis mutandis*, for (5)–(8).

The problem of adverb-adding inferences is solved in an analogous manner. On the wide-scope readings, to infer either (2) or (3) from (4), or to infer (1) from any of these, is to draw an intuitively valid inference.[2] Since, on the simple Neo-Davidsonian schemata, (1)–(4) are analyzed as containing a single event variable, these inferences are invalidated by the fact that $\exists xFx \nvdash \exists x(Fx$ & $Gx)$. But on the more sophisticated analyses, the adverbs are interpreted as contributing predicates applied to the variable for kissing events, and so the inferences are no longer blocked in this way. Likewise, *mutatis mutandis*, for (5)–(8).

In Section 5.2.1, I claimed that a satisfying Neo-Davidsonian approach to negative action sentences should replicate the Deflationist's explanation of why adverb-adding and adverb-dropping inferences seem to be valid and invalid, respectively. It may not be immediately obvious that the sophisticated Neo-Davidsonian approach does this. Negative existential phrases don't occur 'free-standing' in (1$_{\text{SND}}$)–(4$_{\text{SND}}$), but rather as arguments of the predicate, '*Ensure*'. Thus, the adverb-adding inferences aren't *immediately* validated by the rule, $\sim\exists xFx \vdash \sim\exists x(Fx$ & $Gx)$, and the adverb-dropping inferences aren't *immediately* blocked by the fact that $\sim\exists x(Fx$ & $Gx) \nvdash \sim\exists xFx$.

---

[2] I've noted, in Section 4.5, that not all such inferences are equally good, upon reflection.

Fortunately, we can supplement the story with the following, plausible principle:

Closure of Ensuring
Let p and q each be propositions about x's behaviour of either the form '$\exists e(Agent(x)(e)(w)(t)$ & $\varphi_{ND}(e)(w)(t))$' or '$\sim\exists e(Agent(x)(e)(w)(t)$ & $\varphi_{ND}(e)(w)(t))$'. Then, if '$\exists e(Agent(x)(e)(w)(t)$ & $Ensure(e)(p)(w)(t))$' is true, and p entails q, then '$\exists e'(Agent(x)(e')(w)(t)$ & $Ensure(e')(q)(w)(t))$' is true.

That is, if x ensures that she φ-s (or that she doesn't φ), and 'x φ-s' (or 'x doesn't φ') entails 'x ψ-s' (or 'x doesn't ψ'), then x thereby ensures that she ψ-s (or that she doesn't ψ). Given *Closure*, we can give an explanation of why, e.g. (4_{SND}) seems to entail (3_{SND}), which makes indirect appeal to the rule, $\sim\exists xFx \vdash \sim\exists x(Fx$ & $Gx)$: by that rule, the embedded negative existential in (4_{SND}) entails the one in (3_{SND}); by *Closure*, (4_{SND}) entails (3_{SND}). Likewise, we can give an explanation of why (3_{SND}) doesn't entail (4_{SND}), which makes indirect appeal to the fact that $\sim\exists x(Fx$ & $Gx) \nvdash \sim\exists xFx$: the embedded negative existential in (3_{SND}) doesn't entail the one in (4_{SND}), and so we can't infer (4_{SND}) from (3_{SND}) by appeal to *Closure*.

Finally, consider the problem of adverb-conjoining inferences. It seems that (2), (9), and (10) can all be true, with respect to the same world and time:

(3) Alice omitted to kiss Beth in the kitchen.

(9) Alice omitted to kiss Beth in the hallway.

(10) Alice's omission to kiss Beth in the kitchen = Alice's omission to kiss Beth in the hallway.

According to the simple Neo-Davidsonian schemata, (3), (9), and (10) together entail that a single behaviour of Alice's occurs in both the kitchen and the hallway. The sophisticated Neo-Davidsonian schemata avoid this problem, without need of extra principles like *Closure*. The readings of (3) and (9) which make trouble when combined with (10) are the wide-scope ones. According to the sophisticated schemata, (3) and (9) are analyzed, on those readings, as follows:

(3_{SND}) $\exists e(Agent(Alice)(e)$ & $Ensure(e)(\sim\exists e'(Agent(Alice)(e')$ & $Patient(Beth)(e')$ & $Kiss_{ND}(e')$ & $At_L(e')(kitchen))))$

(9_{SND}) $\exists e(Agent(Alice)(e)$ & $Ensure(e)(\sim\exists e'(Agent(Alice)(e')$ & $Patient(Beth)(e')$ & $Kiss_{ND}(e')$ & $At_L(e')(hallway))))$

On these analyses, '$At_L(e')(kitchen)$' and '$At_L(e')(hallway)$' aren't predicated of Alice's omissions, and so the fact that these omissions are identical no longer entails that a single event occurs in both the kitchen and the hallway.

5.3   The Sophisticated Neo-Davidsonian Approach: The Details

I turn now to the task of giving a more precise account of what the predicate '*Ensure*' means, and of the truth-conditions of '*Ensure*(e)(p)(w) (t)'. I begin, in Section 5.3.1, by distinguishing synchronic and diachronic notions of 'ensuring', and argue that only the former is relevant to negative action sentences. In Sections 5.3.2 and 5.3.3, I cash out the notion of 'ensuring' in terms of incompatibility: to ensure that one doesn't φ is to do something which is incompatible, in a certain sense, with φ-ing. In Section 5.3.4, I turn to issues about the 'extent' of a negative action, i.e. of which body parts and/or external objects are involved in a token negative action. I argue there that at least some token negative actions involve body parts beyond the agent's brain; not all negative actions are mental events. In Section 5.3.5, I develop a general account of the extent of a negative action: the body parts and/or external objects involved in x's NEG-φ-ing are those whose behaviour is appropriately relevant to whether one φ-s. In Section 5.3.6, I bring all these discussions together, to provide truth-conditions for '*Ensure*(e)(p)(w)(t)'.

5.3.1   Ensuring and Time

On a diachronic notion of 'ensuring', x can do something at t_1 which ensures that she doesn't φ at a later time, t_2. On a synchronic notion of 'ensuring', the only behaviours of x's which can ensure that she doesn't φ at t are behaviours in which she engages at t. It is the synchronic notion, not the diachronic one, which is relevant to the ensuring-claims communicated by negative action sentences.

Returning to an example from Section 2.2.3, suppose that, at t_1, I throw away a tempting container of ice cream, to help myself stick to my diet. Later, at t_2, I don't eat any of the ice cream, since I've thrown it away. My earlier behaviour ensures, in the diachronic sense, that I don't eat ice cream at t_2, but it seems wrong to describe that behaviour as my refrainment from eating ice cream at t_2. Although 'at t_2' specifies the relevant time at which I don't eat the ice cream, it *also* specifies the time at which my refrainment occurs: the sentence, 'I refrain from eating ice cream at t_2' isn't subject to scope ambiguity. The same holds, *mutatis mutandis*, for other refrainment sentences, omission sentences, and negative action sentences more generally.

Thus, we can place the following necessary condition on the truth of '*Ensure(e)(p)(w)(t)*':

Time Condition
'*Ensure(e)(p)(w)(t)*' is true only if *e* exists in *w* at *t*.

This condition is captured in the sophisticated Neo-Davidsonian schemata: e.g. '*x* NEG-φ' is true with respect to a time *t* only if there occurs, at *t*, an event *e* which ensures that there is no event *e′* of *x* φ-ing at *t*.

5.3.2   Ensuring and Incompatibility 1: In What Sense 'Incompatible'?

In Section 2.2.1, I imposed an 'incompatibility condition' on negative actions: necessarily, if *x* NEG-φ-s at *t*, then *x* doesn't φ at *t*. This condition fits nicely with a view of negative actions as ensuring events. The claim that *x*'s ψ-ing ensures that she doesn't φ is naturally cashed out in terms of incompatibility: for *x* to ensure that she doesn't do something is for her to do something else which is incompatible with it (at least, for her and at the relevant world and time).[3] More generally: to ensure that *p* is true is to do something which is incompatible with the falsity of *p*.

Incompatibility Condition (First Pass)
'*Ensure(e)(p)(w)(t)*' is true only if:

(i)   For some *x* and ψ, *e* is a ψ-ing by *x*; and
(ii) It can't be the case *both* that *x* ψ-s at *t* *and* that *p* is false at *t*.

Clause (ii) is naturally understood as the conjunction of two conditionals: 'If *x* ψ-s at *t*, then *p* is true at *t*'; and 'If *p* is false at *t*, then *x* doesn't ψ at *t*'. Where *p* is the proposition that *x* doesn't φ at *t*, these conditionals capture the idea that ψ-ing at *t* is incompatible with φ-ing at *t*: ψ-ing rules out φ-ing, because if '$\exists e(Agent(x)(e) \ \& \ \psi_{ND}(e))$' is true, then so is the negative existential, '$\sim\exists e(Agent(x)(e) \ \& \ \varphi_{ND}(e))$'; and the only way for *x* to φ is for her to do something other than ψ, because if '$\sim\exists e(Agent(x)(e) \ \& \ \varphi_{ND}(e))$' is false – that is, if '$\exists e(Agent(x)(e) \ \& \ \varphi_{ND}(e))$' is true – then so is '$\exists e(Agent(x)(e) \ \& \ \psi_{ND}(e))$'.

Obviously, we can't understand these conditionals as indicative. Since '*p* & *q*' entails '*p* ⊃ *q*', the latter, indicative conditional doesn't capture the sense that *p* forces the truth of *q*, or that the truth of ~*q* forces the truth of ~*p*. But neither can we understand them as strict conditionals. Consider,

---

[3] Compare Clarke (2010a: 167–172; 2014: 73–85) and note 1.

once again, the case in which I abstain from voting, leaving my hands in my lap. I've suggested that my behaviour of leaving my hands in my lap ensures that I don't vote. But it's not absolutely necessary that, if I leave my hands in my lap at t, then I don't cast a vote at t. There are possible worlds in which the voting procedures dictate that one votes by leaving one's hands down and abstains by raising a hand. If I leave my hands in my lap in such a world, then I cast a vote there.

A better approach is to read our conditionals subjunctively. To say that ψ-ing is incompatible with φ-ing (for x at t) is to say (a) that if x were to ψ then x wouldn't φ and (b) that if x were to φ then x wouldn't ψ. More generally:

Incompatibility Condition (Second Pass)
'*Ensure*$(e)(p)(w)(t)$' is true only if:

(i) For some x and ψ, e is a ψ-ing by x; and
(ii) (a) x ψ-s at t $\square\!\!\rightarrow$ p at t; and
     (b) $\sim\!p$ at t $\square\!\!\rightarrow$ $\sim\!(x\ \psi\text{-s at } t)$.

Adopting the standard semantics for subjunctives developed by Lewis (1973a), Sprigge (1970), and Stalnaker (1968), 'p $\square\!\!\rightarrow$ q' is true with respect to w just in case the closest p-worlds to w – i.e. the worlds in which p is true and which are as similar as possible to w in all other respects – are q-worlds – i.e. worlds in which q is true.[4] Clause (ii.a) no longer requires that p is true at t in *all* worlds in which x ψ-s at t – it merely requires that p is true at t in *the most similar* worlds in which x ψ-s at t. Likewise, *mutatis mutandis*, for (ii.b).

This pass at the *Incompatibility Condition* gets the right result in the voting case, since contingent success-conditions on φ-ing and ψ-ing can play a role in making it the case that x's ψ-ing ensures that x doesn't φ. In general, the most natural readings of 'If x were to ψ then x wouldn't φ' and 'If x were to φ then x wouldn't ψ' are ones on which we hold fixed the actual success-conditions on φ-ing and ψ-ing, when attempting to determine which are the closest worlds in which x ψ-s and which are the closest worlds in which x φ-s. Thus, consider (11) and (12):

(11) If I were to keep my hands in my lap at t, then I wouldn't vote at t.
(12) If I were to vote at t, then I wouldn't keep my hands in my lap.

---

[4] Lewis, Sprigge, and Stalnaker don't all the defend the exact same semantics, but the differences between them – to say nothing of complications arising from later developments – can safely be left aside for our purposes.

The most natural reading of (11) has us looking to worlds in which the voting procedures are the same as in the actual world, and I keep my hands in my lap, and asking whether I cast a vote in any of those worlds. (11) comes out true, because there are no such worlds. Likewise, the natural reading of (12) has us looking to worlds in which the voting procedures are the same as in the actual world, and I cast a vote, and asking whether I keep my hands in my lap in any of those worlds. (12) comes out true, because there are no such worlds.

A note on clause (ii.a). On one way of developing the Lewis-Stalnaker-Sprigge semantics, we adopt the hypothesis of Strong Centering, according to which, if p is true in w, then there is exactly one closest p-world to w – namely w itself. Given Strong Centering, '$p \; \Box\!\!\rightarrow q$' is true if '$p \; \& \; q$' is: if w is the single closest p-world to itself, and '$p \; \& \; q$' is true in w, then the single closest p-world is a q-world. But then, (ii.a) threatens to over-generate ensuring events: if x happens not to φ, then *any* ψ that x does trivially satisfies '$x \; \psi$-s at $t \; \Box\!\!\rightarrow \; \sim\!x \; \varphi$-s at t'.

To see the force of the problem, consider a (slightly modified) example from Clarke (2014: 17). Suppose that I omit to snap the fingers on my right hand, instead drumming them on a table. Suppose further that, as I drum my fingers on the table, I wiggle the toes on my left foot. If we think that negative actions can be identical to bodily events at all, my drumming of my fingers is a good candidate to be my omission: what I do with my fingers is obviously relevant to whether I snap them or not. My wiggling of my toes, by contrast, seems like a very poor candidate: what I do with my toes is obviously *ir*relevant to whether I snap my fingers.

One solution to this problem is to reject Strong Centering in favour of Weak Centering, according to which, even if p is true in w, there may be non-actual p-worlds which count as 'equally close' to w, for the purposes of evaluating '$p \; \Box\!\!\rightarrow q$'. Given Weak Centering, '$p \; \& \; q$' no longer entails '$p \; \Box\!\!\rightarrow q$'. Thus, the subjunctive, 'If I were to wiggle my toes, then I wouldn't snap my fingers' can come out *false*, even if both its antecedent and consequent are true.

The dispute between proponents of Strong Centering and Weak Centering is a thorny one.[5] Fortunately, clause (ii.b) can mitigate the problem of over-generation, even if Strong Centering is true. On the Lewis-Sprigge-Stalnaker semantics, '$p \; \Box\!\!\rightarrow q$' and '$\sim\!q \; \Box\!\!\rightarrow \sim\!p$' aren't equivalent. '$p \; \Box\!\!\rightarrow q$' is true in w just in case the closest p-worlds to w are q-worlds – that is, just in case there are no $\sim\!q$-worlds among the

---

[5] For classic discussion, see Lewis (1973a, 1979) and Stalnaker (1987).

closest *p*-worlds. It doesn't follow from this that '~*q* □→ ~*p*' is true: even if there are no ~*q*-worlds among the *closest p*-worlds, it may be that the closest ~*q*-worlds are, nonetheless, *p*-worlds. Thus, it may be that, while '*x* ψ-s at *t* □→ ~*x* φ-s at *t*'' is true, '*x* φ-s at *t* □→ ~*x* ψ-s at *t*'' is false. Indeed, the relevant instance, in our case, *is* false. It's false that I wouldn't have wiggled my toes if I had snapped my fingers; I might easily have done both. Thus, I'll remain neutral on Strong Centering.

A note on clause (ii.b). Suppose that the relevant thing that *x* doesn't do is something she couldn't possibly have done, e.g. to square the circle. If there is some negative verb 'NEG' such that it can be correct to say that '*x* NEG-(φ)' is true, even if *x* couldn't possibly have φ-ed, then how can we make sense of clause (ii.b)? That is, how can we make sense of the claim that, although *x* couldn't have φ-ed, if she *had*, then she wouldn't have ψ-ed?

We might insist that counterpossibles – i.e. subjunctive conditionals with impossible antecedents – are always false, or at least untrue, and hence that it's *never* correct to say that '*x* NEG-(φ)' is true, if *x* couldn't possibly have φ-ed. However, this view has few defenders. Assuming that '*x* NEG-(φ)' is *sometimes* true, even when φ-ing is impossible, we have two options. First, we might adopt the 'vacuist' view of counterpossibles, according to which they're all trivially true. Typically, a vacuist accepts the Lewis-Sprigge-Stalnaker semantics: '*p* □→ *q*' is true just in case none of the closest possible *p*-worlds are ~*q*-worlds; if there are *no* possible *p*-worlds, this condition is trivially satisfied. Thus, for any choice of *x*, ψ, and *t*, condition (ii.b) is trivially satisfied if *p* is necessarily true.[6] Second, we might adopt the 'non-vacuist' view, on which not all counterpossibles are true. Typically, a non-vacuist revises the Lewis-Sprigge-Stalnaker semantics so that the truth of '*p* □→ *q*' can be sensitive to what goes on at *im*possible worlds, not just possible ones: '*p* □→ *q*' is true just in case all the closest *p*-worlds are *q*-worlds, but there's no requirement that any *p*- or *q*-worlds be possible. Thus, '*p* □→ *q*' is no longer vacuously true if *p* is impossible: even if there are no *possible* p-worlds, we may still have *p*-worlds to work with, and it's not guaranteed that *q* will be true in the closest such worlds.[7] Since the dispute between these approaches to counterpossibles is beyond the scope of this book, I'll assume that the *Incompatibility Condition* is workable, whichever approach we take.

---

[6] For defense of this vacuist position, see Lewis (1973a) and Williamson (2007, 2018).
[7] See, e.g. Berto et al. (2018) and Nolan (1997: 543–567). For detailed discussion of the metaphysics of impossible worlds, see Jago (2014: chs. 4 and 5).

5.3.3   Ensuring and Incompatibility 2: Maximally Precise Behaviours

Sometimes, it seems, x's ψ-ing ensures that x doesn't φ, but ψ-ing isn't incompatible with φ-ing, either in an intuitive sense or in the sense explained in the previous section. Suppose that I'm making pasta for dinner, and I go through all the steps in preparing the sauce except one: I add the onions, the tomatoes, the peppers, the salt . . . I add everything except garlic. Let 'ψ' denote the act of going through all of these steps. ψ-ing certainly *seems* compatible with adding garlic – otherwise, the recipe would be impossible to complete. And, indeed, we can see that ψ doesn't satisfy clause (ii.b) of the *Incompatibility Condition*: the closest worlds in which I add garlic aren't worlds in which I fail to go through all the *other* steps; at least some of them are worlds in which I go through all the other steps *and* add the garlic.[8]

We've seen that a single event can be a doing of many things. Thus, for x's ψ-ing to ensure that x doesn't φ, it's not required that ψ-ing is incompatible with φ-ing; all that's required is that for *some* thing done, χ, x's ψ-ing is a χ-ing, and χ-ing is incompatible with φ-ing. How do we determine, in any given case, what χ is?

Most of the descriptions we have, for how agents act, are less than perfectly precise. For instance, we say, 'Alice raises her arm', without specifying the precise path through which she moves her arm. But whenever an agent acts, there is a precise way in which she does what she does – i.e. some precise way of moving, positioning, or otherwise affecting, the relevant body parts and external objects – and which we can, in principle, specify. The same is true of mere behaviours. We say, for instance, 'Alice's arm rises', without specifying the precise path through which her arm moves. But whenever an agent does something – in the broad sense that covers mere behaviours – there is a precise way in which she does it – i.e. some precise way in which the relevant body parts and external objects are moved, positioned, or otherwise affected – and which we can, in principle, specify.[9] I suggest that, if x's ψ-ing ensures that x doesn't φ, the thing x does which is incompatible with φ-ing is, not necessarily ψ, but rather the precise *way* in which she ψ-s.

---

[8] For the same reason, ψ plausibly fails (ii.a), if we adopt Weak Centering: presumably, at least some nearby worlds in which I go through all the *other* steps are worlds in which I also add the garlic.

[9] On some views, this presumption of maximal specificity will fail: an object may satisfy a predicate 'F' without being F in any maximally specific way. For example, Wilson (2013, 2017) argues that an object may exemplify the determinable property *coloured* without exemplifying any determinates of

This suggestion solves the worry about the pasta sauce case. As I go through all the other steps of making the sauce, I move, position, and otherwise affect various body parts and external objects in certain precise ways – e.g. I don't merely slice the tomatoes (something which can be done in a variety of ways); I manipulate my arm, my hand, the knife, and the tomatoes in a certain precise way, carving a precise path through space and time. What's incompatible with adding garlic is not the act of going through all the other steps, but the precise *way* in which I go through those steps. *This* behaviour satisfies clause (ii.b) of the *Incompatibility Condition*: in order to have added garlic, I would have needed, at some point, to have moved, positioned, or otherwise affected my body otherwise than in the precise way that I actually did.[10]

Thus, I propose to modify the *Incompatibility Condition* as follows:

Incompatibility Condition (Final Pass)
'$Ensure(e)(p)(w)(t)$' is true only if:

(i)   For some x and ψ, e is a ψ-ing by x; and
(ii) For some χ, χ is a maximally precise way of ψ-ing, and e is a χ-ing by x; and
(iii) (a) x χ-s at t $\square\!\!\rightarrow$ p at t; and
      (b) $\sim p$ at t $\square\!\!\rightarrow$ $\sim(x$ χ-s at $t)$.

Incompatibility is understood, as before, in terms of subjunctive conditionals. The new clause (ii) simply restricts our attention to maximally precise ways of behaving.

The behaviours by which agents ensure that they don't do various things may be basic actions (I might stifle a laugh by actively keeping my jaw tight), non-basic actions (I might refrain from taking more hors d'oeuvres by playing with the buttons on my jacket), or mere behaviours (I might unintentionally omit to raise my arm by non-actively leaving it in place). I'll conclude this section by explaining, in turn, how to understand the notion of a precise way of behaving, for behaviours of these different types.

In Section 1.2.3, I defended the view that basic actions, in the sense of things done, are all simply ways of moving, positioning, or otherwise affecting one's body. Where φ is a basic action, all that x does, in φ-ing, is to move, position, or otherwise affect her body in the right way. Thus, to

---

this property (*red, blue*, etc.); see also Calosi and Wilson (2019). If such views are correct, my own view can be refined as the view that there's always a *most* specific way in which an agent φ-s.

[10] For the same reason, this behaviour plausibly satisfies (ii.a), even if we adopt Weak Centering: presumably, there are no nearby worlds in which I do *precisely* what I actually did, and yet I succeed in adding the garlic.

specify the precise way in which an agent performs a basic action, we specify the precise way in which she moves, positions, or otherwise affects her body. If Alice raises her arm throughout the interval t_1–t_n, she moves it through a specific series of positions, P_1–P_n, such that her arm is in exactly one of these positions at each moment in the interval.[11] Thus, instead of saying 'Alice raises her arm through t_1–t_n', we can say 'Alice puts her arm in P_1 at t_1, and Alice puts her arm in P_2 at t_2, and . . .', thereby describing the way in which Alice raises her arm in precise detail. Likewise, if Alice keeps her arm perfectly in place throughout t_1–t_n, then there is a single position such that her arm is in that position at each moment in the interval. Thus, instead of saying 'Alice keeps her arm in place through t_1–t_n', we can say 'Alice keeps her arm in P_1 at t_1, and Alice keeps her arm in P_1 at t_2, and . . .', thereby describing the way in which Alice keeps her arm in place, in precise detail.

Some basic actions are mental actions. We've seen that mental actions aren't obviously bodily movements or non-movements: *something* happens in my brain when I make a decision, but this 'something' doesn't obviously consist in me moving or positioning certain parts of my brain. Fortunately, given that token mental actions may be either changes or non-changes, where 'change' encompass more that movement and 'non-change' encompasses more than non-movement, we may describe mental actions, in the sense of things done, in terms of the changes or non-changes that agents bring about in performing them. If to make a decision is to bring about a certain change in the properties of one's brain, then, if Alice makes a decision throughout an interval t_1–t_n, there is a series of properties P_1–P_n such that Alice makes her brain change from possessing P_1 at t_1 to lacking P_1 to possessing P_2 at t_2 . . . to possessing P_n at t_n. If to make a decision is to maintain certain properties of one's brain, then, if Alice makes a decision throughout an interval t_1–t_n, there is a property P_1 such that Alice makes her brain retain P_1 between t_1 and t_n. Thus, we can specify the changes and non-changes in an agent's brain in precise detail, just as we can specify the overt movements and non-movements of an agent's body.

---

[11] It's not required that Alice's arm be in each of these positions at exactly one time in the interval. If she briefly stops moving her arm, her arm will be in the same position at two moments in the interval. We may say that there exist *two* events of Alice raising her arm, one of which ends when Alice briefly stops moving her arm, and the other of which begins when she starts moving her arm again. But it seems that there is also an arm-raising that occupies the entire interval – including the brief moment at which Alice isn't moving her arm – and which has the two smaller arm-raisings as parts.

Turning to non-basic actions, recall from Section 1.2.3, that I don't assume *By-Action Identity*. Thus, I don't assume that token non-basic actions are all bodily events – that is, I don't assume that they consist entirely in an agent moving, positioning, or otherwise affecting some parts of her body, and involve the movement, position, or affection of no object beyond the boundaries of the agent's body. Nonetheless, there does seem to be a clear difference between basic and non-basic actions, in the sense of things done. Basic actions, in this sense, are all simply ways of moving, positioning, or otherwise affecting one's body. By contrast, not all non-basic actions are simply ways of moving, positioning, or otherwise affecting one's body. Sometimes, where φ-ing is a non-basic action, to φ is, in part, to move, position, or otherwise affect some objects beyond the boundaries of one's body in the right way. Raising a coffee cup is like this: it's not enough, for me to raise my coffee cup, that I move my arm in the right way; I must thereby make my coffee cup rise.

Precise ways of performing such non-basic actions are, in principle, no more difficult to specify than precise ways of performing basic actions. For an agent to perform such an action, two broad conditions must be met: she must move, position, or otherwise affect some parts of her body in some (perhaps less than maximally precise) way; and this actions of hers must result in some external objects being moved, positioned, or otherwise affected in some (perhaps less than maximally precise) way. To specify the precise way in which an agent performs such an action, we need only specify the precise way in which she moves, positions, or otherwise affects her body, and the precise way in which the relevant external objects are moved, positioned, or otherwise affected.

Although some non-basic actions involve moving, positioning, or otherwise affecting external objects, not all do. If my right arm is paralyzed, and I use my left arm to raise it, then raising my arm in this way is a non-basic action: I raise my right arm *by* doing various things with my left. Raising my arm in this way is non-basic, but involves no external objects. To specify the precise way in which an agent performs such an action, we need only specify the precise way in which she moves, positions, or otherwise affects certain parts of her body, and the precise way in which certain *distinct* parts of her body are moved, positioned, or otherwise affected.

Turning, finally, to mere behaviours, these don't consist in an agent actively moving, positioning, or otherwise affecting her body. Some mere behaviours consist entirely in some body parts being moved, positioned, or otherwise affected – e.g. if my right arm rises as the result of an involuntary spasm, or if my left arm rises as the result of an involuntary spasm and thereby causes my right arm to rise. To specify the precise way in which an agent performs such a behaviour, we need only specify the precise way in which certain parts of her body are moved, positioned, or otherwise affected, and, if necessary, the precise way in which certain *distinct* parts of her body are moved, positioned, or otherwise affected as a result. For instance, instead of saying, 'Alice's arm rises though t_1–t_n,', we can say, 'Alice's arm is in P_1 at t_1, and Alice's arm is in P_2 at t_2, and . . .', thereby describing the way in which Alice's arm rises in precise detail.

Other mere behaviours consist both in some body parts being moved, positioned, or otherwise affected, and in some external objects being moved, positioned, or otherwise affected – e.g. if my arm rises as the result of an involuntary spasm, thereby causing my coffee cup to rise, then I have raised my coffee cup, but this is a mere behaviour, not an action. To specify the precise way in which an agent performs such a behaviour, we need only specify the precise way in which certain parts of her body are moved, positioned, or otherwise affected, and the precise way in which certain external objects are moved, positioned, or otherwise affected as a result.

5.3.4   *The Extent of a Negative Action 1: Are Basic Negative Actions Mental Events?*

I've assumed that, if φ is a non-mental behaviour, then any behaviour which ensures that x doesn't φ will itself be non-mental, involving the overt movement, positioning, or affection of certain body parts. If token negative actions are ensuring events, it follows that at least some token negative actions are bodily events which extend beyond the agent's brain.

This consequence is, perhaps, most plausible in cases of non-basic negative action where the positive action by which the agent NEG-φ-s is itself non-mental. When I play with the buttons on my jacket to prevent myself from taking another hors d'oeuvre, it's plausible to suppose that, if my refrainment is an event at all, it extends at least as far as the behaviour of my hands, if not to the event of me playing with my buttons as a whole.

This consequence might seem less plausible in cases of basic negative action. Consider the case where I abstain from voting. I've claimed that what ensures that I don't raise my arm (and thereby cast a vote) is the actual behaviour of my arms, but you might think that my negative action doesn't involve the behaviour of my arms, or the overt affection of *any* body parts beyond my brain. My act of abstaining is an exercise of agency.

Since I don't perform any bodily actions *in order* to abstain, you might think that my agency extends only to what goes on in my brain, in this case. I *decide* not to raise my hand, or *deliberately form the intention* not to raise my hand, and that's that. Generalizing: token basic negative actions are mental events – decisions or volitions – involving the affection of no body parts beyond the agent's brain.

There are three problems with this view. First, it just seems *wrong* to say that, when I refrain from raising my arm, my agency extends no further than the act of deciding not to raise my arm. On the contrary, I exercise my agency over my arm by not raising it. To say otherwise is to say that the behaviour of my arm is merely a *result* of an exercise of agency: my arm's staying in place results from my deciding not to raise it, but while the latter is an exercise of agency, the former isn't. But to say this is incorrect. The voting case doesn't belong in the same category as cases in which some bodily behaviour is clearly the mere result of an exercise of agency – e.g. a case in which my right arm is paralyzed and I use my left arm to raise it.[12]

Second, my account of negative behaviours as ensuring events is intended to apply to mere negative behaviours as well as negative actions proper. Just as the standard Neo-Davidsonian schemata for 'x φ' and 'x φ F-ly' apply whether x *acts* in φ-ing or not, the sophisticated Neo-Davidsonian schemata for 'x NEG-φ', 'x NEG-(φ) F-ly', and 'x NEG-(φ F-ly)' apply whether x *acts* in NEG-φ-ing or not. Thus, a sentence like 'Alice omits to raise her arm' quantifies over ensuring events, whether or not Alice *decides* not to raise her arm, and whether or not she *intentionally* omits to raise her arm. If Alice unintentionally omits to raise her arm, then the event quantified over can't be a mental act of deciding not to raise her arm, since there is no such event. More plausibly, it is bodily event, a token behaviour involving her arm. But if such an event can play the ensuring-role in the case of an unintentional omission, there is no reason to think that, in the case of an intentional omission, that role must instead be played by a decision or the formation of an intention.

Finally, the view renders basic negative actions invisible. My decision not to raise my arm is an event which takes place entirely within my skull, and so it can't be seen by anyone. If my abstention *is* this mental action, then no one can see me abstain from voting. Since people obviously *can* see

---

[12] Buckareff makes a similar point about responsibility: '[W]hen we look at cases of omissions for which an agent is morally culpable, it is not just the *mens rea* of the agent that makes them blameworthy. An agent is blameworthy for some behaviour, namely, their intentionally omitting to act' (2018: 4624).

me abstain from voting, the view is false. More generally: if a basic negative action is visible, it can't be a purely mental action.[13]

In making these arguments, I've focused on a case where the relevant φ (i.e. the thing x doesn't do) is non-mental. If φ involves the overt movement, positioning, or affection of certain body parts, then it's plausible that: (a) if x's NEG-φ-ing is a negative *action*, then x's agency extends beyond the brain; (b) the sentence 'x NEG-φ-s' quantifies over an event which extends beyond x's brain; and (c) people can see x NEG-φ, and so this event must be visible. These arguments are less compelling in cases of basic action where the relevant φ is itself mental. Consider a case where I've been ruminating about an argument with a family member, this behaviour has been preventing me from falling asleep, and so I deliberately refrain from thinking about the argument any further. In this case, it's plausible that my refrainment is a mental action invisible to the naked eye, and that my agency extends only as far as my brain. I have no objection, then, to counting x's NEG-φ-ing as a mental event when φ itself is mental action. However, if φ involves the overt movement, positioning, or affection of body parts beyond x's brain, then x's NEG-φ-ing itself involves body parts beyond x's brain.

5.3.5   *The Extent of a Negative Action 2: Relevance*

We have an intuitive sense that, when x NEG-φ-s, some of what x does might be irrelevant to whether she φ-s. Recall the case from Section 5.3.2 in which, as I omit to snap the fingers on my right hand, I both drum my fingers on the table and wiggle the toes on my left foot. Intuitively, what I do with my fingers is relevant to whether I snap them or not, while what I do with my toes isn't. Thus, if we think that negative actions can be identical to bodily events at all, my drumming of my fingers is a good candidate to be my omission, while my wiggling of my toes isn't. Clause (iii.b) of the *Incompatibility Condition* secures this result: my wiggling of my toes doesn't play the ensuring role, in this case, because I might have snapped my fingers while still wiggling my toes. (Or rather, I might have snapped my fingers while wiggling my toes in the precise way that I actually do.)

However, while the *Incompatibility Condition* allows us to rule out some intuitively poor candidates, it leaves some in. Consider the complex action which consists in *both* drumming one's fingers (in a certain maximally

---

[13] The issue of the visibility of token actions is a familiar one. See Hornsby (1986, 1993) and Steward (2000). I discuss the perception of token actions, and especially token negative actions, in Section 6.2.

specific way) *and* in wiggling one's toes (in a certain maximally specific way). Call this complex action '$\chi_{\&}$'. $\chi_{\&}$ satisfies clause (iii.a) of the *Incompatibility Condition*: all the nearby worlds in which I $\chi_{\&}$ are worlds in which I don't snap my fingers; for, $\chi_{\&}$-ing involves drumming one's fingers (in a certain maximally-specific way), and I can't both drum my fingers (in that way) and snap them. It also satisfies clause (iii.b): all the nearby worlds in which I snap my fingers are worlds in which I don't $\chi_{\&}$; for, in order to snap my fingers, I would have needed to move them otherwise than I actually did, in which case I wouldn't have $\chi_{\&}$-ed. But my $\chi_{\&}$-ing is a poor candidate to be my omission, since it encompasses what I do with my toes, and what I do with my toes is irrelevant.

We can make the problem more acute. At any given time, there's a 'total' maximally specific thing that the agent does, i.e. something which encompasses the movement, position, and affection of every part of her body, and of any external objects with which she interacts at that time. Call this behaviour 'χ_T'. In most cases, x's χ_T-ing is a poor candidate to be x's NEG-φ-ing, since it encompasses a large number of irrelevant behaviours – e.g. the total precise thing I do, when I omit to snap my fingers, includes whatever I do with my toes, *and* whatever I do with my mouth, *and* whatever I do with my eyes, etc. But since χ_T encompasses every other maximally specific behaviour in which x engages, the *Incompatibility Condition* always counts x's χ_T-ing as an event which ensures that x doesn't φ.

We must impose an additional condition on '*Ensure*$(e)(p)(w)(t)$' which will help us to single out, among multiple behaviours which are incompatible with φ-ing, one which is appropriately relevant to whether x φ-s or not. Say that one behaviour 'properly includes' another just in case doing the former would require doing the latter, but not vice-versa:

Proper Inclusion
φ properly includes ψ iff, for any x and any t:

(i) $\Box(x$ φ-s at $t \supset x$ ψ-s at $t)$; and
(ii) $\Diamond(x$ ψ-s at t & $\sim(x$ φ-s at $t))$.

We can now impose the following condition:[14]

Relevance Condition
'*Ensure*$(e)(p)(w)(t)$' is true only if:

(i)   For some x and ψ, e is a ψ-ing by x; and
(ii) For some χ, χ is a maximally-precise way of ψ-ing, and e is a χ-ing by x; and

---

[14] Clauses (iii.a) and (iii.b) are inspired by Yablo's (1992a, 1992b) 'proportionality' constraint on causation. Note that '$p \Diamond\!\!\rightarrow \sim q$' is equivalent to '$\sim(p \Box\!\!\rightarrow q)$'.

(iii) (a) For any χ_+ which properly includes χ, $(x \; \chi\text{-s at } t \; \& \; {\sim}(x \; \chi_+\text{-s at } t))$
$\Box{\rightarrow} \; p$ at t; and

(b) For any χ_- which χ properly includes, $(x \; \chi_-\text{-s at } t \; \& \; {\sim}(x \; \chi\text{-s at } t))$
$\Diamond{\rightarrow} \; {\sim}p$ at t.

According to clause (iii.a), χ is the relevant behaviour only if, for any behaviour χ_+ which properly includes χ, p still would have come out true, if x had χ-ed without χ_+-ing. That is, it doesn't matter that $x \; \chi_+$-s: the most that matters is that $x \; \chi$-s, so any additional behaviours encompassed by χ_+ are irrelevant to whether p is true. According to clause (iii.b), χ is the relevant behaviour only if, for any behaviour χ_- which χ properly includes, p might have come out false, if x had χ_--ed without χ-ing. That is, it really matters that $x \; \chi$-s: it's not enough, for p to come out true, that $x \; \chi_-$-s, so at least one additional behaviour encompassed by χ is relevant to whether p is true. To search for a χ which satisfies both clauses (iii.a) and (iii.b), with respect to the proposition that x doesn't φ, is to search for some maximally precise behaviour which is both the most that's required and the least that's necessary, for x not to φ.

Returning to the case where I omit to snap my fingers, and instead I drum my fingers on the table while wiggling my toes, we can now rule out the complex behaviour $\chi_\&$ as irrelevant. For, $\chi_\&$ fails clause (iii.b): it properly includes the behaviour of drumming one's fingers in the precise way I do, and this behaviour already suffices for me not to snap my fingers; for, if I'd drummed my fingers in that way without wiggling my toes (and hence without $\chi_\&$-ing) I *still* wouldn't have snapped my fingers.

Similarly, in most cases where an agent NEG-φ-s, the 'total' maximally precise thing the agent does, χ_T, will fail (iii.b). Typically, not *all* of one's maximally precise behaviour is required, in order for one not to φ; some behaviour properly included in it suffices.

Another kind of case is of interest in illustrating the *Relevance Condition*, namely, the kind in which the thing I omit to do (refrain from doing, etc.) is disjunctive. Suppose that I'm expected *both* to snap my fingers *and* to tap my toes, but I do neither. Letting 'φ_1' and 'φ_2' denote these behaviours, respectively, one thing I omit to do in this case is $(\varphi_1 \lor \varphi_2)$.[15] Now suppose, as before, I drum my fingers on the table while wiggling my toes, in certain precise ways, and call these behaviours 'χ_1' and 'χ_2', respectively.

---

[15] In Section 1.3.5, I argued against the existence of sparse disjunctive properties. However, as noted there, I'm not committed to thinking that all the things we do are sparse properties, so my view allows for disjunctive behaviours.

Neither of these behaviours, on its own, is incompatible with $(\varphi_1 \vee \varphi_2)$-ing: I might drum my fingers in the precise way I do while also tapping my toes, in which case I φ_2 and therefore $(\varphi_1 \vee \varphi_2)$; and I might wiggle my toes in the precise way I do while also snapping my fingers, in which case I φ_1 and therefore $(\varphi_1 \vee \varphi_2)$. What does the ensuring is (a token of) the conjunctive behaviour $(\chi_1 \ \& \ \chi_2)$.[16] This behaviour satisfies clause (iii.b) of the *Relevance Condition*: $(\chi_1 \ \& \ \chi_2)$ properly includes both χ_1 and χ_2, and each of these is such that, if I had done it without doing the other – and hence without $(\chi_1 \ \& \ \chi_2)$-ing – then I might have $(\varphi_1 \vee \varphi_2)$-ed. Thus, what ensures that I neither snap my fingers nor tap my toes is (a token of) the conjunctive behaviour of drumming my fingers and wiggling my toes (in the precise ways I do).

You might worry that, although the *Relevance Condition* rules out some poor candidates for ensuring events, it also rules out some *good* candidates. In the case where I omit to snap my fingers, you might think, what ensures that I don't snap my fingers is my drumming of them. But the *Relevance Condition* doesn't secure this result. The behaviour of drumming one's fingers (in the precise way I do) doesn't satisfy (iii.b), since it properly includes some behaviours which already suffice for me not to snap my fingers. Consider the maximally precise way in which I move just my middle finger. I can't move that finger in the way I do, and also snap my fingers. Moreover, as long as I move that finger in the way I do, it doesn't matter what I do with the rest of my fingers: even if I keep them still, and simply tap the one finger on the table, I won't snap my fingers. Thus, according to the *Relevance Condition*, my drumming of my fingers – a behaviour which involves all of my fingers, not just one – is *not* what ensures that I don't snap them; at most, a token behaviour involving only one finger does the ensuring.

While I agree that my drumming my fingers is an intuitively good candidate to be my omission, it's not clear that it's the *only* good candidate, and that the behaviour of my middle finger is a *bad* candidate. Thus, I'm willing to accept this result, as the price to be paid for an otherwise plausible account which rules out behaviours which are, more plausibly, bad candidates. That is, while I've spoken so far of my token drumming of my fingers as being the event which ensures that I don't snap them, I'm willing to accept that this is, strictly speaking, false.

[16] To see that this conjunctive behaviour satisfies the *Incompatibility Condition*, note that, if I were to $(\chi_1 \ \& \ \chi_2)$, then I wouldn't $(\varphi_1 \vee \varphi_2)$, since χ_1 and χ_2 are incompatible with φ_1 and φ_2, respectively. For the same reason, if I were to $(\varphi_1 \vee \varphi_2)$, then I wouldn't $(\chi_1 \ \& \ \chi_2)$.

Of course, this move will leave us, in any given case, with several events competing to be x's omission to φ (refrainment from φ-ing, etc.). For example, in the case where I omit to snap my fingers, both the behaviour of my middle finger *and* the behaviour of my thumb are candidates. However, I already noted in Section 1.3.2, that we generally face a problem of referential indeterminacy when it comes to event nominals. Whenever Alice kisses Beth, there's a range of candidates to be the referent of 'Alice's kissing of Beth', each of which differs from the others in its 'extent'. Thus, it should come as no surprise if an account of ensuring events leaves us with a range of candidates to be x's omission to φ (refrainment from φ-ing, etc.).

5.3.6   Putting It Together

I submit that the *Time*, *Incompatibility*, and *Relevance* conditions are, not just individually necessary, but jointly sufficient for the truth of '*Ensure*(e) $(p)(w)(t)$'. Together, they provide an account of the conditions an event must meet to play the ensuring role, and hence be identified with x's NEG-φ-ing (*modulo* concerns of referential indeterminacy).

Truth-Conditions for '$Ensure(e)(p)(w)(t)$'
'$Ensure(e)(p)(w)(t)$' is true iff:

(i) e exists in w at t;
(ii)   For some x and ψ, e is a ψ-ing by x;
(iii) For some χ, χ is a maximally precise way of ψ-ing, and e is a χ-ing by x; and
    (a) x χ-s at t $\square\!\!\rightarrow$ p at t;
    (b) $\sim\!p$ at t $\square\!\!\rightarrow$ $\sim\!(x$ χ-s at $t)$;
    (c)   For any χ_+ which properly includes χ, $(x$ χ-s at t & $\sim\!(x$ χ_+-s at $t))$ $\square\!\!\rightarrow$ p at t; and
    (d)   For any χ_- which χ properly includes, $(x$ χ_--s at t & $\sim\!(x$ χ-s at $t))$ $\lozenge\!\!\rightarrow$ $\sim\!p$ at t.

The token behaviour which ensures that x doesn't φ at, and hence is to be identified with x's NEG-φ-ing, is x's χ-ing, where χ is some maximally precise behaviour which x performs at t, which is incompatible with φ-ing, and which, among all the maximally precise things x does at t, is the most that's required and the least that's necessary for x not to φ at t.

5.4   Negation and Positive Action Sentences

Before concluding this chapter, I'll consider a worry you might have about the sophisticated Neo-Davidsonian approach.

According to Deflationism, negative action sentences don't quantify over events. Rather, they express negative existentials: 'x NEG-φ' reports the absence of events in which x φ-s. On this view, a negative action sentence, 'x NEG-φ', is, at its core, simply the negation of a corresponding positive action sentence, 'x φ'. Likewise, a negated negative action sentence, '~(x NEG-φ)' is, at its core, equivalent (by double-negation elimination) to 'x φ'. Thus, the Deflationist accepts – and seems to be in a position to explain – the following equivalences:

x NEG-φ- iff ~(x φ)
~(x NEG-φ) iff x φ

On the sophisticated Neo-Davidsonian view, the relationship between negative action sentences and positive ones is more complicated. 'x NEG-φ' doesn't merely report the absence of events in which x φ-s, and so it isn't simply the negation of 'x φ'. Likewise, '~(x NEG-φ)' reports the absence of an event which ensures that x doesn't φ. On this view, the equivalences don't hold.

For concreteness, consider the following sentences, along with (what I claim to be) their Neo-Davidsonian analyses:

(4)   Alice omitted to kiss Beth.
(4_{SND}) $\exists e(Agent(Alice)(e)$ & $Ensure(e)(\sim\exists e'(Agent(Alice)(e')$ & $Patient$ $(Beth)(e')$ & $Kiss_{ND}(e'))))$

(13)   Alice didn't kiss Beth.
(13_{SND}) $\sim\exists e(Agent(Alice)(e)$ & $Patient(Beth)(e)$ & $Kiss_{ND}(e))$

(4~)   Alice didn't omit to kiss Beth.
($4\sim_{SND}$) $\sim(\exists e(Agent(Alice)(e)$ & $Ensure(e)(\sim\exists e'(Agent(Alice)(e')$ & $Patient$ $(Beth)(e')$ & $Kiss_{ND}(e')))))$

(13~)   Alice kissed Beth.
($13\sim_{SND}$) $\exists e(Agent(Alice)(e)$ & $Patient(Beth)(e)$ & $Kiss_{ND}(e))$

(4_{SND}) implies (13_{SND}), as it should. The *Incompatibility Condition* developed in the previous section secures the intuitive result that ensuring is factive: e ensures that p only if p is true; thus, e ensures that Alice didn't kiss Beth only if Alice didn't kiss Beth. More generally, 'x NEG-φ' implies '~(x φ)', and so conversely, 'x φ' implies '~(x NEG-φ)'. However, ($4\sim_{SND}$) doesn't imply ($13\sim_{SND}$). Consider a time after both Alice and Beth have ceased to exist. At that time, there exist no events of which Alice is the agent, and hence no events of which she is the agent and which ensure that she doesn't kiss Beth. Thus, ($4\sim_{SND}$) is true. But, for the same reason, ($13\sim_{SND}$) is *false*: there exist no events of which Alice is the agent, and no event of Alice kissing Beth. The same case shows that (13_{SND}) doesn't imply (4_{SND}): in this case, (13_{SND}) is true but (4_{SND}) is false. Thus, we don't have it that '$\sim(x \text{ NEG-}\varphi)$' implies '$x \varphi$' or that '$\sim(x \varphi)$' implies '$x \text{ NEG-}\varphi$'.

The sophisticated Neo-Davidsonian should bite this particular bullet. First, attention to the differences between merely not doing something, on one hand, and various kinds of negative actions, on the other, shows that the equivalences don't *generally* hold. Consider: even by the Deflationist's lights, 'Alice didn't kiss Beth' can be true while 'Alice refrained from kissing Beth' is false; in order to *refrain* from kissing Beth, Alice must *intentionally* fail to kiss her, but she can fail to kiss Beth without forming any relevant intention.

Second, we can do justice to our sense that '$x \text{ NEG-}\varphi$' and '$\sim(x \varphi)$' are equivalent, in cases where that equivalence seems more plausible (e.g. in cases involving omission sentences[17]). Consider: Although ($4\sim$) doesn't *imply* ($13\sim$), on the sophisticated Neo-Davidsonian view, the following subjunctive will hold in any ordinary case in which Alice omits to kiss Beth:

(14) If Alice hadn't omitted to kiss Beth, then she would have kissed Beth.

Equivalently: if ($4\sim$) had been true, then ($13\sim$) would have been true. We've seen that there are cases in which ($4\sim$) is true and ($13\sim$) is false, namely, cases in which Alice doesn't exist. But if (14) is assessed from a world in which (4) is true, then the closest worlds in which ($4\sim$) is true are, presumably, worlds in which Alice *exists*, and is the agent of some event(s), but none of these events ensures that she doesn't kiss Beth. This requires, at minimum, that no maximally precise behaviour of hers be incompatible with kissing Beth. The only way for that requirement to be met, it seems, is for her to kiss Beth.

Likewise, although (13) doesn't *imply* (4), on the sophisticated Neo-Davidsonian view, the following subjunctive will hold in any ordinary case in which Alice kisses Beth (and she was supposed or expected to do so):

(15) If Alice hadn't kissed Beth, then she would have omitted to kiss Beth.

Equivalently: if (13) had been true, then (4) would have been true. If (15) is assessed from a world in which ($13\sim$) is true, then the closest worlds in

---

[17] I've argued that 'x omits to φ' merely presupposes that x is supposed or expected to φ, rather than having this as part of its semantic content. Thus, it's at least *prima facie* plausible that, although (4) and (13) aren't equivalent in the sense that one is entitled to assert the former just in case one is entitled to assert the latter, they're equivalent in the sense that the *content* of the former is true just in case the *content* of the latter is.

which (13) is true are, presumably, worlds in which Alice exists, but doesn't kiss Beth. But if Alice doesn't kiss Beth, then she must perform some maximally precise behaviour which is incompatible with kissing Beth. Assuming that we can, in principle, specify some such behaviour which is not only incompatible with kissing Beth, but also appropriately relevant to whether Alice kisses Beth, the only way for Alice to fail to kiss Beth is for some token behaviour of hers to *ensure* that she doesn't do so.

Thus, the sophisticated Neo-Davidsonian can deny that 'x NEG-φ' and '$\sim(x\ \varphi)$' are equivalent in the sense that one is always true if and only if the other is, but insist that they're equivalent in the sense that, in any ordinary case, one *will be* true if and only if the other is, or *would have been* true if and only if the other had been.

5.5 Conclusion

I've developed an approach to the analysis of negative action sentences on which these sentences don't simply express negative existentials, but existentially quantify over events. If successful, this approach allows us to reject (PNA 3), and claim that negative actions are events, just as positive ones are. I've shown that the approach has the resources to answer the case for Deflationism from Chapter 4, since it avoids the problems that plagued the simple Neo-Davidsonian approach. However, it's one thing to show that the sophisticated Neo-Davidsonian approach avoids the problems facing the simple approach; it's another to show that it ought to be accepted over Deflationism. It's to this task that I now turn.

CHAPTER 6

The Logical Form of Negative Action Sentences III
The Approach Defended

6.1 Introduction

In this chapter, I offer positive arguments for adopting the sophisticated Neo-Davidsonian approach to negative action sentences. In Section 6.2, I argue that this approach explains linguistic data regarding the interaction of negative action sentences and perceptual locutions. I consider various ways in which the Deflationist might accommodate this data, and argue that they're unsatisfactory. In Section 6.3, I return to the topic of adverbs. We saw in Chapters 4 and 5 that, while Deflationism has trouble allowing for the existence of narrow-scope readings of adverbially modified negative action sentences, the sophisticated Neo-Davidsonian approach handles them quite easily. In this section, I defend the existence of such readings. Finally, in Section 6.4, I consider two recent approaches to the analysis of negative action sentences which differ both from Deflationism and from my own approach. I argue that both alternatives face serious problems.

6.2 Perceptual Locutions

6.2.1 Perceptual Locutions and Positive Action Sentences

In Section 4.2.2, I sketched two arguments for taking a Neo-Davidsonian approach to positive action sentences: the approach explains why seemingly valid adverb-dropping inferences are valid, by assimilating them to the form, '$\exists x(Fx \ \& \ Gx)$; therefore, $\exists xFx$'; and it explains why seemingly invalid adverb-adding inferences are invalid, by assimilating them to the form, '$\exists xFx$; therefore, $\exists x(Fx \ \& \ Gx)$'. There's another source of evidence for the Neo-Davidsonian approach: that approach makes the best sense of sentences in which ordinary action phrases – i.e. phrases of the form '$x \ \varphi$', where 'φ' is taken to denote a positive action or behaviour rather than a negative one – interact with perceptual locutions.

138

The argument draws on pairs of sentences of the forms, '*x* sees *y* φ' and '*x* sees that *y* φ-s'/'*x* sees that *y* is φ-ing', e.g.:[1]

(1) Charlie saw Alice kiss Beth.
(2) Charlie saw that Alice was kissing Beth.

Sentences of the first form report that some agent stands in a perceptual relation to some aspect of the external world – e.g. (1) reports that Alice kissed Beth and that Charlie saw this happen. Sentences of the second form, by contrast, report that an agent stands in a certain cognitive relation to some proposition – e.g. (2) reports that Charlie stood in the relation of seeing-that to the proposition *Alice is kissing Beth*. It's difficult to say precisely what seeing-that amounts to, but I take it that seeing-that *p* is a way of knowing that *p* (Williamson 2000: 33–41). (2) reports that, at the relevant time, Charlie possessed perceptual knowledge that Alice was kissing Beth at that time.

For the purposes of the argument, there are two important facts about (1) and (2). First, the names 'Alice and Beth' occur in a transparent context in (1) and in an opaque context in (2). Co-referring terms and descriptions can be substituted *salva veritate* in (1). For instance, if Alice is the tallest person in the room, then (1) entails (3).

(3) Charlie saw the tallest person in the room kiss Beth.

By contrast, co-referring terms and descriptions can't be substituted *salva veritate* in (2). Even if Alice is the tallest person in the room, (2) doesn't entail (4).

(4) Charlie saw that the tallest person in the room was kissing Beth.

The reason is that (2) might be true even if Charlie didn't know that Alice was the tallest person in the room.

Second, neither (1) nor (2) entails the other. (1) doesn't entail (2) because, again, '*x* sees that *p*' entails '*x* knows that *p*'. Charlie might see Alice kiss Beth without knowing that it's Alice and Beth he's seeing, and so without knowing that Alice is kissing Beth.

Why doesn't (2) entail (1)? The answer, roughly, is that Charlie can have perceptual knowledge that Alice is kissing Beth without actually seeing Alice kiss Beth. A complete defense of this claim would require an account of perceptual knowledge, and I have none to offer. I'll rest content

---

[1] The argument is based on Parsons (1990: 15–17), although I develop it differently than Parsons does.

with the claim that x sees that p just in case x comes to know p as a sufficiently direct result of visual perceptual experience. It's not always clear when a bit of knowledge is a 'sufficiently direct' result of visual perceptual experience to count as an instance of seeing-that.[2] But it's plausible that Charlie's knowledge that Alice is kissing Beth can be a sufficiently direct result of visual perceptual experience, even if he doesn't see Alice and Beth kiss (e.g. in a case where he only sees their shadows).

A Neo-Davidsonian can accommodate the data as follows. First, we give the action sentence 'Alice kissed Beth' the Neo-Davidsonian treatment:

(5)   Alice kissed Beth.
(5_{ND}) $\exists e(Agent(\text{Alice})(e)\ \&\ Patient(\text{Beth})(e)\ \&\ Kiss_{\text{ND}}(e))$

(5) reports that an event of a certain kind – a kissing of Beth by Alice – occurred. We then take (1) to report that Charlie saw an event of that kind – in Neo-Davidsonian terms, that there occurred a seeing-event whose agent is Charlie and whose patient is an event of Alice kissing of Beth:

(1_{ND}) $\exists e\exists e'(Agent(\text{Charlie})(e)\ \&\ Patient(e')(e)\ \&\ Seeing_{\text{ND}}(e)\ \&\ Agent(\text{Alice})(e')\ \&\ Patient(\text{Beth})(e')\ \&\ Kiss_{\text{ND}}(e'))$

By contrast, we take (2) to report that Charlie had a certain attitude towards the proposition, *Alice is kissing Beth*:[3]

(2_{ND})   Sees-that(Charlie)(Alice is kissing Beth)

This approach explains why 'Alice' and 'Beth' occur in a transparent context in (1) but an opaque one in (2). 'Alice' and 'Beth' figure, in (1), in the description of the event Charlie saw. Now, substitution of co-referring terms and/or descriptions for 'Alice' and/or 'Beth' plausibly results not in a description of a new event, but a new description of the old one: e.g. if Alice is the tallest person in the room, then the event of Beth being kissed by Alice *is* the event of Beth being kissed by the tallest

---

[2] Can I see that it's currently midnight in Dubai by looking at a clock in the Toronto airport that says so? That seems plausible. At least, it seems *as* plausible as the claim that I can see that it's currently midnight wherever I am by looking at a clock. There's little by way of inference or calculation in either case; I simply see what the time is in the relevant place. Can I see that it's currently midnight in Dubai by looking at a clock that says it's 4:00pm in Toronto, given that I know that Dubai is eight hours ahead of Toronto? That seems less plausible – there's certainly more by way of inference and calculation – but I know of no way to give a precise demarcation of 'sufficiently direct' which will yield a verdict one way or the other.

[3] Here, I ignore the issue of how progressive aspect is to be understood in a Neo-Davidsonian framework. Rather than provide an analysis of *Alice is kissing Beth*, I simply use the English label for this proposition. Nothing in what follows hinges on the correct treatment of progressive aspect.

person in the room. But in general, if $x = y$, then 'z sees x' entails 'z sees y'. Thus, in the right circumstances, (1_{ND}) entails (3_{ND}):

(3_{ND}) $\exists e \exists e' (Agent(\text{Charlie})(e)$ & $Patient(e')(e)$ & $Seeing_{ND}(e)$ & $Agent(\text{the tallest person in the room})(e')$ & $Patient(\text{Beth})(e')$ & $Kiss_{ND}(e'))$

By contrast, assuming that (2) is to be read *de dicto* rather than *de re* (i.e. it isn't to be read as equivalent to 'Charlie had perceptual knowledge, of Alice, that she was kissing Beth') we should expect that co-referring terms and descriptions for Alice and Beth can't be substituted *salva veritate* in (2), since *de dicto* propositional attitude reports quite generally don't allow such substitutions. Thus, (2_{ND}) doesn't entail (4_{ND}) in any circumstance:

(4_{ND}) Sees-that(Charlie)(The tallest person in the room is kissing Beth)

The approach also explains why neither (1) nor (2) entails the other. (1_{ND}) doesn't entail (2_{ND}) because (2_{ND}) reports perceptual knowledge that a certain kind of event is unfolding, and Charlie can easily see an event of a certain kind without knowing that it *is* (or will be, upon completion) an event of that kind. (2_{ND}) doesn't entail (1_{ND}) because (2_{ND}) merely reports that Charlie had perceptual knowledge of a certain proposition, and carries no information about how he obtained it – that is, (2_{ND}) carries no information about what Charlie saw, and which allowed him to know that Alice was kissing Beth.

A proponent of the traditional approach to action sentences sketched in Section 4.2.1 might try to accommodate the data in a different way. On that approach, (5) is analyzed as (5_T):

(5_T) *Kiss*(Alice)(Beth)

How, then, is (1) to be analyzed? What does (1) report Charlie as seeing, if not an event? A natural answer is that it reports Charlie as seeing *Alice*. More specifically, it reports that Charlie saw Alice as she kissed Beth:[4]

(1_T) *Sees*(Charlie)(Alice) & *Kiss*(Alice)(Beth)

Since I've left the proposition *Alice is kissing Beth* unanalyzed, (2) can be analyzed as (2_{ND}) as before. This approach seems to explain why 'Alice' and 'Beth' occur in an opaque context in (1), since there's no reason to think that either '*Sees*' or '*Kiss*' generates an opaque context. And it seems to explain why neither (1) nor (2) entails the other: that Charlie saw Alice

[4] Note that, since we're currently considering a non-Davidsonian view, 'sees' is no longer taken to contribute an event-variable.

while she kissed Beth doesn't entail that he knew either that it was Alice he was seeing or that what she was doing is kissing Beth; and, as before, (2) reports that Charlie has perceptual knowledge of a certain proposition without containing information about how he obtained it.

There are reasons to prefer the Neo-Davidsonian approach to the traditional one. First, consider how (1) relates to (6):

(1) Charlie saw Alice kiss Beth.
(6) Charlie saw Alice kiss Beth, and David saw it, too.

It seems that (1) reports that Charlie saw something, and that (6) adds that David saw that same thing: 'it' in (6) seems to function anaphorically, referring back to some object introduced in (1). This is no problem on the Neo-Davidsonian approach: (1) reports that Charlie saw an event of Alice kissing of Beth, and (6) adds that David saw that same event.

(6$_{ND}$) $\exists e \exists e' \exists e''$ (*Agent*(Charlie)(*e*) & *Patient*(*e'*)(*e*) & *Seeing*$_{ND}$(*e*) & *Agent* (Alice)(*e'*) & *Patient*(Beth)(*e'*) & *Kiss*$_{ND}$(*e'*) & *Agent*(David)(*e''*) & *Patient*(*e'*)(*e''*) & *Seeing*$_{ND}$(*e''*))

By contrast, on the traditional approach, (1) reports that Charlie saw Alice while she kissed Beth, and so (6) should presumably add that David saw her, too.

(6$_T$) *Sees*(Charlie)(Alice) & *Kiss*(Alice)(Beth) & *Sees*(David)(Alice)

But if (6) reports that Charlie and David saw the same *person*, rather than that they saw the same *event*, the presence of the impersonal pronoun 'it' is odd. We should expect (6$_T$) to be expressed in English with a personal pronoun ('he', 'she', 'they') and for the use of the impersonal 'it' to be objectionable. But (6) sounds fine as it is.

Second, (1$_T$) and (6$_T$) get the truth-conditions for (1) and (6) wrong. (1$_T$) says that Charlie saw Alice while she kissed Beth. But Charlie can see Alice while she kisses Beth, even if he doesn't actually see her kiss Beth. Suppose that Alice and Beth are standing next to a table when the kiss occurs, and suppose that Charlie is a small child hiding under the table. Charlie can see Alice's legs, and hence he can see Alice, but his view is obstructed from roughly her waist up. In such a case, it seems that (1$_T$) is true but (1) is false: Charlie sees Alice while she kisses Beth, but he doesn't actually see her kiss Beth. A similar argument shows that (6$_T$) can be true while (6) is false. (Simply add David under the table.)

The Neo-Davidsonian can explain why (1) is false, in the case described above. In order for Charlie to see Alice kiss Beth, he must see the kiss itself, an *event*. But, since Charlie's view is obstructed roughly from Alice's waist up, he can't see this event. For, kissing Beth is something that Alice does by moving and positioning various parts of her body, none of which is located below her waist. The kiss consists in Alice moving and positioning parts of her body that are out of Charlie's view, and so the event itself is out of his view. Thus, (1_{ND}) is false in this case. A similar argument shows that, in the case where David is also under the table, (6_{ND}) is false. Thus, while the traditional approach gets the truth-conditions of (1) and (6) wrong, the Neo-Davidsonian approach seems to get them right.

Wyner (1989) and Landman (2000: 27–30) worry that the Neo-Davidsonian approach will validate intuitively invalid inferences. Suppose that Charlie saw Alice leave the house and that, unbeknownst to Charlie, Alice had a knife hidden under her coat. It's plausible that the event of Alice leaving the house is identical to the event of her leaving the house with a knife hidden under her coat. Thus, just as the Neo-Davidsonian approach validates the inference from (1) to (3), it validates the inference from (7) to (8):[5]

(7)   Charlie saw Alice leave the house.

(7_{ND}) $\exists e \exists e' (Agent(\text{Charlie})(e)\ \&\ Patient(e')(e)\ \&\ Seeing_{ND}(e)\ \&\ Agent(\text{Alice})(e')\ \&\ Patient(\text{house})(e')\ \&\ Leave_{ND}(e'))$

(8)   Charlie saw Alice leave the house with a knife hidden under her coat.

(8_{ND}) $\exists e \exists e' (Agent(\text{Charlie})(e)\ \&\ Patient(e')(e)\ \&\ Seeing_{ND}(e)\ \&\ Agent(\text{Alice})(e')\ \&\ Patient(\text{house})(e')\ \&\ Leave_{ND}(e')$
    $\&\ \exists x(Knife(x)\ \&\ With(e')(x)))$

But Wyner and Landman think that, while (7) is true in this case, (8) is false: Charlie sees Alice leave the house, but doesn't see her leave the house with a knife hidden under her coat.

Of course, there's *something* odd about asserting (8) in this case, but we can explain this while allowing that (8) is true. I've distinguished the locutions '*x* sees *y* φ' and '*x* sees that *y* is φ-ing'. In general, the former locution doesn't entail the latter. Thus, (8) can be true while (9) is false.

(9)   Charlie saw that Alice was leaving the house with a knife hidden under her coat.

Nonetheless, an utterance of (8) can be heard as *suggesting* that (9) is true. (More generally, an utterance of '*x* sees an *F*' can be heard as suggesting

---

[5] '*With*' denotes a thematic role. Roughly, '$With(e)(x)(w)(t)$' is true if, whatever *e* is a doing of, the agent of *e* does that thing with *x*. I ignore the complexity of the phrase, '*x* is hidden under *y*'s coat', and let '$\exists x(Knife(x)(w)(t)\ \&\ With(e)(x)(w)(t))$' stand in for the contribution of 'with a knife hidden under her coat'.

that x sees-that *There is an F.*) If it's heard in that way, then an utterance of (8) is objectionable, because (9) is false: for, it was stipulated that Charlie has no knowledge of the knife hidden under Alice's coat. Thus, (8) sounds bad, even though it's true.

To see that this explanation is correct, consider how Charlie should reply, if asked whether he saw Alice leave the house with a knife hidden under her coat. Obviously, he shouldn't say 'Yes'. But he shouldn't say 'No', either. His answer should be the more qualified 'I don't know'. (If he's feeling snippy, he might reply, 'How should I know, if the knife was *hidden?*') This is because, given that Charlie saw Alice leave her house, *if* she had a knife hidden under her coat, *then* he saw her leave with a knife hidden under her coat. Thus, if Charlie says that he didn't see Alice leave with a knife hidden under her coat, he thereby commits himself to the claim that she didn't have a knife hidden under her coat. Since he's in no position to know that, he must neither affirm nor deny (8), but simply say, 'I don't know'.

Summing up: the Neo-Davidsonian approach to action sentences does better than the traditional approach at capturing the truth-conditions of 'x sees y φ' and the relationships between that locution and the 'x sees that y is φ-ing' locution; and we can adopt this approach without validating intuitively invalid inferences.

6.2.2   *Perceptual Locutions and Negative Action Sentences*

I've just argued that, when 'φ' denotes a positive action or behaviour, a sentence of the form 'x sees y φ' should be analyzed as reporting that x sees the event of y φ-ing. But the 'x sees y φ' locution is acceptable in cases where 'φ' denotes a *negative* action or behaviour as well. Consider:

   (10) Charlie saw Alice omit to kiss Beth.
   (11) Charlie saw Alice refrain from kissing Beth.

(10) and (11) are just as acceptable as (1) is. And the arguments for a Neo-Davidsonian approach to (1) apply to (10) and (11), as well.

Focusing on (10), first note that 'Alice' and 'Beth' occur in a transparent context in (10) but an opaque one in (12):

   (12) Charlie saw that Alice was omitting to kiss Beth.

If Alice is the tallest person in the room, then (13) follows from (10), but (14) doesn't follow from (12):

   (13) Charlie saw the tallest person in the room omit to kiss Beth.
   (14) Charlie saw that the tallest person in the room was omitting to kiss Beth.

Second, note that neither (10) nor (12) entails the other. Charlie might see Alice omit to kiss Beth without seeing that Alice is omitting to kiss Beth, since he might not know that it's Alice and Beth he's seeing. And Charlie might see that Alice is omitting to kiss Beth even if he doesn't actually see Alice omit to kiss Beth – e.g. in a case where he only sees their shadows.

Finally, compare (10) with (15):

(15) Charlie saw Alice omit to kiss Beth, and David saw it, too.

It seems that (10) reports that Charlie saw something, and that (15) adds that David saw that same thing: 'it' in (21) seems to function anaphorically, referring back to some object introduced in (15).

If we adopt the sophisticated Neo-Davidsonian schemata for negative action sentences developed in Chapter 5, we can give an explanation of these facts which parallels the explanation given in Section 6.2.1. Given those schemata, (16) is analyzed as (16_{SND}):

(16)   Alice omitted to kiss Beth.
(16_{SND}) $\exists e(Agent(\text{Alice})(e)$ & $Ensure(e)(\sim\exists e'(Agent(\text{Alice})(e')$ & $Patient$ $(\text{Beth})(e')$ & $Kiss_{ND}(e'))))$

(16) reports the occurrence of an event in which Alice ensures that she doesn't kiss Beth. We can therefore take (10) to report that Charlie saw an event of this kind:

(10_{SND}) $\exists e \exists e'(Agent(\text{Charlie})(e)$ & $Patient(e')(e)$ & $Seeing_{ND}(e)$ & $Agent$ $(\text{Alice})(e')$ & $Ensure(e')(\sim\exists e''(Agent(\text{Alice})(e'')$ & $Patient(\text{Beth})(e'')$ & $Kiss_{ND}(e''))))$

Given this analysis, we can explain why 'Alice' and 'Beth' occur in a transparent context in (10): (10) reports that Charlie sees an event of a certain kind, and 'Alice' and 'Beth' figure in the description of the event seen; thus, substitution of co-referring terms and/or descriptions for 'Alice' and 'Beth' simply results in a new description of the same event; that's why (10) entails (13).

We can also explain why neither (10) nor (12) entails the other: (10) doesn't entail (12) because (12) reports perceptual knowledge that a certain kind of event is unfolding, and Charlie can easily see an event of a certain kind without knowing that it is (or will be, upon completion) an event of that kind; and (12) doesn't entail (10) because (10) merely reports that Charlie had perceptual knowledge of a certain proposition, and carries no information about how he obtained it.

Finally, we can explain what's going on in (15): (10) says that Charlie saw an event of a certain kind, and (15) adds that David saw that same event.

(15$_{\text{SND}}$) $\exists e \exists e' \exists e''$(Agent(Charlie)(e) & Patient(e')(e) & Seeing$_{\text{ND}}$(e) & Agent(Alice)(e') & Ensure(e')($\sim\exists e'''$(Agent(Alice)(e'') & Patient (Beth)(e'') & Kiss$_{\text{ND}}$(e'''))) & Agent(David)(e') & Patient(e')(e') & Seeing$_{\text{ND}}$(e'))

The Deflationist will have a harder time accommodating and explaining the data. The Neo-Davidsonian approach works by taking the '*x* sees *y* φ' locution to report that *x* sees an event of the kind whose occurrence is reported by the simpler, '*y* φ-s' locution. According to the Deflationist, however, the latter locution doesn't report the occurrence of an event at all, if 'φ' denotes a negative action or behaviour. Apparently, there *is* no object that Charlie can be taken to see when he sees Alice omit to kiss Beth. Thus, just as facts about perceptual locutions support the Neo-Davidsonian approach to positive action sentences against a more traditional approach, those same facts support the sophisticated Neo-Davidsonian approach to negative action sentences against Deflationism.

6.2.3 Deflationist Responses

How might the Deflationist reap the benefits of treating '*x* sees *y* NEG-φ' as a report of object-perception? What does (10), 'Charlie saw Alice omit to kiss Beth', report Charlie as seeing?

The Deflationist might claim that (10) reports, not that Charlie saw an omission of Alice's (considered as an event), but that he saw *Alice*, as she omitted to kiss Beth.

(10$_{\text{DEF1}}$) $\exists e$(Agent(Charlie)(e) & Patient(Alice)(e) & Seeing$_{\text{ND}}$(e) & $\sim\exists e'$ (Agent(Alice)(e') & Patient(Beth)(e') & Kiss$_{\text{ND}}$(e')))

This proposal fails for the same reasons that the corresponding proposal regarding positive action sentences failed in Section 6.2.1. First, if (10) reports that Charlie saw a person, then the presence of the impersonal pronoun 'it' in (15) should be objectionable, but it isn't. Second, (10$_{\text{DEF1}}$) gets the truth-conditions of (10) wrong. (10$_{\text{DEF1}}$) says that Charlie saw Alice while she omitted to kiss Beth. But Charlie might see Alice while she omits to kiss Beth, even if he doesn't actually see her omit to kiss Beth. Suppose that Alice and Beth are standing next to a table when the omission occurs, and suppose that Charlie is a small child hiding under the table. Charlie can see Alice's legs, and hence he can see Alice but his view is obstructed from roughly her waist up. In such a case, it seems that (10$_{\text{DEF1}}$) is true but (10) is false: Charlie sees Alice while she omits to kiss Beth, but he doesn't see her omit to kiss Beth.

(Note that the sophisticated Neo-Davidsonian can explain why (10) is false, in this case. (10) reports that Charlie sees an event of a certain kind, an omission by Alice to kiss Beth. According to the account of Chapter 5, this is an event in which Alice does some maximally precise χ which is incompatible with kissing Beth. Plausibly, the relevant χ is the maximally precise way in which Alice moves, positions, or otherwise affects the parts of her body that would, or might, have been involved, if she had kissed Beth: it's *those* parts that she would have needed to move, position, or affect differently than she actually did, if she were to kiss Beth; and any behaviour which involves those body and parts and more besides will fail the *Relevance Condition*, since it includes a χ which suffices, on its own, for Alice not to kiss Beth. Since those body parts are out of Charlie's view, the omission is out of his view, too.)

As an alternative, the Deflationist might attempt to 'piggy-back' on the sophisticated Neo-Davidsonian approach, claiming that while negative action sentences don't quantify over ensuring events, sentences of the form 'x sees y NEG-φ' do. That is, she might claim that while (16), 'Alice omitted to kiss Beth', expresses a negative existential, (10) is to be analyzed as (10_{SND}), just as I've argued.

This view violates a plausible compositionality constraint on semantic theorizing: roughly, if α is a complex phrase and β_1–β_n are its constituents, then the denotation of α is a function of the denotations of β_1–β_n. This suggests that, if 'x sees y NEG-φ' quantifies over, and hence contains a variable for, ensuring events, then that variable must be contributed by one of this phrase's constituents. On the sophisticated Neo-Davidsonian view, this variable is contributed by 'y NEG-φ'. The Deflationist, of course, can't give this explanation. She owes us an alternative, and none is obviously forthcoming.

Finally, the Deflationist might claim (10) reports that Charlie saw an absence of a certain kind, namely, an absence of events in which Alice kisses Beth. Thus, (10) is analyzed as (something like) (10_{DEF2}):[6]

(10_{DEF2}) $\exists e \exists x (\textit{Agent}(\text{Charlie})(e) \ \& \ \textit{Patient}(x)(e) \ \& \ \textit{Seeing}_{\text{ND}}(e) \ \& \ \textit{Absence}(x))$

Of course, if we're skeptical of absences *qua* entities – as I argued we should be in Section 2.3.4 – this will seem like an unattractive analysis. However, the Deflationist might point out that believers in absences have

---

[6] For simplicity, I let the '*Absence*$(x)(w)(t)$' stand in for the proposition that x is an absence of events in which Alice kisses Beth in w at t.

defended their position precisely by appealing to perceptual locutions: according to them, we can *see* absences, just as we can see ordinary objects.

Taylor (1952: 444–445) considers a case in which I'm confronted with an image of two circles. One of these circles has a dot at its centre, the other is empty. According to Taylor, when I look at the second circle, I perceive, not only the circle, but the absence of dots at its centre. I don't need to *infer* that a dot is absent; I simply see that there's no dot (445).

Recalling Section 6.2.1, it's easy to see where the argument goes wrong. When I look at the circle, I see *that* there's no dot; or, as Taylor would put it, I see *that* dots are absent, or that there's an absence of dots. But when '*x* sees an *F*' is a literal report of object perception, it's neither equivalent to, nor entailed by, '*x* sees that there is an *F*'. Thus, even leaving aside the concern that the quantification over absences in (17) may be best understood non-seriously, it isn't equivalent to, and doesn't entail, (18), if (18) is understood as a literal report of object perception.

(17) I see that there's an absence of dots./I see that dots are absent.
(18) I see an absence of dots.

The distinction between 'I see that dots are absent' and 'I see an absence of dots', so understood, is no doubt obscured by the fact that believers in absences tend to think of them as facts or state of affairs, and to talk about them in those terms. Indeed, Taylor (1952: 433–434) presents his argument in the context of a general ontology of states of affairs, which later discussions have also assumed (Kukso 2006; Molnar 2000). Thus, the claim that I see an absence of dots is presented as the claim that I see 'the fact that there is no dot in the circle' (Taylor 1952: 445) or 'the negative fact that the circle is empty of dots' (Molnar 2000: 79), or perhaps that I have the 'perception of the dot's being absent' (Kukso 2006: 31). These ways of speaking only serve to confuse the claim that I see *that* there's no dot (which is acceptable) with the claim that I see an absence of dots (which I reject).

Of course, we often use sentences like (18), but I suggest that the '*x* sees an absence of *F*s' locution, like any other locution which apparently quantifies over absences, should be taken as a figurative shorthand.

To see why, consider that (17) and (18), as they would ordinarily be used, are interchangeable: I can appropriately be said to 'see the absence of dots' only if I see *that* there are no dots. To illustrate this, Molnar (2000: 80) points out that, in Taylor's case, the second circle isn't merely empty of dots; it's also empty of dashes, squares, triangles, etc. If I can simply *see* the absence of dots, I should be able to see these absences, as well. And yet, it seems wrong to say, 'I see the absence of dashes (squares, triangles, etc.)'. The reason, it seems, is that I don't see *that* there are no dashes (squares, triangles, etc.). In general, I can be said to 'see the absence of *F*s' on a given occasion only if the fact that there are no *F*s is salient to me, on that occasion (e.g. if I was looking for an *F* and found none). As Taylor's case is set up, the first circle contains a dot, and so the fact that the second circle contains no dots is made salient to me. But the fact that the second circle contains no dashes (squares, triangles, etc.) isn't made salient, and so it's wrong to say, 'I see the absence of dashes (squares, triangles, etc.)'.[7]

So, as the locutions '*x* sees that there is an absence of *F*s/*x* sees that there are no *F*s' and '*x* sees an absence of *F*s' are ordinarily used, they're interchangeable. If the latter were used as a literal report of object perception, in which the quantification over absences was taken ontologically seriously, this would be mysterious; in general, '*x* sees that there is an *F*' and '*x* sees an *F*' aren't equivalent. The mystery dissolves, however, if the '*x* sees an absence of *F*s' locution is understood not as a literal report of object perception, but as a figurative shorthand for '*x* sees that there are no *F*s'.[8]

If the preceding discussion is correct, the perceptual argument for realism about absences fails: it's never *literally* true that there's an x and y such that x is an absence of *F*s and y sees x. Thus, the analysis of (10) as (10_{DEF2}) gets no support from this argument.

There are two further problems with the analysis. First, there's a compositionality problem. If '*x* sees *y* NEG-φ' quantifies over, and hence contains a variable for, absences, then that variable must be contributed by one of this phrase's constituents. But according to the Deflationist, the

---

[7] Compare the discussion of (8), 'Charlie saw Alice leave the house with a knife hidden under her coat', and (9), 'Charlie saw *that* Alice was leaving the house with a knife hidden under her coat'. Although (8) can be heard as suggesting (9), I argued that (8) can be heard as true even when (9) is false. The same doesn't seem to be true of (18) and (17): it doesn't seem sensible to say that I saw the absence of dots unless I saw *that* there were no dots.

[8] Molnar (2000: 80) draws a different conclusion. He recognizes that, as they're ordinarily used, (18) is true iff (17) is. He also recognizes the oddity of this, given the ontologically serious reading of (18). Thus, he denies that (17) is true and, more generally, denies that any sentence of the form '*x* sees that there is absence of *F*s/*x* sees that there are no *F*s' is ever true. In Molnar's view, knowledge that there are no *F*s is always *inferred* – typically, I infer that there are no *F*s from the fact that I don't see any – and so doesn't count as an instance of seeing-that. But this is incorrect. My knowledge that there's no dot in the circle can be just as direct and non-inferential as my knowledge that it's 4:00pm, gained from a glance at a clock. My own view, on which (18) is only equivalent to (17) when read non-seriously, accounts for this.

Kukso (2006: 31) reads Molnar as arguing that absences are mind-dependent, and points out that, even if *perception* of the absence *F*s depends on certain mental states of the perceiver (e.g. the perceiver's *looking* for *F*s, or *expecting to see* an *F*), it doesn't follow that the *existence* of that absence depends on those mental states. But Molnar doesn't think that absences are mind-dependent; he thinks they *don't exist*.

denotation of 'y NEG-φ' is a negative existential, containing no variable for absences. Thus, it's mysterious how such a variable gets into the denotation of 'x sees y NEG-φ'.

Second, the account gets the truth-conditions of sentences like (10) wrong. Consider (19):

(19) Charlie saw Alice omit to kiss Beth in the kitchen.

Give the embedded phrase 'omit to kiss Beth in the kitchen' the wide-scope reading, on which 'in the kitchen' modifies what Alice doesn't do, rather than her omission to do it. On the Deflationist view being considered, (19) reports that Charlie saw an absence of a certain kind, namely, an absence of events in which Alice kisses Beth in the kitchen. If (19) is true, then Charlie must have had perceptual access to the spatial location of that absence. Where is that? The most plausible answer is that this absence is located in the kitchen: if there are such things as absences, then an absence of Fs is located in the relevant place where there are no Fs; and the relevant place where there are no kissings-of-Beth-by-Alice is the kitchen. Thus, on the Deflationist view being considered, (19) is true only if Charlie had perceptual access to the kitchen, e.g. if he looked into the kitchen and the absence of kissings-of-Beth-by-Alice there.

But now, suppose that Charlie and Alice are sitting at the dining room table, and that neither can see inside the kitchen. It seems that Charlie can see Alice omit to kiss Beth in the kitchen, and so (19) can be true, in such a case. But the Deflationist analysis predicts that (19) is false, and so it gets the truth-conditions wrong.

I see no other way for the Deflationist to accommodate the data regarding the interaction of negative action phrases and perceptual locutions. Thus, this data supports the sophisticated Neo-Davidsonian approach over Deflationism.

6.3   Adverbs Again

In Section 4.3, I distinguished wide- and narrow-scope readings of adverbially modified negative action sentences. On the wide-scope reading of 'x NEG-φ F-ly', 'F-ly' modifies what x doesn't do, rather than what she does: 'NEG' takes scope over the whole phrase, 'φ F-ly'. On the narrow-scope reading, 'F-ly' modifies what x does, rather than what she doesn't do: 'NEG' takes scope, not over 'φ F-ly', but only over 'φ'. The Deflationist schemata introduced in Chapter 4 capture the wide-scope readings, but not the narrow-scope ones. By contrast, the sophisticated Neo-Davidsonian schemata introduced in Chapter 5 capture both readings.

Deflationist Schemata (Negative Action Sentences)

$[\![x \ \text{NEG-}\varphi]\!]_{<w, \ t>}$ $= \sim\exists e(Agent(x)(e)(w)(t) \ \& \ \varphi_{ND}(e)(w)(t))$

$[\![x \ \text{NEG-}(\varphi) \ \text{F-ly}]\!]_{<w, \ t>}$ $= ???$

$[\![x \ \text{NEG-}(\varphi \ \text{F-ly})]\!]_{<w, \ t>}$ $= \sim\exists e(Agent(x)(e)(w)(t) \ \& \ \varphi_{ND}(e)(w)(t) \ \& \ F(e)(w)(t))$

Sophisticated Neo-Davidsonian Schemata (Negative Action Sentences)

$[\![x \ \text{NEG-}\varphi]\!]_{<w, \ t>}$ $= \exists e(Agent(x)(e)(w)(t) \ \& \ Ensure(e)(\sim\exists e'(Agent(x)(e')(w)(t)$ $\& \ \varphi_{ND}(e')(w)(t)))(w)(t))$

$[\![x \ \text{NEG-}(\varphi) \ \text{F-ly}]\!]_{<w, \ t>} = \exists e(Agent(x)(e)(w)(t) \ \& \ F(e)(w)(t) \ \& \ Ensure(e)(\sim\exists e'(Agent$ $(x)(e')(w)(t) \ \& \ \varphi_{ND}(e')(w)(t)))(w)(t))$

$[\![x \ \text{NEG-}(\varphi \ \text{F-ly})]\!]_{<w, \ t>} = \exists e(Agent(x)(e)(w)(t) \ \& \ Ensure(e)(\sim\exists e'(Agent(x)(e')(w)(t)$ $\& \ \varphi_{ND}(e')(w)(t) \ \& \ F(e')(w)(t)))(w)(t))$

As I noted in Section 4.3, the wide-scope readings tend to be the more natural ones, and for many adverbs, the narrow-scope readings appear to be simply unavailable. However, there are adverbially modified negative action sentences which are true on the narrow-scope reading, and which the Deflationist can't easily account for.

6.3.1 Locative Adverbs

Consider (20):

(20) Alice omitted to kiss Beth in the kitchen.

The natural reading of (20) is the wide-scope one, on which it says that what Alice omitted to do is *kiss Beth in the kitchen*. On this reading, (20) doesn't entail (16):

(16) Alice omitted to kiss Beth.

(For, Alice might fail to kiss Beth in the kitchen, and still kiss her somewhere else.) However, there's also a narrow-scope reading of (20), on which it says that what Alice did is *omit to kiss Beth*, and that she did it in the kitchen. On this reading, (20) *does* entail (16): if *omit to kiss Beth* is one of the things Alice did in the kitchen, it follows that it's one of the things she did *simpliciter*.

As additional evidence for this reading, notice that there are two ways to attribute presuppositions to (20), corresponding to the wide- and narrow-scope readings. 'x omits to φ' presupposes that x is supposed, or expected, to φ (at the relevant time). On the natural reading, (20) presupposes, not only that Alice was supposed to kiss Beth, but that she was supposed to do it *in the kitchen*. This presupposition projects into the negation of (20): 'Alice didn't omit to kiss Beth in the kitchen' presupposes not only that Alice was supposed to kiss Beth, but that she was supposed to do it *in the kitchen*. It's also revealed by the 'Hey, wait a minute!' test: you can object to (20) by saying, not only 'I didn't know Alice was supposed to kiss Beth', but 'I didn't know Alice was supposed to kiss Beth *in the kitchen*'. Thus, on this reading, the whole phrase, 'kiss Beth in the kitchen' is in the scope of 'omit'.

However, there's a reading of (20) on which it presupposes not that Alice was supposed to kiss Beth *in the kitchen*, but simply that she was supposed to kiss Beth. This presupposition can be projected into the negation of (20): there's a reading of 'Alice didn't omit to kiss Beth in the kitchen' on which it presupposes only that Alice was supposed to kiss Beth, not that she was supposed to do it *in the kitchen*. It can also be revealed by the 'Hey, wait a minute!' test: there's a reading of (20) to which you can object by saying, 'I didn't know Alice was supposed to kiss Beth', but *not*, 'I didn't know Alice was supposed to kiss Beth *inthe kitchen*'. Thus, on this reading, only 'kiss Beth' is in the scope of 'omit'.

The sophisticated Neo-Davidsonian captures the wide- and narrow-scope readings using $(20_{\text{SND-W}})$ and $(20_{\text{SND-N}})$, respectively:

$(20_{\text{SND-W}})$ $\exists e(Agent(\text{Alice})(e)$ & $Ensure(e)(\neg\exists e'(Agent(\text{Alice})(e')$ & $Patient(\text{Beth})(e')$ & $Kiss_{\text{ND}}(e')$ & $At_{\text{L}}(e')(\text{kitchen}))))$

$(20_{\text{SND-N}})$ $\exists e(Agent(\text{Alice})(e)$ & $At_{\text{L}}(e)(\text{kitchen})$ & $Ensure(e)(\neg\exists e'(Agent(\text{Alice})(e')$ & $Patient(\text{Beth})(e')$ & $Kiss_{\text{ND}}(e'))))$

In $(20_{\text{SND-W}})$, the denotation of 'in the kitchen' modifies 'e', the variable for kissing events. This reflects the fact that, on the wide-scope reading, 'in the kitchen' modifies what Alice doesn't do, and it can't be dropped to yield (16). In $(20_{\text{SND-N}})$, the denotation of 'in the kitchen' modifies 'e' the variable for ensuring events. This reflects the fact that, on the narrow-scope reading, 'in the kitchen' modifies what Alice does, and it can be dropped to yield (16).

By contrast, it seems that the only analysis the Deflationist can give for (20) is (20_{DEF1}), which captures the wide-scope reading:

(20_{DEF1}) $\neg\exists e(Agent(\text{Alice})(e)$ & $Patient(\text{Beth})(e)$ & $Kiss_{\text{ND}}(e)$ & $At_{\text{L}}(e)(\text{kitchen}))$

The Deflationist countenances no event variable for which Alice's omission could be a value, and so apparently can't give an analysis of the narrow-scope reading of (20).

The Deflationist might agree that there's a reading of (25) on which 'in the kitchen' isn't in the scope of 'omit', but object to my claim that, on that reading, 'in the kitchen' modifies what Alice *does*. She might claim, instead, that 'in the kitchen' modifies *Alice*. If that's right, then there's no need to posit an event variable which can take omissions as values, in order to capture the narrow-scope reading of (20). Instead, we can analyze it as (20_{DEF_2}):

> (20_{DEF_2}) $\neg\exists e(Agent(\text{Alice})(e)$ & $Patient(\text{Beth})(e)$ & $Kiss_{ND}(e))$ & $At_L(\text{Alice})$
> (kitchen)

(20_{DEF_2}) doesn't explicitly locate any token behaviour of Alice's in the kitchen: instead, it reports that Alice was in the kitchen when she didn't kiss Beth.

The discussion of Section 6.2 shows why this analysis is incorrect. Consider (19) again:

> (19) Charlie saw Alice omit to kiss Beth in the kitchen.

In Section 6.2.3, I considered only the reading of (19) on which the embedded phrase, 'Alice omit to kiss Beth in the kitchen', is given its wide-scope reading. But there's also a reading on which that phrase is given its narrow-scope reading. If the narrow-scope reading of (20) is analyzed as (20_{DEF_2}), then the narrow-scope reading of (19) should be analyzed as (19_{DEF}):

> (19_{DEF}) $\exists e(Agent(\text{Charlie})(e)$ & $Patient(\text{Alice})(e)$ & $Seeing_{ND}(e))$ & $\neg\exists e'$
> $(Agent(\text{Alice})(e')$ & $Patient(\text{Beth})(e')$ & $Kiss_{ND}(e'))$ & $At_L(\text{Alice})$
> (kitchen)

On this analysis, (19) reports that Charlie saw Alice at the time she was in the kitchen and omitted to kiss Beth. But this analysis fails, for familiar reasons. It makes the unproblematic presence of the impersonal pronoun 'it', in (21), mysterious:

> (21) Charlie saw Alice omit to kiss Beth in the kitchen, and David saw it, too.

And it gets the truth-conditions of (19) wrong: Charlie can see Alice, while she's in the kitchen omitting to kiss Beth, without actually seeing her omit to kiss Beth; recall the case where Charlie is under the table, and his view is obstructed from Alice's waist up.

The narrow-scope reading of (20) is best understood as on the sophisticated Neo-Davidsonian approach: on that reading, 'in the kitchen' contributes a predicate of events, and this predicate is applied to a variable for token omissions, considered as events.

6.3.2 'Intentionally'

Compare (22) and (23):

(22) Alice intentionally kissed Beth.
(23) Alice intentionally omitted to kiss Beth.

In (22), 'intentionally' modifies 'kissed Beth': it reports that one of the things Alice did intentionally was to kiss Beth. Likewise, it seems, 'intentionally' modifies 'omitted to kiss Beth' in (23): it reports that one of the things Alice did intentionally was to omit to kiss Beth. The sophisticated Neo-Davidsonian can accommodate this by analyzing (22) and (23) as (something like) (22_{SND}) and (23_{SND}), respectively:[9]

(22_{SND}) $\exists e(Agent(\text{Alice})(e) \mathrel{\&} Patient(\text{Beth})(e) \mathrel{\&} Kiss(e) \mathrel{\&} Intentional(e))$

(23_{SND}) $\exists e(Agent(\text{Alice})(e) \mathrel{\&} Intentional(e) \mathrel{\&} Ensure(e)(\neg\exists e'(Agent(\text{Alice})$
        $(e') \mathrel{\&} Patient(\text{Beth})(e') \mathrel{\&} Kiss_{ND}(e'))))$

On this approach, 'intentionally', like manner adverbs and locative adverbs, contributes a predicate of events: (22) reports that there was an intentional kissing of Beth by Alice, and (23) reports that there was an intentional omission to kiss Beth by Alice.

The Deflationist can't treat 'intentionally', as it occurs in (23), as contributing a predicate of events. The only event variable in (23), in her view, is a variable for kissing events, which is within the scope of '$\neg\exists$'. Thus, if 'intentionally' contributes a predicate of events, then (23) can only be analyzed as (something like) (23_{DEF1}):

(23_{DEF1}) $\neg\exists e(Agent(\text{Alice})(e) \mathrel{\&} Patient(\text{Beth})(e) \mathrel{\&} Kiss(e) \mathrel{\&} Intentional(e))$

But this is incorrect. (23_{DEF1}) merely reports that there occurred no *intentional* kissing of Beth by Alice. Thus, unlike (23), it can be true even if Alice unintentionally omitted to kiss Beth.

The Deflationist might claim that 'intentionally', as it occurs in (23), is a phrase adverb rather than a mode adverb (recall Section 4.2.2): just as

---

[9] These analyses are simplified: events are (un)intentional, not *simpliciter*, but only relative to descriptions, and a satisfying analysis must reflect this (recall Section 4.5.3). However, those details are irrelevant for the present purposes.

'Alice bravely kissed Beth' is equivalent to 'It was brave of Alice to kiss Beth', 'Alice intentionally omitted to kiss Beth' is equivalent to 'It was intentional of Alice that she omitted to kiss Beth'. On this approach, (23) is analyzed as (something like) (23$_{\mathrm{DEF_2}}$):

(23$_{\mathrm{DEF_2}}$) It is intentional of Alice that: $\sim\!\exists e(Agent(\mathrm{Alice})(e) \mathrel{\&} Patient(\mathrm{Beth})$
(e) $\&$ *Kiss*(e))

There's some precedent for this view. Davidson himself refuses to classify 'intentionally' as a mode adverb, even when it occurs in positive action sentences, and proposes that 'x intentionally φ-s' is to be understood as equivalent to 'It is intentional of x that x φ-s' (1967a: 121–22; 1985a: 218–219). Despite its pedigree, however, the view has little to motivate it.

First, what's at issue is how 'intentionally' functions in English: if 'intentionally' is a mode adverb, then 'x φ-s intentionally' is equivalent, *in ordinary English*, to 'x's φ-ing is intentional'; if it's a phrase adverb, then 'x φ-s intentionally' is equivalent, *in ordinary English*, to Davidson's phrase, 'It is intentional of x that x φ-s'. But the latter equivalence doesn't hold: 'It was intentional of Alice that she omitted to kiss Beth' is not an acceptable paraphrase, in ordinary English, of 'Alice intentionally omitted to kiss Beth'.

Second, Davidson's explicit argument that 'intentionally' can't be a mode adverb is uncompelling. He writes, 'It is obvious, I hope, that the adverbial form must be in some way deceptive; intentional actions are not a class of actions, or, to put the point a little differently, doing something intentionally is not a manner of doing it' (1967a: 121).[10] On one reading of the phrase, Davidson is justified in claiming that 'intentional actions are not a class of actions'. According to him, *every* action is intentional under *some* description (1971), and so intentional actions aren't a *subclass* of actions. But it's hard to see how this view implies *anything* about the semantic function of 'intentionally'.

Davidson might have the following argument in mind:

(α) If 'F-ly' modifies 'φ', then φ-ing F-ly is a manner of φ-ing.

(β) If φ-ing F-ly is a manner of φ-ing, then it's possible for some x to φ without φ-ing F-ly.

---

[10] He goes on to write, 'To say someone did something intentionally is to describe the action in a way that bears a special relation to the beliefs and attitudes of the agent; and perhaps further to describe the action as having been caused by those beliefs and attitudes. But of course to describe the action of the agent as having been caused in a certain way does not mean that the agent is described as performing any further action' (ibid.). But this passage is a *non sequitur*. Davidson is right that to φ intentionally (as opposed to intentionally bringing it about that one φ-s; recall Section 3.3.3) isn't to perform a *further* action. But to treat 'intentionally' as a mode adverb is not, in and of itself, to make this mistake (consider 'quickly' and 'slowly').

(γ) If φ-ing is a way of acting, then it's not possible for any x to φ without φ-ing intentionally. (If φ is a way of acting, then to φ *is* to φ intentionally.)

(δ) ∴ If φ-ing is a way of acting, then 'intentionally' doesn't modify 'φ'.

If φ-ing is a way of acting – or, as Davidson would put it, the verb 'φ' 'imputes agency' (1967a: 121) – then to φ just *is* to φ intentionally; φ-ing intentionally isn't one way of φ-ing among others (γ). By (β), φ-ing intentionally isn't a manner of φ-ing, and so by (α), 'intentionally' can't modify 'φ'.

There are (at least) two problems with this argument. First, even if it's true that all token actions are intentional under some description, it's *not* true that any verb 'φ' which describes a way of acting is equivalent to 'φ intentionally'. (Consider 'startled': Alice can exercise her agency by intentionally startling Beth, but she may also do it accidentally.) So, (γ) is false. Second, (β) is highly questionable. While there may be *some* acceptable use of the phrase 'manner of φ-ing' on which φ-ing F-ly is a manner of φ-ing only if it's one among many, it's not clear why the use of that phrase which is relevant to semantics should be beholden to this constraint. That 'F-ly' functions as a mode adverb entails that it applies to, or modifies, a verb, but not that it applies non-redundantly.

Taylor (1983: 106–108) gets a bit further than Davidson. Consider (24):

(24) Alice intentionally didn't kiss Beth.

Taylor claims that (24) is an acceptable English sentence. But it's difficult to see how 'intentionally' can be functioning as a mode adverb, here, since the required paraphrase, 'Alice's didn't kissing Beth was intentional'/ 'Alice's not-kissing Beth was intentional', is either nonsense or highly awkward.

In response, I deny that (24) is an acceptable English sentence. Consider: if x φ-s intentionally, then one of the things x does intentionally is φ; but it's hardly acceptable to say that one of the things Alice does intentionally is *not kiss Beth*. What *is* acceptable is (23), 'Alice intentionally omitted to kiss Beth'; it's perfectly sensible to say that one of the things Alice does intentionally is *omit to kiss Beth*. But there's no reason to think that 'intentionally' doesn't function as a mode adverb in (23).

The claim that 'intentionally' is a phrase adverb rather than a mode adverb lacks any clear motivation. 'Intentionally' functions as a mode adverb in both positive and negative action sentences, and so, *contra* the Deflationist, it contributes a predicate of events in sentences of both kinds.

Summing up this section: adverbs occurring in narrow scope are best analyzed as contributing predicates of events. This is something that the sophisticated Neo-Davidsonian schemata can accommodate, but which the Deflationist ones can't. Thus, whereas the behaviour of adverbs in negative action sentences seemed, in Chapter 4, to provide an argument for Deflationism, it actually provides a powerful argument *against* Deflationism, and in favour of the sophisticated Neo-Davidsonian approach. That approach accommodates the wide-scope readings of negative action sentences as well as Deflationism does, but it has the advantage of accommodating the narrow-scope readings, as well.

6.4 Comparison to Alternatives

6.4.1 Schaffer and Narrow-Scope Negation

Schaffer (2012: 417–423) suggests an approach to negative action sentences which, like mine, is designed to justify the claim that negative actions are events rather than absences. He agrees with the Deflationist that the difference between '$x \varphi$' and 'x NEG-φ' comes down to the presence of a negation operator in the latter. But whereas the Deflationist thinks that '$\sim$' must take scope over '$\exists e$', so that a negative action sentence always has the form, '$\sim\exists x F x$', Schaffer claims that, in context, we can force '$\exists e$' to take scope over '$\sim$'. On such a reading, a negative action sentence reports the occurrence of an event, but describes it in negative terms: it says that there occurs some event which isn't of a certain type.[11]

Given that a positive action sentence '$x \varphi$' is analyzed as quantifying over an event which satisfies a *conjunctive* description – at minimum, it reports that an event is a φ-ing *and* that that event has x as its agent – we have a choice to make, when deciding how far past '$\exists e$' to push '$\sim$'. Schaffer's first suggestion is that '$\sim$' occurs just past '$\exists e$', and so takes scope over the entire description. Schematically:

Schafferian Schemata (Negative Action Sentences – First Pass)

$[\![x \text{ NEG-}\varphi]\!]_{<w, \ t>} = \exists e \sim (Agent(x)(e)(w)(t) \ \& \ \varphi_{\text{ND}}(e)(w)(t))$

$[\![x \text{ NEG-}(\varphi) \text{ F-ly}]\!]_{<w, \ t>} = \ ???$

$[\![x \text{ NEG-}(\varphi \text{ F-ly})]\!]_{<w, \ t>} = \exists e \sim (Agent(x)(e)(w)(t) \ \& \ \varphi_{\text{ND}}(e)(w)(t) \ \& \ F(e)(w)(t))$

---

[11] In my view, it's better to say that a negative action describes an event in *functional* terms: it describes that event, not in terms of what it *isn't*, but in terms of what it *does*. See Section 7.2.

As the reader can see, this suggestion has some hope of capturing the wide-scope reading of negative action sentences, but not the narrow-scope reading. Recall, on the wide-scope reading, 'F-ly' modifies what x doesn't do, and 'x NEG-φ F-ly' doesn't entail 'x NEG-φ'. This is apparently captured on these schemata by the fact that the entire description occurs within the scope of '$\sim$', and by the fact that $\exists x \sim (Fx \ \& \ Gx) \nvDash \exists x \sim Fx$. However, if '$\sim$' can only take scope either over '$\exists e$' or over the entire description, we're left without an analysis of the narrow-scope reading, on which 'F-ly' modifies what x does, and 'x NEG-φ F-ly' *does* entail 'x NEG-φ'.

A natural modification, which is in the spirit of Schaffer's discussion, is that when we intend the narrow-scope reading, we force '$\sim$' to take scope over the description *minus the contribution of 'F-ly'*:

Schafferian Schemata (Negative Action Sentences – Second Pass)

$\llbracket x \ \text{NEG-}\varphi \rrbracket_{<w, \ t>}$ $= \exists e \sim (Agent(x)(e)(w)(t) \ \& \ \varphi_{\text{ND}}(e)(w)(t))$

$\llbracket x \ \text{NEG-}(\varphi) \ \text{F-ly} \rrbracket_{<w, \ t>} = \exists e (\sim (Agent(x)(e)(w)(t) \ \& \ \varphi_{\text{ND}}(e)(w)(t)) \ \& \ F(e)(w)(t))$

$\llbracket x \ \text{NEG-}(\varphi \ \text{F-ly}) \rrbracket_{<w, \ t>} = \exists e \sim (Agent(x)(e)(w)(t) \ \& \ \varphi_{\text{ND}}(e)(w)(t) \ \& \ F(e)(w)(t))$

Thus, on the narrow-scope reading, 'x NEG-φ F-ly' reports the occurrence of an event which is F, and adverb-dropping inferences are validated by the rule, $\exists x (Fx \ \& \sim Gx) \vdash \exists x Fx$.

Nonetheless, these schemata face serious problems. First, there are problems regarding consistency and inconsistency. The schema for bare negative action sentences renders 'x NEG-φ' consistent with 'x φ', since '$\exists x \sim Fx$' is consistent with '$\exists x Fx$'. Specifically, 'Alice omitted to kiss Beth (at a certain time, t)', analyzed as (16_{S1}), is now consistent with 'Alice kissed Beth (at t)', analyzed as (5_{ND}).

> (16_{S1}) $\exists e \sim (Agent(\text{Alice})(e) \ \& \ Patient(\text{Beth})(e) \ \& \ Kiss_{\text{ND}}(e))$
> (5_{ND}) $\exists e (Agent(\text{Alice})(e) \ \& \ Patient(\text{Beth})(e) \ \& \ Kiss_{\text{ND}}(e))$

This is a bad result: you can't both do something and omit to do it at the same time, so 'Alice omitted to kiss Beth (at t)' should be inconsistent with 'Alice kissed Beth (at t)'.

The schemata for adverbially modified negative action sentences face similar problems. Consider, first, the wide-scope reading, 'x NEG-(φ F-ly)'. The schema for this reading renders 'x NEG-φ F-ly' consistent with 'x φ F-ly', since '$\exists x \sim (Fx \ \& \ Gx)$' is consistent with '$\exists x (Fx \ \& \ Gx)$'. Specifically, 'Alice omitted to kiss Beth in the kitchen (at t)', analyzed as ($20_{\text{S1-W}}$), is consistent with 'Alice kissed Beth in the kitchen (at t)', analyzed as (25).

(20$_{\text{SI-W}}$) $\exists e$-(*Agent*(Alice)(e) & *Patient*(Beth)(e) & *Kiss*$_{\text{ND}}$(e) & *At*$_{\text{L}}$(e)
(kitchen))

(25) $\exists e$(*Agent*(Alice)(e) & *Patient*(Beth)(e) & *Kiss*$_{\text{ND}}$(e) & *At*$_{\text{L}}$(e)
(kitchen))

This is a bad result: you can't both do something and omit to do it at the same time, so 'Alice omitted to kiss Beth in the kitchen (at t)', on the wide-scope reading, should be inconsistent with 'Alice kissed Beth in the kitchen (at t)'.

Now consider the narrow-scope reading, 'x NEG-(φ) F-ly'. The schema for this reading renders 'x NEG-φ F-ly' consistent with 'x NEG-φ', since '$\exists x(Fx$ & $\sim Gx)$' is consistent with '$\exists xGx$'. Specifically, 'Alice omitted to kiss Beth in the kitchen (at t)', analyzed as (20$_{\text{SI-N}}$), is consistent with 'Alice kissed Beth (at t)', analyzed as (5$_{\text{ND}}$):

(20$_{\text{SI-N}}$) $\exists e$($\sim$(*Agent*(Alice)(e) & *Patient*(Beth)(e) & *Kiss*$_{\text{ND}}$(e)) & *At*$_{\text{L}}$(e)
(kitchen))

(5$_{\text{ND}}$) $\exists e$(*Agent*(Alice)(e) & *Patient*(Beth)(e) & *Kiss*$_{\text{ND}}$(e))

This is a bad result: on the narrow-scope reading, 'Alice omitted to kiss Beth in the kitchen (at t)' entails 'Alice omitted to kiss Beth (at t)', and so it should be inconsistent with 'Alice kissed Beth (at t)'.

In addition to these problems, the schemata face a problem with negation related to the one I raised for the sophisticated Neo-Davidsonian view in Section 5.4. Consider the object-level negation of 'Alice omitted to kiss Beth':

(16$\sim$) Alice didn't omit to kiss Beth.

Since what's being objected to here is the *semantic content* of (16), rather than the use of the word 'omit', (16$\sim$) intuitively implies (5), 'Alice kissed Beth'.[12] I showed that this implication doesn't hold on the sophisticated Neo-Davidsonian view, but argued that we can bite the bullet on this point. Schaffer doesn't face this problem. According to the Schafferian schemata, (16$\sim$) is analyzed as (16$\sim$$_{\text{SI}}$):

(16$\sim$$_{\text{SI}}$) $\sim\exists e$-(*Agent*(Alice)(e) & *Patient*(Beth)(e) & *Kiss*$_{\text{ND}}$(e))

(16$\sim$$_{\text{SI}}$) entails (5$_{\text{ND}}$), since '$\sim\exists x$-$Fx$' entails '$\exists xFx$' (or at least, it does unless we assume a free logic).

---

[12] Recall the discussion, in Section 2.2.2, of the difference between object-level and meta-linguistic negations of omission sentences.

But of course, this advantage comes at a serious cost. '$\neg\exists x \sim Fx$' is equivalent to '$\forall x Fx$', so (16$\sim_{S_I}$) is equivalent to '$\forall e(Agent(\text{Alice})(e)$ & $Patient(\text{Beth})(e)$ & $Kiss_{ND}(e))$', or '*Every* event is a kissing of Beth by Alice'. This gets the truth-conditions of (16$\sim$) wrong: in any ordinary case in which (16$\sim$) is true, there will be plenty of events which aren't kissings of Beth by Alice.

The schema for the wide-scope reading of 'x NEG-φ F-ly' faces a similar problem. The object-level negation of 'Alice omitted to kiss Beth in the kitchen', on this schema, is analyzed as (20$\sim_{S_I-W}$):

(20$\sim_{S_I-W}$) $\neg\exists e \sim (Agent(\text{Alice})(e)$ & $Patient(\text{Beth})(e)$ & $Kiss_{ND}(e)$ & $At_L(e)$
(kitchen))

This is equivalent to '$\forall e(Agent(\text{Alice})(e)$ & $Patient(\text{Beth})(e)$ & $Kiss_{ND}(e)$ & $At_L(e)(\text{kitchen}))$', or '*Every* event is a kissing of Beth by Alice and occurs in the kitchen'. This gets the truth-conditions of 'Alice didn't omit to kiss Beth in the kitchen' wrong.

Finally, the schemata generate a serious problem of referential indeterminacy. On these schemata, (16), 'Alice omitted to kiss Beth', merely reports the occurrence of an event which isn't a kissing of Beth. But then, *any* event which isn't a kissing of Beth by Alice – e.g. the spinning of an electron on the other side of the planet – can serve as a witness to (16), and so becomes a candidate referent of 'Alice's omission to kiss Beth'. The reference of that nominal is massively indeterminate.[13]

Of course, I noted in Section 1.3.2 that event nominals, like all referring phrases, are referentially indeterminate to some degree. Schaffer notes this, too, and attempts to use this fact to mitigate the problem: 'language is sometimes indeterminate. The fact that a reading would make for indeterminacy simply cannot exclude that reading as a possibility' (2012: 422). But the problem isn't merely that the referent of 'Alice's omission to kiss Beth' is rendered indeterminate; the problem is that it's rendered *massively* indeterminate, beyond all plausibility. We *know* that the spinning of an electron on the other side of the plant isn't a candidate referent, but the Schafferian schemata do nothing to rule it out.[14]

---

[13] Moore (2009: 439) introduces this as a problem for *any* theory on which a negative action is an ordinary event described in negative terms, rather than as a problem specific to Schaffer's view.

[14] Notice that my own view doesn't face *this* problem of referential indeterminacy. Given the sophisticated Neo-Davidsonian schemata, x's NEG-φ-ing is guaranteed to be an event with x as its agent, and so the spinning of an electron isn't a candidate to be Alice's omission to kiss Beth. Moreover, the account of ensuring events given in Section 5.3 provides a suitably determinate account of which events ensure that x doesn't φ, and hence of which events are candidate referents of 'x's NEG-φ-ing'.

Attempting to reduce the indeterminacy, Schaffer suggests that '~' needn't take scope over the whole description, in bare and wide-scope negative action sentences, after all. Rather, we can allow '~' to take scope over '$\varphi_{ND}(e)$' (and perhaps '$F(e)$') while leaving other aspects of the description (specifically, '$Agent(x)(e)$' and '$Patient(y)(e)$') outside its scope (2012: 419, 422). Schematically:

Schafferian Schemata (Negative Action Sentences – Third Pass)

$[\![x \text{ NEG-}\varphi]\!]_{<w,\ t>} = \exists e(Agent(x)(e)(w)(t) \ \& \ \text{-}\varphi_{ND}(e)(w)(t))$

$[\![x \text{ NEG-}(\varphi) \text{ F-ly}]\!]_{<w,\ t>} = \exists e(Agent(x)(e)(w)(t) \ \& \ \text{-}\varphi_{ND}(e)(w)(t) \ \& \ F(e)(w)(t))$

$[\![x \text{ NEG-}(\varphi \text{ F-ly})]\!]_{<w,\ t>} = \exists e(Agent(x)(e)(w)(t) \ \& \ \text{-}(\varphi_{ND}(e)(w)(t) \ \& \ F(e)(w)(t)))$

On these schemata, (16) doesn't merely report the occurrence of an event which isn't a kissing of Beth by Alice. Rather, it reports an event in which Alice does *something* to Beth, but which isn't a kiss:

(16_{S2}) $\exists e(Agent(\text{Alice})(e) \ \& \ Patient(\text{Beth})(e) \ \& \ \text{-}Kiss_{ND}(e))$

The spinning of an electron is no longer a candidate to be Alice's omission, and indeed, the indeterminacy has been drastically reduced.

Problems remain, however. First, (16_{S2}) gets the truth-conditions of (16) wrong. Intuitively, Alice can omit to kiss Beth without doing anything *else* to her; there needn't be any event of which Alice and Beth are the agent and patient, as (16_{S2}) requires. The same argument applies, *mutatis mutandis*, to (20), whose narrow- and wide-scope readings are now analyzed, respectively, as ($20_{S2\text{-}N}$) and ($20_{S2\text{-}W}$):

($20_{S2\text{-}N}$) $\exists e(Agent(\text{Alice})(e) \ \& \ Patient(\text{Beth})(e) \ \& \ \text{-}Kiss_{ND}(e) \ \& \ At_L(e)$
(kitchen))

($20_{S2\text{-}W}$) $\exists e(Agent(\text{Alice})(e) \ \& \ Patient(\text{Beth})(e) \ \& \ \text{-}(Kiss_{ND}(e) \ \& \ At_L(e)$
(kitchen)))

Each of these requires that Alice do *something* to Beth other than kiss her. But (20) doesn't require this, on either reading.

Moreover, since '$\exists x(Fx \ \& \ \text{-}Gx)$' is consistent with '$\exists x(Fx \ \& \ Gx)$', '$x$ NEG-φ' is *still* consistent with '$x \ \varphi$'. For the same reason, the narrow-scope reading of 'x NEG-φ F-ly' is consistent with '$x \ \varphi$', and the wide-scope reading is consistent with '$x \ \varphi$ F-ly'.

Finally, Schaffer still faces a problem with negation. (16~) is now analyzed, on its object-level reading, as (16-_{S2}):

(16-_{S2}) $\text{-}\exists e(Agent(\text{Alice})(e) \ \& \ Patient(\text{Beth})(e) \ \& \ \text{-}Kiss_{ND}(e))$

In English: there is no event of which Alice and Beth are the agent and patient, respectively, and which isn't a kiss. But now, (16~) no longer entails (5). Consider a case where Alice doesn't do *anything* to Beth. In this case, (16~$_{S_2}$) is true (if there's no event of which Alice and Beth are the agent and patient, then, *a fortiori*, there is no such event which isn't a kiss), but (5) is false.

Schaffer might adopt my own solution to this problem: although (16~) doesn't entail (5), it's still the case that if (16~) had been true, then (5) would have been as well. But this subjunctive conditional is uncompelling, given the analysis of (16~) as (16~$_{S_2}$). For, it's easy to see how (16~$_{S_2}$) might have been true and (5) false: Alice might not have done *anything* to Beth.

6.4.2   Bernstein and De Re Modality

Bernstein (2014b) presents an account of what she calls 'omission sentences', where an 'omission' is an absence which plays some causal role. In her view, a sentence with the surface form 'x NEG-φ' expresses a negative existential proposition, just as the Deflationist says, provided that x's NEG-φ-ing isn't claimed, in the conversational context, to have caused anything. However, if x's NEG-φ-ing *is* claimed to have caused something, then 'x NEG-φ' expresses not a negative existential proposition, but a *de re* modal proposition. Specifically, it expresses that there occurs some event which might have been a φ-ing by x (2014b: 8–9). Since I'm not concerned, here, with issues of causation, I'll consider whether Bernstein's approach might be extended to negative action sentences generally (although my criticisms should still apply to negative action sentences in causal contexts).

To begin, consider just the schema for bare negative action sentences:[15]

Bernsteinian Schemata (Negative Action Sentences – First Pass)
$[\![x \text{ NEG-}\varphi]\!]_{<w,\, t>}$ $= \exists e \Diamond (Agent(x)(e)(w)(t) \,\&\, \varphi_{ND}(e)(w)(t))$
$[\![x \text{ NEG-}(\varphi) \text{ F-ly}]\!]_{<w,\, t>} = ???$
$[\![x \text{ NEG-}(\varphi \text{ F-ly})]\!]_{<w,\, t>} = ???$

We can already see that Bernstein's proposal faces a problem regarding consistency and inconsistency, like the one that plagued Schaffer's. The schema renders 'x NEG-φ (at t)' consistent with 'x φ (at t)', since '$\exists x \Diamond Fx$' is

---

[15] Bernstein prefers to translate the language of quantified modal logic into Lewis's (1968) language of counterpart theory, but none of my arguments hinge on which language we use.

consistent with '$\exists x F x$'. Specifically, 'Alice omitted to kiss Beth (at t)', analyzed as (16_{B_I}), is consistent with 'Alice kissed Beth (at t)', analyzed as (5_{ND}).

(16_{B_I}) $\exists e \Diamond (Agent(\text{Alice})(e) \ \& \ Patient(\text{Beth})(e) \ \& \ Kiss_{ND}(e))$
(5_{ND}) $\exists e (Agent(\text{Alice})(e) \ \& \ Patient(\text{Beth})(e) \ \& \ Kiss_{ND}(e))$

In fact, the problem is even worse for Bernstein. '$\exists x F x$' is not merely consistent with, but *entails* '$\exists x \Diamond F x$': if x is actually F, then x is possibly F. Thus, on Bernstein's proposal, '$x \ \varphi$ (at t)' entails 'x NEG-φ (at t)', and so 'Alice kissed Beth (at t)' entails 'Alice omitted to kiss Beth (at t)' (provided the required presupposition is in place).

Relatedly, the schema faces a problem with negation. Consider (16-):

(16-)   Alice didn't omit to kiss Beth.

Intuitively, '$\text{-}(x$ NEG-$\varphi)$', on its object-level reading, implies '$x \ \varphi$', so (16-) is true only if Alice kissed Beth (i.e. only if (5_{ND}) is true). But the negation of (16_{B_I}) is (16-_{B_I}):

(16-_{B_I}) $\text{-}\exists e \Diamond (Agent(\text{Alice})(e) \ \& \ Patient(\text{Beth})(e) \ \& \ Kiss_{ND}(e))$

Now, since '$\exists x F x$' entails '$\exists x \Diamond F x$', '$\text{-}\exists x \Diamond F x$' entails '$\text{-}\exists x F x$': if nothing is possibly F, then nothing is actually F. Thus, (16-_{B_I}) entails (5-_{ND}):

(5-_{ND}) $\text{-}\exists e (Agent(\text{Alice})(e) \ \& \ Patient(\text{Beth})(e) \ \& \ Kiss_{ND}(e))$

That is, (16-_{B_I}) is true only if (5_{ND}) is *false*, and so it gets the truth-conditions of (16-) quite wrong.[16] More generally, the schema yields the result that '$\text{-}(x$ NEG-$\varphi)$', on its object-level reading, entails '$\text{-}(x \ \varphi)$', which it shouldn't.

Now consider how adverbially modified negative action sentences should be analyzed, in Bernstein's approach. How should we distinguish the narrow- and wide-scope readings of such sentences, given that we have only one event variable to work with? The natural suggestion is that the difference between narrow- and wide-scope readings is to be reflected in the scope of the modal operator, '$\Diamond$'. Recall that, on the narrow-scope reading, 'x NEG-(φ) F-ly', 'F-ly' modifies what x does, while on the wide-scope reading, 'x NEG-(φ F-ly)', it modifies what x doesn't do. In Bernstein's proposal, it seems, for 'F-ly' to modify what x doesn't do is for it to modify what x might have done (or, if we take the modal claim to

---

[16] Clearly, an appeal to subjunctives won't help, here. If (16-_{B_I}) entails (5-_{ND}), then '(16-_{B_I}) $\Box\!\!\to$ (5_{ND})' is false.

be *de re* rather than *de dicto*, it's for 'F-ly' to modify how x's actual behaviour might have been). This suggests that, in the analysis of 'x NEG-(φ) F-ly', 'F' should occur outside the scope of '$\Diamond$', thus describing how the event quantified over *actually* is, while in the analysis of 'x NEG-(φ F-ly)', 'F' should occur inside the scope of '$\Diamond$', thus describing how the event quantified over *might* have been:

Bernsteinian Schemata (Negative Action Sentences – Second Pass)

$[\![x \text{ NEG-}\varphi]\!]_{<w,\,t>}$ $= \exists e \Diamond(Agent(x)(e)(w)(t) \ \& \ \varphi_{ND}(e)(w)(t))$

$[\![x \text{ NEG-}(\varphi) \text{ F-ly}]\!]_{<w,\,t>} = \exists e(F(e)(w)(t) \ \& \ \Diamond(Agent(x)(e)(w)(t) \ \& \ \varphi_{ND}(e)(w)(t)))$

$[\![x \text{ NEG-}(\varphi \text{ F-ly})]\!]_{<w,\,t>} = \exists e \Diamond(Agent(x)(e)(w)(t) \ \& \ \varphi_{ND}(e)(w)(t) \ \& \ F(e)(w)(t))$

But his won't work. Recall that, with respect to the narrow-scope reading, adverb-dropping inferences are valid and adverb-adding inferences are invalid – 'x NEG-(φ) F-ly' entails 'x NEG-φ', while 'x NEG-φ' doesn't entail 'x NEG-(φ) F-ly' – while the situation is reversed for the wide-scope reading, where adverb-dropping inferences are invalid and adverb-adding inferences are valid – 'x NEG-(φ F-ly)' doesn't entail 'x NEG-φ', but 'x NEG-φ' entails 'x NEG-(φ F-ly)'. However, according to the Bernstein schemata, the situation is the same for both readings: on both readings, adverb-dropping inferences are valid and adverb-adding inferences are invalid. On the narrow-scope reading, 'x NEG-(φ) F-ly', 'F' is outside the scope of '$\Diamond$', so adverb-dropping inferences are validated by the rule, $\exists x(Fx \ \& \ Gx) \vdash \exists x Fx$, while adverb-adding inferences are blocked by the fact that $\exists x Fx \nvdash \exists x(Fx \ \& \ Gx)$. On the wide-scope reading, 'x NEG-(φ F-ly)', 'F' is inside the scope of '$\Diamond$', so adverb-dropping inferences are validated by the rule, $\exists x \Diamond(Fx \ \& \ Gx) \vdash \exists x \Diamond Fx$ (if x might have been both F and G, it follows that x might have been F) while adverb-adding inferences are blocked by the fact that $\exists x \Diamond Fx \nvdash \exists x \Diamond (Fx \ \& \ Gx)$ (that x might have been F doesn't entail that x might have been both F and G). Thus, these schemata can't capture the crucial difference between the narrow- and wide-scope readings of 'x NEG-φ F-ly'.

We can mitigate some of these problems if we complicate Bernstein's proposal in a seemingly natural way. On a more complex proposal, 'x NEG-φ' reports *both* the negative existential proposition that no actual event was a φ-ing by x *and* the *de re* modal proposition that some actual event *might* have been a φ-ing by x:[17]

---

[17] Note that, in the schema for 'x NEG-(φ F-ly)', I assume that 'F' occurs both within the scope of '$\neg \exists e$' and within the scope of '$\exists e$'. I take this to be the most natural way of developing the proposal: on the wide-scope reading, 'x NEG-φ F-ly' reports, and doesn't merely entail, that x doesn't φ F-ly.

Bernsteinian Schemata (Negative Action Sentences – Third Pass)

$\llbracket x$ NEG-$\varphi \rrbracket_{<w,\ t>}$ = $\neg\exists e(Agent(x)(e)(w)(t)$ & $\varphi_{ND}(e)(w)(t))$ & $\exists e'\Diamond(Agent(x)$
$(e')(w)(t)$ & $\varphi_{ND}(e')(w)(t))$

$\llbracket x$ NEG-(φ) F-ly$\rrbracket_{<w,\ t>}$ = $\neg\exists e(Agent(x)(e)(w)(t)$ & $\varphi_{ND}(e)(w)(t))$ & $\exists e'(F(e')(w)(t)$
& $\Diamond(Agent(x)(e')(w)(t)$ & $\varphi_{ND}(e')(w)(t)))$

$\llbracket x$ NEG-$(\varphi$ F-ly$)\rrbracket_{<w,\ t>}$ = $\neg\exists e(Agent(x)(e)(w)(t)$ & $\varphi_{ND}(e)(w)(t)$ & $F(e)(w)(t))$ &
$\exists e'\Diamond(Agent(x)(e')(w)(t)$ & $\varphi_{ND}(e')(w)(t)$ & $F(e')(w)(t))$

Given these schemata, 'x NEG-φ (at t)' is neither consistent with nor entailed by 'x φ (at t)'. Specifically, 'Alice omitted to kiss Beth (at t)', now analyzed as (16_{B2}), is no longer consistent with or entailed by 'Alice kissed Beth (at t)', analyzed as (5_{ND}).

(16_{B2}) $\neg\exists e(Agent(Alice)(e)$ & $Patient(Beth)(e)$ & $Kiss_{ND}(e))$ & $\exists e'\Diamond(Agent$
(Alice)(e') & $Patient(Beth)(e')$ & $Kiss_{ND}(e'))$

This is because the first conjunct of (16_{B2}), $\neg\exists e(Agent(Alice)(e)$ & $Patient$ (Beth)(e) & $Kiss_{ND}(e))$' is the negation of (5_{ND}).

Moreover, the new schema for 'x NEG-$(\varphi$ F-ly)' blocks adverb-dropping inferences, as it should. Since '$\neg\exists x(Fx$ & $Gx)$' doesn't entail '$\neg\exists xFx$', the conjunction '$\neg\exists x(Fx$ & $Gx)$ & $\exists y\Diamond(Fy$ & $Gy)$' doesn't entail the conjunction '$\neg\exists xFx$ & $\exists y\Diamond(Fy)$', either.

However, problems remain. First, while the new schema for bare negative action sentences solves the original problem of negation – that '$\neg(x$ NEG-$\varphi)$' implies '$\neg(x \varphi)$' – it gives rise to a new one. According to the new schema, $(16\neg)$ is analyzed as $(16\neg_{B2})$:

($16\neg_{B2}$) $\neg(\neg\exists e(Agent(Alice)(e)$ & $Patient(Beth)(e)$ & $Kiss_{ND}(e))$ & $\exists e'\Diamond$
$(Agent(Alice)(e')$ & $Patient(Beth)(e')$ & $Kiss_{ND}(e')))$

$(16\neg_{B2})$ is equivalent to the disjunction (26):

(26) $\exists e(Agent(Alice)(e)$ & $Patient(Beth)(e)$ & $Kiss_{ND}(e))$ $\vee$ $\neg\exists e'\Diamond(Agent$
(Alice)(e') & $Patient(Beth)(e')$ & $Kiss_{ND}(e'))$

In English: *either* Alice kissed Beth, *or* no actual behaviour of Alice's was a possible kissing of Beth. Now, we no longer get the result that $(16\neg)$ implies $(5\neg_{ND})$: the proposition that no event is a possible kissing of Beth by Alice, which entails $(5\neg_{ND})$, is only one disjunct of (26), and $p \vee q \nvdash p$. But for the same reason, $(16\neg)$ doesn't imply (5_{ND}), either: (5_{ND}) is only one disjunct of (26).

Of course, as discussed in Sections 5.4, and 6.4.1, (16~) doesn't imply (5_{ND}) on the sophisticated Neo-Davidsonian view. I argued that we can bite the bullet, and rest content with a subjunctive conditional: in any ordinary case, (5_{ND}) would be true if (16~) were. Bernstein might attempt the same move, with respect to (5_{ND}) and (26). Suppose that *any* event of which Alice is the agent could have been an event in which she kisses Beth: if Alice does *anything at all*, then the event of her doing it might have been a kissing of Beth. If so, then the closest worlds in which the disjunct '~∃*e*′◊ (*Agent*(Alice)(*e*′) & *Patient*(Beth)(*e*′) & $Kiss_{ND}$(*e*′))' is true are worlds in which Alice doesn't exist. But presumably, worlds in which Alice exists and kisses Beth are closer to actuality than any such world. Thus, Bernstein might argue, the closest worlds in which (26) is true are worlds in which the disjunct '∃*e*(*Agent*(Alice)(*e*) & *Patient*(Beth)(*e*) & $Kiss_{ND}$(*e*))' is true, and so (5_{ND}) would be true if (26) were.

Unfortunately, the supposition that *any* event of which Alice is the agent could have been an event in which she kisses Beth is one which we have no clear reason to accept. Moreover, alternative modal hypotheses don't secure the desired result. We might suppose that only an event in which Alice does something *to Beth* could have been an event in which she kisses her. But then, in a case where Alice doesn't do *anything* to Beth, the closest worlds in which (26) is true are worlds in which the disjunct '~∃*e*′◊(*Agent*(Alice)(*e*′) & *Patient*(Beth) (*e*′) & $Kiss_{ND}$(*e*′))' is true (since, according to our modal hypothesis, that disjunct is *actually* true). But since ~∃*x*◊*Fx* ⊢ ~∃*xFx*, we have it that the closest worlds in which (26) is true are worlds in which '~∃*e*(*Agent*(Alice)(*e*) & *Patient*(Beth)(*e*) & $Kiss_{ND}$(*e*))' is true. In short, if (26) were true, then (5_{ND}) would be *false*.

Second, although the new schema for '*x* NEG-(φ F-ly)' blocks intuitively bad adverb-dropping inferences, it fails to validate intuitively good adverb-adding inferences. The conjunction '~∃*xFx* & ∃*y*◊(*Fy*)' doesn't entail the conjunction '~∃*x*(*Fx* & *Gx*) & ∃*y*◊(*Fy* & *Gy*)', since '∃*y*◊(*Fy*)' doesn't entail '∃*y*◊(*Fy* & *Gy*)'.

6.5   Conclusion

This completes my defense of the sophisticated Neo-Davidsonian approach to negative action sentences. In addition to accommodating the data about adverbs from Chapter 4, it also accommodates data regarding the interaction of negative action phrases and perceptual locutions, and data regarding the behaviour of adverbs that occur outside the scope of 'NEG', which Deflationism doesn't. The approach also avoids a host of problems that are faced by Schaffer's and Bernstein's alternative proposals.

On the best analysis of negative action sentences, those sentences quantify over events which play what I've called the 'ensuring' role: they report the *occurrence* of an event, not the *absence* of one. Thus, the justification for believing that token positive actions are events extends to token negative actions. If we accept (PNA 2), then we can, and should, reject (PNA 3): negative actions are events, not absences thereof. With (PNA 3) rejected, the problem of negative actions is solved.

CHAPTER 7

Realizer-Functionalism and the Metaphysics of Events

7.1 Introduction

I've argued that negative action sentences express existential quantifications over events that play what I've called the 'ensuring role'. Moreover, I've argued that ordinary, positive events – i.e. events which consist in an agent *doing* something – play this role. If we identify negative actions with the ensuring-events quantified over in these sentences, we can identify them with ordinary, positive events. This is the view I'll defend in the remainder of the book.

In Section 7.2, I flesh out this view in more detail, contrasting it with an alternative on which negative actions are *realized* by, not *identical* to, ensuring-events. In Section 7.3, I raise a familiar problem for my view and, indeed, for any view on which negative actions are identical to positive events. Such views appear to be incompatible with a popular theory of what events are, the 'Property-Exemplification Theory'. In Section 7.4, I provide my solution to this problem: the identity of negative actions with positive events isn't in conflict with the Property-Exemplification Theory per se, but only with a widespread assumption about how that theory is to be developed. I argue that this assumption should be rejected on independent grounds, and provide a sketch for a version of the theory which doesn't incorporate it.

7.2 A Tale of Two Functionalisms

I claim that negative action sentences quantify over events that play a certain role, and that our negative actions just *are* the events which play that role. This view is an analogue of 'token realizer-functionalism' in the philosophy of mind.

Functionalist theories of mind are united by the thought that mental states are to be understood in terms of the role they play in a person's psychology: for any mental state-type M, there is a role, R, associated with M, such that x is in a token state of type M just in case x is in a token state which plays R. For example, the state-type *pain* is associated with a certain role – it's produced by certain external stimuli, like my placing my hand on a hot stove, and produces further mental states and/or behaviours, like my pulling my hand away from the stove – and I am in pain just in case some token state of mine plays that role. What distinguishes token realizer-functionalism is the claim that token mental states just *are* those states that play the roles associated with the corresponding mental state-types. To describe an event or token state in mental terms – i.e. as a *pain*, a *belief that snow is white*, etc. – is to describe it in functional terms.

Token realizer-functionalism is opposed to 'token role-functionalism'. According to the latter view, a token M-state, m, isn't to be identified with whatever token state plays the associate role, R. Rather, m is a token of the *higher-level* state, *being in a state which plays R*. That is, m itself doesn't play R; it's a state that one is in by virtue of being in a *distinct* state which *does* play R.

Token realizer-functionalism is attractive to a reductive physicalist. For, given realizer-functionalism, if she can show that a token physical state plays the role associated with a given mental state-type, M, she can thereby show that that physical state is a token of M (e.g. if some token state of my brain plays the role associated with pain, then that token physical state *is* my token pain state). By contrast, token role-functionalism is attractive to a non-reductive physicalist, who thinks that token mental states are 'grounded' in certain physical states without being identical to them. On this view, the token physical state which plays the role associated with M realizes, but is nonetheless distinct from, the corresponding token M-state.

My view of negative behaviours is a functionalist one. In my view, negative behaviours are understood in terms of the ensuring-role, since to describe x as NEG-φ-ing is to report the occurrence of an event which plays that role. Given this broadly functionalist view, we can distinguish analogues of token realizer- and token role-functionalism:

Token Realizer-Functionalism (Negative Actions)
e is a NEG-φ-ing by x iff e is an event of which x is the agent, and which ensures that x doesn't φ.

Token Role-Functionalism (Negative Actions)
e_1 is a NEG-φ-ing by x iff e_1 is an event of which x is the agent, and e_1 is the higher-level event of there being a numerically distinct e_2 of which x is the agent, and which ensures that x doesn't φ.

The role-functionalist view has affinities with some views that have been explicitly defended in the literature. In the literature on causation, Tiehen

(2015) defends a view of absences inspired by role-functionalist theories in the philosophy of mind. And in the literature on negative actions, Palmer (2020) defends the view that negative actions are *constituted by* (but not *identical to*) positive events, where constitution is a relation analogous to realization.[1]

By contrast, I opt for the realizer-functionalist view. On my view, our negative actions just *are* the events over which we quantify in negative action sentences, and which play the ensuring-role. To describe an event as an omission to φ (refrainment from φ-ing, etc.) is to describe it in functional terms.[2]

There are two arguments for taking token realizer-functionalism to be the default view. The first is the *argument from symmetry*. The dispute between realizer- and role-functionalists can be cast, at one level of semantic ascent, as a dispute about which events are denoted by perfect nominals like 'my omission to φ', 'my refrainment from φ-ing', etc. In Section 1.3.2, I noted that a perfect nominal derived from positive action sentences denotes that event which serves as the value of the bound event-variable, and hence witnesses that sentence. (Here, as usual, I leave aside the concerns about indeterminacy of reference raised there.) For example, (1) is analysed as (1_{ND}), and so the nominal 'Alice's kissing of Beth' (or, if we wish to avoid the appearance of imperfection, 'the kiss Alice gave to Beth') denotes, if anything, that event which serves as the value of 'e' in (1_{ND}).

(1)   Alice kissed Beth.
(1_{ND}) $\exists e(Agent(\text{Alice})(e) \ \& \ Patient(\text{Beth})(e) \ \& \ Kiss_{ND}(e))$

Now, I've argued that (2) must be analyzed as (2_{SND}):

(2)   Alice omitted to kiss Beth.
(2_{SND}) $\exists e(Agent(\text{Alice})(e) \ \& \ Ensure(e)(\sim\exists e'(Agent(\text{Alice})(e') \ \& \ Patient(\text{Beth})(e') \ \& \ Kiss_{ND}(e'))))$

---

[1] Roughly, a certain *F* realizes a certain *G* just in case (i) for there to be a *G* just is for there to be something which plays role *R* and (ii) that *F* plays *R*. Likewise, a certain *F* constitutes a certain *G* just in case (i) for there to be a *G* just is for there to be an *F* in circumstances *C* and (ii) that *F* is in *C*.

[2] Compare this to the view that (some) negative actions are positive events described in *negative* terms – Davidson (1985a: 219), Schaffer (2012: 418), Silver (2018: 41), and Vermazen (1985: 95). To describe something in negative terms is to describe in terms of what it *isn't* – e.g. as a non-*F*. To think of negative action sentences and derived nominals this way is to adopt Schaffer's (2012) analyses, which we saw fail in Section 6.4.1. By contrast, to describe something in functional terms is to describe it in terms of what it *does*. Thus, while negative action sentences contain a negative element in my view – i.e. they contain negative existential phrases – it's wrong to say that negative actions are positive events described in negative terms.

In the absence of any reason to think that perfect nominals derived from negative action sentences behave differently from those derived from positive ones, we should think that 'Alice's omission to kiss Beth' denotes, if anything, the event which serves as the value of 'e'. That is, we should think that it denotes the event which ensures that Alice doesn't kiss Beth, not the higher-level event of there being such an event.

The second, related argument is the *argument from perceptual locutions*. Sentences like (3), which report that one agent saw another agent perform a negative action, report that an agent saw an ensuring-event:

(3)   Charlie saw Alice omit to kiss Beth.

(3_{SND}) $\exists e \exists e'(Agent(\text{Charlie})(e)$ & $Patient(e')(e)$ & $Seeing_{ND}(e)$ & $Agent(\text{Alice})(e')$ & $Ensure(e')(\neg\exists e''(Agent(\text{Alice})(e'')$ & $Patient(\text{Beth})(e'')$ & $Kiss_{ND}(e'''))))$

If to see Alice omit to kiss Beth just is to see that event which ensures that Alice doesn't kiss Beth, then we should think that that event just *is* Alice's omission. For, it's not clear how seeing that ensuring-event could amount to seeing Alice omit to kiss Beth, if Alice's omission were a distinct, higher-level event. Certainly, if Charlie was aware that the event he was seeing played the ensuring-role, he might thereby come to know that Alice was omitting to kiss Beth, and so it might be correct to say that he saw *that* Alice omitted to kiss Beth. But, as shown in Chapter 6, 'x saw y φ' and 'x saw that y φ-ed' aren't equivalent. Thus, a role-functionalist will have trouble explaining the interaction of negative action sentences and perceptual locutions.

Now, just as token realizer-functionalism in the philosophy of mind allows us to identify mental states with physical ones, my realizer-functionalist view allows us to identify negative actions – and token negative behaviours more generally – with positive events. Returning to Vermazen's (1985: 95–96) case, if my act of playing with my buttons ensures that I don't take a second helping of hors d'oeuvres, then my refrainment *is* my act of playing with my buttons. This is a case in which a negative action is identical to a positive one. Or, in the case where I intentionally omit to cast a vote, it's plausible that the event of my hands being in my lap ensures that I don't vote, even if that event isn't intentional under that description. Thus, in my view, my omission *is* that event. This is a case in which a negative action is identical to a positive 'mere event'. Finally, consider the variant on the voting case, in which I'm not paying attention to the meeting, and my omission to vote is unintentional. In this case, it's still plausible that the event of my hands being in my lap ensures that I don't vote, and hence, in my view, that my omission *is* that event. This is a case in which a 'mere negative behaviour' is identical to a positive 'mere event'.

Prima facie, this is an advantage of the realizer-functionalist view. We can be *realists* about token negative behaviours – i.e. we can think that there really are such things, and that they're denoted by phrases like '*x*'s omission to φ', '*x*'s refrainment from ψ-ing', etc. – without believing in such troublesome entities as absences (recall Section 2.3.4), and indeed without adding *any* new entities to our ontology. For, the positive events with which token negative behaviours are identical are perfectly ordinary events, which we believe in anyway (or at least, which we believe in if we believe in events at all).

However, as we'll now see, the identification of negative actions with positive events can appear to be not an advantage of realizer-functionalism, but a liability.

7.3   A Problem for Realizer-Functionalism

7.3.1   The Property-Exemplification Theory of Events

The Property-Exemplification Theory of events (PET) is most prominently defended by Goldman (1970) and Kim (1973, 1976). On the most simple, straightforward construal of this theory, an event is a complex particular with an object x, a property F, and a time t as its constituents, and which exists just in case x possesses F at t. Thus, an event is an entity which consists in an object exemplifying a certain property at a certain time, a 'property-exemplification'. We can refer to such entities using the construction, '*x*'s exemplification of F at t' or, borrowing Kim's notation, '$[x, F, t]$'.[3]

Some complications of this simple construal are in order. First, we shouldn't assume that every event has a single constitutive object. There

---

[3] It's sometimes worried that objects, properties, and times can't be construed as parts/constituents of events, as PET requires. According to Classical Extensional Mereology (CEM), the mereological sum of some things, xx, exists just in case those things exist; thus, if x, F, and t are parts of the event $[x, F, t]$, that event exists just in case x, F, and t exist. But this result seems wrong: there is (thankfully) no event of me exploding at the present moment, even though the property of exploding, the present moment, and I all exist (Bennett 1988: 90–91).

Fortunately, we needn't think of property-exemplifications as *mereological sums* of their constituents (at least not if mereological sums are taken to obey the axioms and theorems of CEM). Property-exemplifications are like Armstrong's (1997) states of affairs, the constituents of which are *not* bound together by a classically-understood parthood relation. Indeed, Kim (1976) draws no distinction between events and states of affairs.

may be properties which are irreducibly plural. That is, there may be a polyadic property F which is collectively exemplified by some x and y, but not by either x or y individually, and which can't be reduced to, or eliminated in favour of, some monadic properties G_1 and G_2 which are exemplified by x and y, respectively (Bohn 2018, 2019). But if there are such properties, it would be odd to assume that they can't be constituents of property-exemplifications, i.e. that there can be no such event as x and y's exemplification of F at t. Likewise, it would be odd to assume that *relational* properties can't be constituents of property-exemplifications. Thus, we should allow, in principle, for events with more than one constitutive object, in the sense that the 'constitutive object' role is filled by many objects collectively, and by no single object individually.

Similarly, we shouldn't assume that every event has a single constitutive time. There may be temporally extended properties. That is, there may be a property F which is exemplified by x across an interval $t_1 - t_n$, but which is not itself exemplified by x at any t_i within that interval, and which isn't reducible to, or eliminable in favour of, any properties which are so exemplified.[4] While I'll consider some reasons we might have to be skeptical of such properties in Section 7.4.2, their non-existence shouldn't be built into PET, and so we should allow that they can be constituents of events, if they exist. Thus, we should allow for events with more than one constitutive time. Using plural variables for objects and times, 'xx' and 'tt', we can now refer to events using the construction, 'xx's exemplification of F at tt' or, in Kimian notation, '$[xx, F, tt]$'.

You might think that what goes for objects and times goes for properties as well: 'If an event can consist in some *things* being a certain way at a certain time, or in something being a certain way at some *times*, why can't it consist in a something being certain *ways* at a certain time?' However, while I have some idea of how a single property could irreducibly be possessed by many things, or at many times, it's less clear how multiple properties could be irreducibly possessed by a single thing. If x exemplifies both F and G at t, it's difficult to see how this could fail to reduce to the facts that x exemplifies F at t and that x exemplifies G at t. Instead of a single property-exemplification with two constitutive properties, $[x, FG, t]$,

---

[4] The label 'temporally extended properties' comes from Perovic (2018). Parsons (2004) uses the label 'distributional properties' to apply to properties which are neither possessed at, nor reducible to properties possessed at, point-sized sub-regions of any region of either time or space – e.g. he argues that *being polka-dotted* is possessed across a region of space, neither possessed at, nor reducible to properties possessed at, point-sized regions of space.

we seem to have two distinct property-exemplifications, $[x, F, t]$ and $[x, G, t]$ (and, perhaps, their mereological sum).

We can offer more by way of argument. According to Kim (1991: 642), the technical expression, 'x's exemplification of F at t', is meant to serve as a functor: plug in terms for some object(s), some property, and some time(s), and the resulting expression refers, if at all, to the exemplification, by that object (or those objects), of that property at that time (or those times). Now, it seems that, if xx is/are F at tt, then 'xx's exemplification of F at tt' ought to refer to something, that is, that there ought to be such an event as $[xx, F, tt]$. But if we allow that the 'constitutive property' role can be played by F and G collectively without being played by either of them individually, then there's no such guarantee: there may be such an event as $[x, FG, t]$, but no such event as $[x, F, t]$.

MacDonald and MacDonald (2006) argue that there can be a single property-exemplification with two or more distinct constitutive properties:

> That this is possible is evident from determinate/determinable examples, such as that of being coloured and being red. The most natural understanding of the relation between these properties is that for an object to instance the latter (being red) just is for it to instance the former (being coloured): nothing further is required, once the latter is instanced, for the former to be instanced. (MacDonald & MacDonald 2006: 561)

This argument is naturally read as an appeal to (something like) truthmaker theory together with the principle that we ought not to multiply truthmakers beyond necessity. So understood, the argument goes like this: Suppose that 'a is red' is true, and that we posit a state of affairs of a being red (call it 'a's being red') to serve as its truthmaker. From the fact that 'a is red' is true, it follows that 'a is coloured' is true, and so we must posit a truthmaker for *it*, namely the state of affairs of a being coloured (call it 'a's being coloured'). But since the truth of 'a is coloured' simply follows from the truth of 'a is red', it seems odd that we should have to posit a distinct truthmaker for it – after all, the existence of a's being red already suffices for the truth of 'a is coloured'. Thus, we should *identify* a's being red with a's being coloured: this state has *two* constitutive properties, namely *red* and *coloured*, and so the existence of this single state suffices both the truth of 'a is red' and 'a is coloured'.

Even if we adopt truthmaker theory, we should find this argument uncompelling. The MacDonalds begin by assuming that a certain state of affairs, a's being coloured, is required to serve as the truthmaker for 'a is coloured'. Finding that a's being red already suffices for the truth of this sentence, they conclude that those two states of affairs are identical. The more natural conclusion, however, is that the original assumption is false: a's being coloured *isn't* required to make '*a* is coloured' true, since it's already made true by a's being red. (Compare: it would be odd to posit a disjunctive state of affairs as the truthmaker for '*Fa* ∨ *Ga*', and then identify it with the state of affairs of a's being F when we realize that only the latter is needed to explain why '*Fa* ∨ *Ga*' is true; the more natural response to deny the need for the disjunctive state of affairs in the first place.)

Thus, while I'll allow that the 'constitutive object(s)' and 'constitutive time(s)' roles can be collectively filled by many object and times, respectively, I won't allow that the 'constitutive property' role can be collectively filled by many properties.

One last complication. I noted above that, if x exemplifies both F and G at t, then we may want to allow the mereological sum of $[x, F, t]$ and $[x, G, t]$ into our ontology. It's plausible that the mereological sum of two or more events is itself an event. Recall the example of the temporally scattered lecture from Section 1.3.1: a lecture with a 10-minute break in the middle is, plausibly, an event which is made up of two smaller events separated by that 10-minute interval. (And indeed, these two smaller events are plausibly made up of further events, involving various behaviours of mine and of my students.) Thus, PET should *not* be understood as requiring that every event is itself a property-exemplification. Rather, the theory should allow that an event may be the mereological sum of two or more property-exemplifications. (We'll see further reasons to allow this in Section 7.4.2.)

7.3.2 Arguments for the Theory

Perhaps the most popular alternative to PET is the *Sui Generis* Theory of events (SGT), defended primarily by Davidson (1969, 1970a). According to SGT, events form a 'fundamental ontological category' (Davidson 1969: 180), not explicable in terms of entities in other categories. We can say what events are by gesturing at very general differences between them and other kinds of thing – e.g. we can say that events are *happenings* or *occurrences* – but, beyond this, no more informative account can be given. The best arguments for PET point to certain advantages of that theory, over SGT.

First, PET promises to give an illuminating and ecumenical account of the nature of events. If we already have objects, properties, and times in our ontology, it's both illuminating and ecumenical to understand events in terms of them. SGT, because it places events in a fundamental category of their own, offers no such account.

This point extends from the general category of events to specific *types* of events. PET promises to give illuminating and ecumenical accounts of the nature of events of various types by way of the constitutive properties of these events, which are, allegedly, understood independently of those event-types: we gain insight into the nature of events of the type *explosion* by seeing them as exemplifications of the allegedly better-understood property *exploding*; we gain insight into the nature of events of the type *arm-raising* by seeing them as exemplifications of the allegedly better-understood property *raising one's arm*, etc.

Second, facts about which events occur – or at least, facts about which *kinds* of events occur – seem to supervene on facts about which objects possess which properties at which times. Once you fix the distribution of properties across objects and times, you thereby fix which (kinds of) events occur. For example, once you fix the precise position of my arm across an interval, you thereby fix whether it remains in place (and hence an event of its remaining in place occurs) or moves in a certain way (and hence an event of its moving in that way occurs).[5] PET seems to explain this: since events are just exemplifications of properties at times (or mereological sums thereof), it makes perfect sense that facts about which (kinds of) events occur supervene on facts about which properties are exemplified by which objects at which times. By contrast, SGT must take supervenience as a basic, unexplained fact.

Finally, PET promises to shed light on the identity-conditions of events. For, it's natural to think that property-exemplifications are identical just in case their constitutive objects, properties, and times are (Kim 1976: 35); if e just *is* the exemplification of F by x at t_1, it's difficult to see how it could be identical to an exemplification of some distinct G, or an exemplification by some distinct y, or an exemplification at some distinct t_2 (or all three). More generally:

Identity-Conditions for Property-Exemplifications

(ICPE1) $[xx, F, tt_1] = [yy, G, tt_2]$ only if $xx = yy$, $F = G$, and $tt_1 = tt_2$.
(ICPE2) If $xx = yy$, $F = G$, and $tt_1 = tt_2$, then if $[xx, F, tt_1]$ exists, $[yy, G, tt_2]$ exists and $[xx, F, tt_1] = [yy, G, tt_2]$.[6]

---

[5] See Bennett (1988: 12), Kim (1991: 461), Lombard (1986: ch. 8), and Savellos (1995).
[6] Notice that we can't adopt the simpler, biconditional statement, '$[xx, F, tt_1] = [yy, G, tt_2]$ iff $xx = yy$, $F = G$, and $tt_1 = tt_2$', as Kim (1976: 35; 1991: 642) does. For, the right-to-left direction assumes that a

By contrast, SGT sheds no clear light on the identity-conditions of events.[7]

It's perhaps worth noting that, although Kim proposed (something like) these identity-conditions in his (1976), he later became skeptical of them. In particular, he became skeptical of (ICPE1). (ICPE2), he says, follows from the fact that the phrase 'the exemplification of *F* by *xx* at *tt*' – or, in Kimian notation, '[*xx*, *F*, *tt*]' – is intended to be a functor (recall Section 7.3.1). It's a condition on well-behaved functions that they always yield the same output(s) given the same input(s), and so it must be that 'the exemplification of *F* by *xx* at *tt*' always yields a name for the same property-exemplification, given the same input of object(s), property, and time(s); hence (ICPE2). But (ICPE1) does *not* follow from the behaviour of 'the exemplification of *F* by *xx* at *tt*', since it's *not* a condition on well-behaved functions that different inputs can never yield the same output(s). Thus, he says, (ICPE1) isn't a commitment of PET (1991: 642).

This argument is uncompelling. The mere fact that we can't 'read off' (ICPE1) from the fact that 'the exemplification of *F* by *xx* at *tt*' is intended to be a function is no reason to doubt that that condition actually holds. (If it were, the argument would generalize to *any* putatively necessary conditions on the identity of property-exemplifications, since *no* such conditions can be 'read off' in this way.) Thus, I'll assume that a defender of PET should adopt both (ICPE1) and (ICPE2).[8,9]

You might think that, since I've defended a Neo-Davidsonian approach to action sentences, I ought to reject PET outright, in favour of Davidson's

property-exemplification exists if its constituents do, which a defender of PET ought to deny (see note 3).

[7] Davidson (1969) originally proposed that $e_1 = e_2$ iff e_1 and e_2 have exactly the same causes and effects, but this condition is unhelpful: we can only tell if e_1 and e_2 have the same causes and effects if we have some way of identifying/distinguishing *those* events, which is what Davidson's condition was supposed to provide (Lowe 1989a, 1989b). Davidson (1985b) eventually despaired of providing identity-conditions for events.

[8] You might think that we ought to reject (ICPE1) *anyway*, given that we allow a single property-exemplification to have more than one constitutive object and/or time. But recall, what's allowed is that many objects can *collectively* occupy the 'constitutive object(s)' role and that many times can *collectively* occupy the 'constitutive time(s)' role. This is perfectly consistent with (ICPE1). We would only be required to reject it if we allowed that some *xx* collectively occupy the 'constitutive object(s)' role while some distinct *yy* also collectively occupy that role (and likewise, *mutatis mutandis*, for times).

[9] In Section 7.3.1, I interpreted MacDonald and MacDonald's (2006: 561) view that a single event may be the exemplification of many properties as the view that many properties can *collectively* fill the 'constitutive property' role. So understood, the view is consistent with (ICPE1). (Compare the previous note on objects and times.) Perhaps the MacDonalds intend, rather, that many properties can *individually* fill that role. So understood, the view is inconsistent with (ICPE1). However, my reasons for being skeptical of the view apply on either interpretation.

SGT. However, the fact that action sentences quantify over events tells us nothing, on its own, about what events are like and, in particular, it doesn't commit us to taking events to form a basic ontological category.[10]

PET has a lot going for it. Unfortunately, my realizer-functionalist view of negative actions appears to be incompatible with it.

7.3.3   The Problem

According to PET, a negative action is an exemplification of the property of NEG-ϕ-ing, for some choice of ϕ: my omission to raise my arm is an exemplification of the property *NEG-(raise one's arm)*; Alice's omission to kiss Beth is an exemplification of the property *NEG-(kiss Beth)*; etc. It seems, then, that with a few possible exceptions, no negative action can be identical to any positive event. For, according to PET, a positive event is an exemplification of some positive property, ψ: my scratching of my leg is an exemplification of the property *scratching one's leg*; Alice's chewing of gum is an exemplification of the property *chewing gum*; etc. Thus, x's NEG-ϕ-ing is identical to x's ψ-ing only if the properties of NEG-ϕ-ing and of ψ-ing are identical. And, with a few possible exceptions, this is never the case.

The properties F and G are identical only if it's impossible for any object to possess one without possessing the other. That is, F and G are identical only if possession of each is necessary and sufficient for possession of the

---

[10] Davidson (1970b: 146–147) makes this point; his motivation for rejecting PET isn't that his analyses of action sentences rule it out, but rather that it apparently requires us to distinguish events he thinks are identical (1969: 170–171).

While Davidson doesn't take his approach to action sentences to provide direct support for his metaphysics of events, he does occasionally trace *resistance* to his metaphysics to the acceptance of a bad semantic theory of action sentences. He reads Kim and others as thinking that a sentence of the form 'x ϕ-s at t' functions as a *name* for a certain event, and that its components function as names for the constituents of that event. This thought is, of course, false: action sentences *quantify over*, but don't *name* events. Making a helpful comparison, Davidson writes, 'if I say, "There is an elephant in the bathtub", you are no doubt justified in supposing that one elephant at most is in the bathtub, but you are confused if you think my sentence contains a singular term that refers to a particular elephant if any' (1969: 168).

It's unclear whether Kim ever held the view that action sentences function as names for events. That interpretation is suggested, though not forced, by his claim that 'we often take singular sentences of the form "x has F at t" as referring to, describing, representing, or specifying an event' (1973: 8). (On one reading, Kim takes 'referring to', 'describing', etc. as equivalent, suggesting that he adopts the sentences-as-event-names view.) But even if he held that view in 1973, he had abandoned in by 1976 – see especially Kim (1976: 39–41), where he defends the compatibility of PET with Davidson's approach to action sentences (without, however, noting the consequences of combining these views; see Section 7.4.1). Thanks to David Liebesman and Jessica Wilson for discussion on these points.

other. But, for most choices of φ and ψ, it's simply not the case that ψ-ing is both necessary and sufficient for NEG-φ-ing.

We encountered the non-sufficiency point in Section 5.3.3. Where ψ is a behaviour of the sort for which natural language provides a ready-made verb phrase, it's hardly ever true that ψ-ing suffices for me (or anyone else) to NEG-φ: scratching my leg doesn't suffice for omitting to vote, since the voting procedures could have been different; the things I do as I go through the process of making a pasta sauce don't suffice for not adding the garlic, since I could have done all those things *and* added the garlic; etc. But likewise, it's hardly ever true that ψ-ing is *necessary* for me (or anyone else) to NEG-φ: I needn't have scratched my leg in order to have omitted to vote, since I could have kept my hands in my lap, or drummed my fingers on the table, instead; I needn't have gone through all the other steps of the recipe, in order to have omitted to add the garlic, since I could have done fewer of them, or even omitted to make the sauce altogether; etc.

As I said, there may be exceptions. Borrowing Clarke's (2014: 22) example, it may be that 'remaining still' denotes a positive behaviour. But if it does, then this is a positive behaviour which is both necessary and sufficient for not moving, and so a proponent of PET could conceivably agree that *remaining still* and *NEG-(moving)* are the same property, and hence that an exemplification of one could be – and indeed *must* be – an exemplification of the other. But in general, PET suggests that negative actions must be distinct from positive events.

Notice that the problem still arises if we claim, as I did in Chapter 5, that the event which ensures that *x* doesn't φ is an event which consists in *x* moving or positioning some parts of her body and/or external objects in some specific ways, or an event which consists merely in those body parts and/or objects being moved or positioned in those ways. Suppose that, instead of raising my arm to cast a vote, I scratch my leg. Suppose further that the event which ensures that I don't vote is an exemplification not of the property *scratching one's leg*, but of the maximally specific *way* in which I scratch my leg. Still, exemplification of this property isn't *necessary* for me (or anyone else) to omit to vote: I might have scratched my leg in a slightly different way, thereby failing to exemplify that property, and still omitted to vote. Neither is exemplification of this property *sufficient* for me (or anyone else) to omit to vote: if the voting procedures had been different, and the way to cast a vote was to scratch one's leg, I could have exemplified this property and still voted.

In some cases, the non-sufficiency point is less obvious. For example, in the case where I omit to add garlic to the pasta, it's not clearly possible for me to go through all the other steps, in the maximally specific way I do, and still add the garlic. But even in such cases, the non-necessity claim remains plausible – e.g. I could still have omitted to add the garlic, even if I had gone through the other steps in a slightly different, maximally specific way. Thus, it will remain true that, with a few possible exceptions, no negative action is identical to a positive event.

So, it seems that PET is incompatible with token realizer-functionalism, and indeed with *any* view on which negative actions are identical to ordinary positive events. By contrast, it seems to be perfectly compatible with token role-functionalism. For, that view brings with it no commitment to the identity of negative actions and positive events, and so no commitment to the identity of their constitutive properties.[11]

Indeed, if we adopt my generally functionalist approach to negative behaviours, and we adopt PET, it seems that token role-functionalism is the more natural view to take. Recall, according to that view, a negative action – or negative behaviour more generally – is a higher-level event, an event which consists in there existing some *other* event which plays the ensuring role. This is just what we'd expect, given PET. For, according to PET, a negative action is an exemplification of the property of NEG-φ-ing, for some choice of φ. Since the property of NEG-φ-ing is the higher-level property of there being an event which ensures that one doesn't φ, x's NEG-φ-ing is the higher-level event of there being an event which ensures that x doesn't φ.

Thus, it seems that to accept realizer-functionalism, and the identity of negative actions with positive events, would require us to reject an attractive theory of events.

7.4   Solving the Problem

7.4.1   *The Troublesome Assumption*

The argument against realizer-functionalism rests on the following principle:

Property-Exemplification Principle
If 'x φ_V-s' is true with respect to t, then the perfect nominal 'x's φ_N' denotes, with respect to t, the exemplification at t, by x, of the property denoted by 'φ_V'.

---

[11] Something like this argument against the identity of negative actions and ordinary, positive events appears in Silver (2018: 38) – although Silver also appeals to arguments to be considered in Chapter 8. Similarly, Tiehen (2015: 507–509) combines his role-functionalist theory of absences with a version of PET on the ground that PET rules out the identity claims to which a realizer-functionalist theory is committed, and which are apparently false.

(Here, the subscripts 'V' and 'N' serve to clarify that what's at issue are a verb phrase, a corresponding derived noun phrase, and the denotations thereof.) For example, recalling an example from Section 1.2.2, if 'Quisling betrayed Norway' is true, then the derived nominal 'Quisling's betrayal of Norway' denotes Quisling's exemplification of the property *betraying Norway*. Likewise, the *Principle* tells us that if 'Alice scratches her leg' and 'Alice omits to raise her arm' are both true, then 'Alice's scratching of her leg' and 'Alice's omission to raise her arm' denote, respectively, Alice's exemplification of the property of *scratching one's leg* and her exemplification of the property *omitting to raise one's arm* (or, more properly, *NEG-(raise one's arm)-ing*). That's why these events seem to have distinct constitutive properties.

While the *Property-Exemplification Principle* is generally accepted by defenders of PET – and taken by that theory's opponents as something that *would* be true, if the theory were true[12] – I submit that a defender of PET should reject it. She should allow that an event which falls under the type denoted by 'φ_N' can be an exemplification of a property other than the one denoted by 'φ_V'.

First, the *Principle* says that any *doing* of a certain thing has that *thing done* as its constituent property. As argued in Section 1.3.3, the things we do are higher-level properties which we possess by virtue of being related to certain events – e.g. the property *raising one's arm* is the property *being an x such that there is an e such that x is the agent of e and e is a raising of x's arm*. And, as argued in Section 1.3.5, higher-level properties are abundant, not sparse properties: they aren't 'worldly' properties which make real contributions to the natures of objects, explain similarities between them, or bestow causal powers on them. If events are worldly entities – and, in particular, if they occupy space and time, enter into causal relations, and can be perceived – then there's a presumption against positing events with higher-level properties as constituents. Or at least, there's a presumption against treating exemplifications of higher-level properties as occupying space and time, entering into causal relations, and being capable of being perceived, as actions are.

Second, the *Principle* threatens to undermine one of the arguments for PET. Recall, PET promises to give an illuminating account of the nature of events, by explaining the nature of events in terms of properties. This account can only be illuminating, however, if the property F through which we understand events of type G is explicable other than in terms of G itself. If we explain what it is for an object to be F in terms of G – e.g. by saying that x is F iff a G-event occurs – then the account is ultimately circular. But, given the arguments of Chapter 1, the *Principle* enjoins us to give accounts that are circular in precisely this way. The property of φ_V-ing is explicated as the property of being the agent of a φ_N-event; that is, the *thing done* is explicated in terms of the corresponding *doing-type*. If the only account we can give of the nature of φ_N-events is that they're exemplifications of the property of φ_V-ing – and, hence, the *doing-type* is explicated in terms of the *thing done* – the account is circular. In order to give an illuminating account of the nature of φ_N-events, a defender of PET must claim that they're exemplifications of some *other* property, which can be explicated independently of quantification over events of that same type.

Finally, the defender of PET ought to reject the *Principle* on the ground that it commits her – via arguments which parallel the argument for role-functionalism – to claiming that x's φ-ing is distinct from x's ψ-ing, in cases where this is highly implausible.

To see this, note first that the *Principle* commits us to certain non-identity claims due to the fact that a verb phrase 'φ_V' may be adverbially modified. Consider our example sentences from Chapter 4:

(4) Alice kissed Beth quickly in the kitchen.
(5) Alice kissed Beth quickly.
(6) Alice kissed Beth in the kitchen.
(7) Alice kissed Beth.

It seems to me that, if (4)–(7) are all true (with respect to the same time), then we have four ways of referring to the exact same event: we may refer to it as 'Alice's kissing of Beth', 'Alice's kissing of Beth in the kitchen', 'Alice's quick kissing of Beth', or 'Alice's quick kissing of Beth in the kitchen';[13] these nominals all refer to the same event, and differ only in the amount of descriptive information they contain. However, the *Property-Exemplification Principle*, taken in full generality, rules this out. We have, here, four verb phrases: 'kissed Beth', 'kissed Beth in the kitchen', 'kissed Beth quickly', and 'kissed Beth quickly in the kitchen'. Since none of the properties denoted by theses phrases is identical to any of the others, the

---

[13] If some of the constructions seem strained, there are natural alternatives available. For example, instead of 'Alice's quick kissing of Beth in the kitchen', we may use 'The quick kiss Alice gave Beth in the kitchen'. While the latter lacks the straightforward structure of some other perfect nominals, I assume it's intended to behave as other perfect nominals are, i.e. as denoting the event (if any) quantified over in (4).

Principle tells us that (4)–(7) report the occurrence of four distinct events, with distinct constitutive properties.[14]

We could avoid this problem by revising the *Principle*, so that bare, unmodified verbs denote the constitutive properties of events, while adverbially modified ones don't.

Property-Exemplification Principle (First Revision)

(i) If 'x φ_V-s' is true with respect to t, and 'φ_V' isn't an adverbially-modified verb phrase of the form 'ψ_V-s *F*-ly', then the perfect nominal 'x's φ_N' denotes, with respect to t, the exemplification at t, by x, of the property denoted by 'φ_V'.

(ii) If 'x φ_V-s' is true with respect to t, and 'φ_V' is an adverbially-modified verb phrase of the form 'ψ_V-s *F*-ly', then the perfect nominal 'x's φ_N' (equivalently, 'x's *F* ψ_N') denotes, with respect to t, the exemplification at t, by x, of the property denoted by 'ψ_V'.

We could then adopt the Neo-Davidsonian view that adverbs denote properties of *events*, rather than making any contribution to the constitutive properties of events, which are properties of their *agents* and *patients*. E.g. by clause (ii), 'Alice's quick kissing of Beth' denotes an exemplification, by Alice, of the property *kissing Beth* (or perhaps the exemplification, by Alice and Beth, of the relation *kissing*); we're free to say that 'quick' denotes a property of the kissing.

Kim resists this revision to the *Principle*, but his argument is uncompelling. He writes,

> Whatever else events might be, they were intended to be entities that enter into causal relations with one another, and that can be objects of explanations. But it is clear that we may want to explain not only why [Alice kissed Beth, i.e., Alice's kissing of Beth], but also why [she kissed Beth quickly, i.e., her quick kissing of Beth]. Under the approach being considered, the second explanation would be of why [Alice's kiss was quick]; we would be explaining why a certain event had a certain property, not why a certain event occurred. (Kim 1976: 45)

Evidently, Kim thinks that an explanation of why Alice kissed Beth quickly must be an explanation of why a particular event (Alice's quick kissing of Beth) occurred, and hence that it can't be an explanation of why a particular event (Alice's kissing of Beth) had a certain property (being quick). However, *neither* of these views is correct. To explain why Alice

---

[14] Kim (1976: 45–46) explicitly accepts this consequence.

kissed Beth quickly isn't to explain why *this* particular event had a certain property, but neither is it to explain why *this* particular event occurred, rather than *that* one. Rather, it's to explain why at least one event *of a certain kind* (a quick kissing of Beth) occurred. To think otherwise is to forget the Neo-Davidsonian analysis of 'Alice kissed Beth quickly'. This account of how the explanation functions is perfectly consistent with the revised *Principle*.

However, while the revised *Principle* is defensible, it doesn't fully solve the problem. For, *both* principles commit us to implausible non-identity claims which have nothing to do with the role of adverbs in action sentences. Consider an event in which I raise my arm. As I raise my arm, I do so in a maximally specific way, χ: I move it first into *this* position, then into *this* one, etc. Now, the property *raising one's arm* is distinct from the property of χ-ing (since I could exemplify the former without the latter), and so both principles imply that my raising of my arm is distinct from my χ-ing. But this is highly implausible. To give a more precise description of the way in which I raise my arm is to give a more detailed description of *my raising of my arm*. To say that I χ-ed is to describe my arm-raising in more detail, not to report the occurrence of a separate event.

Thus, we have good reason to reject both the original *Property Exemplification Principle* and the revised version. But what can we put in its place? What *are* the constitutive properties of our doings?

7.4.2   Alternatives

Recall a point I made in Section 5.3.3. Whenever an agent does something, we can describe what she does in more or less detail. But there seems to be, at least in principle, a maximally precise description available: in the case of acts, there is some maximally precise way in which the agent moves, positions, or otherwise affects the relevant body parts and external objects; and in the case of mere behaviours, there is some maximally precise way in which the relevant body parts and external objects move, are positioned, or are affected. In Section 7.4.1, I noted the plausibility of identifying, e.g. my raising of my arm with the event of my raising my arm *in the maximally specific way that I do*. Given that these two events are identical, they must, according to PET, be exemplifications of the same property. Thus, as a first pass, I suggest that my raising of my arm is an exemplification, not of *raising one's arm*, but of χ, the maximally precise *way* in which I raise my arm. Generalizing:

Property-Exemplification Principle (Second Revision)

(i) If 'x φ_V-s' is true with respect to t, and 'φ_V' isn't an adverbially-modified verb phrase of the form 'ψ_V-s F-ly', then the perfect nominal 'x's φ_N' denotes, with respect to t, the exemplification at t, by x, of χ, the maximally precise way in which x φ_V-s.

(ii) If 'x φ_V-s' is true with respect to t, and 'φ_V' is an adverbially-modified verb phrase of the form 'ψ_V-s F-ly', then the perfect nominal 'x's φ_N' (equivalently, 'x's F ψ_N') denotes, with respect to t, the exemplification at t, by x, of χ, the maximally precise way in which x ψ_V-s.

Our doings are exemplifications, not of the things we do, but of the maximally specific ways in which we do those things.[15]

This revision to the *Principle* allows us to answer the argument for role-functionalism and, indeed, it fits well with realizer-functionalism. On the latter view, my omission to raise my arm is an event which ensures that I don't raise my arm. As argued in Chapter 5, the best candidates to play the ensuring-role are doings of maximally specific things. Thus, a defender of PET should think that ensuring-events are exemplifications of these maximally specific behaviours, just as this revision to the *Principle* suggests.

There's a problem, however. Most behaviours, whether maximally specific or not, take time to perform; that is, they're temporally extended properties. *Prima facie*, temporally extended properties are equivalent to 'conjunctive' properties, i.e. properties denoted by predicates of the form '$\lambda x.(Fx \,\&\, Gx)$'. (For example, for my arm to move in a certain way is for my arm to be in *this* position, then *that* position, etc. By stringing all these positional properties together, we generate a conjunctive property that corresponds to the specific way in which my arm moves.) But it's not always appreciated that the concerns about disjunctive and negative properties discussed in Chapters 1 and 2, respectively, apply to conjunctive properties, too.

Conjunctive properties, construed as sparse rather than abundant, aren't needed to explain why the corresponding conjunctive predicates are true of objects. If a exemplifies both F and G, then '$Fa \,\&\, Ga$' is true, and it

---

[15] Given this revision to the *Principle*, there may be no unique answer to the question, 'What is the constitutive property of a φ_N-event?' For, if there's more than one maximally specific way of φ-ing, then there's more than one property which may serve as the constitutive property of such an event (e.g. there are many specific ways in which I can raise my arm, and thus many properties which can serve as constituents of arm-raisings). In such cases, that question has no unique answer. And in such cases, the answer to the more specific question, 'What is the constitutive property of *this particular φ_N-event*?' is to be determined, not a priori, but by investigation of how, exactly, x went about φ-ing.

trivially follows that '$\lambda x.(Fx \ \& \ Gx)$' is true of a. Nor are they needed to explain why objects which satisfy conjunctive predicates are genuinely similar. If a exemplifies both F and G, and b does too, then there are two respects in which they're similar: they're both F and they're both G. It's hard to see that there's any similarity left unaccounted for, which could be accounted for by the existence of a sparse conjunctive property, $\lambda x.(Fx \ \& \ Gx)$.[16]

So much might be obvious. But it's sometimes thought that, while negative properties aren't suited to bestow causal powers at all, and disjunctive powers can't bestow any powers not already bestowed by their 'disjuncts', conjunctive powers are needed to bestow powers not already bestowed by their 'conjuncts'. Borrowing Armstrong's (1989: 84) example, while *having charge C or mass M* may not bestow any powers not already bestowed by *having charge C* and *having mass M* alone, it seems that *having charge C and mass M* might very well bestow powers not bestowed by those non-conjunctive properties – for, an object with both C and M might be capable of doing things that it couldn't do, if it had either C or M alone.

Unfortunately, this argument ignores the possibility that a causal power may be bestowed, not by a single property, but by multiple properties working in tandem. Suppose that an object which has both C and M can do things it couldn't do if it had either C or M alone. We needn't say that, because neither C nor M bestows these powers, there must be a third property which does. We may say, instead, that those powers are bestowed by C and M collectively, though not individually. Indeed, considerations of simplicity suggest that we *should* say this, unless given reason not to.

Of course, just as there's no obstacle to positing negative and disjunctive properties, considered as *abundant* rather than sparse, there's no obstacle to positing conjunctive properties, so considered: the denotations of words like 'square' and 'bachelor' may be best understood as conjunctive functions. But if we're resistant to positing *sparse* negative and disjunctive properties, and to allowing such properties as constituents of worldly events, we should be equally resistant to positing sparse conjunctive properties.

Faced with this concern, there are three ways we might go. First, we might reject the identification of temporally extended properties with conjunctive properties. Rather than treat, e.g. a maximally specific way of moving as the conjunction of several maximally specific positions, we

---

[16] Of course, if 'F' and 'G' are themselves either disjunctive or negative, joint satisfaction of these predicates won't make for genuine similarity, either.

might insist that this temporally extended property is *basic*, and not reducible to the conjunction of several instantaneous properties.[17] This approach requires no further revision to the *Property-Exemplification Principle*.

Second, we might accept the identification of temporally extended properties with conjunctive properties, and so deny that such properties can be the constitutive properties of events. The only 'worldly' properties there are, in this view, are the instantaneous ones.

How, in this view, can we fit maximally specific behaviours into PET? Recall, PET can allow that some events are not property-exemplifications, but mereological sums thereof. The natural move, then, is to claim that maximally specific behaviours are mereological sums of events. For example, when Alice's arm moves in a certain way, and so she exemplifies a series of distinct positions, F_1–F_n, across an interval of instants, t_1–t_n, the movement of her arm is the mereological sum of a series of property-exemplifications, $[Alice, F_1, t_1]$–$[Alice, F_n, t_n]$. This approach, in contrast to the first, *does* require further revision to the *Principle*:

Property-Exemplification Principle (Third Revision)

(i)   If 'x φ_V-s' is true with respect to t, and 'φ_V' isn't an adverbially-modified verb phrase of the form 'ψ_V-s F-ly', then 'φ_V' denotes either an instantaneous property or a temporally-extended conjunctive property all the 'conjuncts' of which are instantaneous properties. If the former, then the perfect nominal 'x's φ_N' denotes, with respect to t, the exemplification at t, by x, of χ, the maximally precise way in which x φ_V-s. If the latter, then the perfect nominal 'x's φ_N' denotes the mereological sum of $[x, \chi_1, t_1]$–$[x, \chi_n, t_n]$, where t_1–t_n are all instants within t, and $\lambda y.(\chi_1 \ \& \ \ldots \ \& \ \chi_n)$ is the maximally specific way in which x φ_V-s.

(ii) If 'x φ_V-s' is true with respect to t, and 'φ_V' is an adverbially-modified verb phrase of the form 'ψ_V-s F-ly', then 'ψ_V' denotes either an instantaneous property or a temporally-extended conjunctive property all the 'conjuncts' of which are instantaneous properties. If the former, then the perfect nominal 'x's φ_N' (equivalently, 'x's F ψ_N')

---

[17] Perovic (2018), while not outright endorsing irreducibility, argues against some attempted reductions in the context of four-dimensionalist theories of persistence. Parsons (2004: 176–177) argues that *spatially* extended properties may be irreducible in this way, on the ground that space might not be made up of extentionless points (in which case, spatially extended properties can't be reduced to, or eliminated in favour of, properties possessed at such points). The same argument could be run for temporally extended properties, on the assumption that time is suitably space-like to admit the question of whether it is made up of extentionless points.

denotes, with respect to t, the exemplification at t, by x, of χ, the maximally precise way in which x ψ_V-s. If the latter, then the perfect nominal 'x's φ_N' denotes the mereological sum of $[x, \chi_1, t_1]-[x, \chi_n, t_n]$, where t_1-t_n are all instants within t, and $\lambda y.(\chi_1 \& \ldots \& \chi_n)$ is the maximally specific way in which x ψ_V-s.

Finally, we might split the difference, and insist that while some temporally-extended properties can be identified with conjunctive properties, others can't. This approach, like the previous one, requires that we adopt the third revision of the *Principle*. It's also interesting because it potentially has different consequences for different theories of actions.

Suppose you think that ways of moving, in the intransitive sense of 'moving', are reducible to conjunctions of instantaneous positions: for my arm to *move* in a certain maximally specific way is for it to be in *this* position at one instant, then in *this* position at the next instant, and so on. Suppose, further, you think that ways of *causing* movement aren't reducible in this way: causation takes time, and so a pair of objects can't stand in this relation at an instant, but only across an interval. This combination of views affects different theories of action differently.

Recall, on traditional versions of both the Event-Causal Theory (CTA) and the Agent-Causal Theory (ACT), when I move my body in a certain way, my action is identical to a bodily movement in the intransitive sense of 'movement'. For example, my raising of my arm and the rising of my arm are identical: the rising counts as a raising, rather than a *mere* rising, by virtue of its causal history. If ways of moving, in the intransitive sense, are conjunctions of instantaneous properties, then bodily movements, in both the transitive and intransitive senses (e.g. arm-raisings and mere arm-risings) can be treated as mereological sums of exemplifications of instantaneous properties.

Compare the versions of CTA and ACT on which bodily movements, in the transitive sense of 'movement', are distinct from bodily movements in the intransitive sense (e.g. my raising of my arm isn't identical to the rising of my arm, but is rather a *causing* of the latter). On these views, at least some bodily movements, in the transitive sense, are property-exemplifications rather than mereological sums thereof. Suppose I move my arm during an interval t_1-t_n, where this interval is sufficiently short that my causing of *this* movement isn't reducible to, or eliminable in favour of causings of several distinct, smaller movements. Then, on these versions of CTA and ACT, my moving of my arm is the exemplification of a temporally extended property, rather than the mereological sum of several exemplifications, either of instantaneous properties or of properties possessed across smaller intervals.

Here, I won't adjudicate between these three reactions to the problem with temporally-extended properties, and so I won't commit myself to either the second or third revisions of the *Property-Exemplification Principle*. The important point, for our purposes, is that each of these reactions is compatible with realizer-functionalism.

7.5 Conclusion

In this chapter, I've addressed the apparent incompatibility of PET with realizer-functionalism, and indeed with *any* theory on which negative actions are positive events. I've argued that the incompatibility is *only* apparent, and arises from an assumption that a defender of PET needn't, and shouldn't, accept. Thus, if you accept that theory of events, you needn't reject my realizer-functionalist view.[18]

My defense of realizer-functionalism isn't complete, however. In recent years, a slew of arguments have appeared in the literature which purport to show – sometimes within the scope of a few sentences – that *no* view on which negative actions are identical to positive events can be correct. It's to these arguments that I now turn.

---

[18] A similar problem can be posed, and a similar solution provided, within the context of the Trope Theory of events, according to which events are properties, thought of as particulars (Bennett 1988; Campbell 1990; Ehring 1997, 2011; Williams 1953a, 1953b). According to trope-based theories of properties, there are no universals. Talk of 'general properties' is explicated in terms of trope-types. Moreover, it's natural to delineate a trope-type F according to the way any object must be, in order to be F: F is that type all and only tokens of which make a certain contribution to their possessors. But then, if F and G are distinct 'general properties', then the exact contributions made by F-tropes and G-tropes must be distinct, and so nothing can be a trope of both types. (Wilson (2011b: 145, 152 n.27) makes a similar argument, focusing specifically on the causal powers that a trope bestows on its possessor.) This is a problem for realizer-functionalism, assuming we accept the following principle:

Trope Principle

If 'x φ_V-s' is true with respect to t, then the perfect nominal 'x's φ_N' denotes an instance of the general property denoted by 'φ_V', and which x possesses at t.

Fortunately, we needn't do so. We can allow that, if x possesses the general property of φ_V-ing (i.e. the higher-level property of there being a φ_N-event of which x is the agent), then x possesses a trope which is an instance of that property. But we needn't say that x's φ_N, the event in which x φ_V-s, is itself an instance of that property. We may say, instead, (i) that x's φ_N is an instance of a distinct property, i.e. the maximally specific *way* in which x φ_V-s, and (ii) that, at the same time, x possesses a distinct, higher-level trope, which *is* an instance of the general property of φ_V-ing.

CHAPTER 8

Objections

8.1 Introduction

In the previous chapters, I've articulated a realizer-functionalist view of negative actions: negative actions are events which play a certain role; this role is played by ordinary, positive events; and, so, negative actions are identical to the positive events which play that role. In this chapter, I defend the identity of negative actions and positive events against a range of objections that have appeared in the literature in recent years.

In Section 8.2, I consider arguments to the effect that identifying negative actions with positive events yields strange results about their locations in space and time. In Section 8.3, I consider arguments to the effect that negative actions typically have different modal profiles than the positive events with which I claim they're identical. In Section 8.4, I consider arguments to the effect that negative actions typically have different causal roles than the positive events with which I claim they're identical. Finally, in Section 8.5, I consider arguments which appeal to alleged differences between negative actions and positive events, but which don't hinge on issues about spatiotemporal location, modality, or causation. In each case, I show that the argument is uncompelling; in some cases, I note that the argument applies with equal or greater force against metaphysical views which are opposed to mine, and which the argument is used to support.

8.2 Spatiotemporal Location

8.2.1 Space

It's sometimes thought that, if x's NEG-φ-ing is located in space at all, then it must be located at the relevant place (if any) where x doesn't φ (Clarke 2014: 26). Putting it another way: we saw in Section 6.3.1 that locative adverbs like 'in the kitchen' are subject to a scope ambiguity in negative action sentences: they can modify either what the agent *does* (omit to φ, refrain from φ-ing, etc.) or what she *doesn't* do (φ). The thought under consideration is that, when 'x NEG-φ-s at r' is given the latter, wide-scope reading, the spatial location of x's NEG-φ-ing (if it can be said to have such a location at all) is given by the adverb 'at r'. This thought makes trouble for realizer-functionalism.

Borrowing an example from Clarke (2014: 37–38), suppose that Alice promises to go for a jog in Central Park with Beth, but omits to do so, and instead goes for a walk in High Park with Charlie. Then (1) is true, on its wide-scope reading:

(1) Alice omitted to go for a jog with Beth in Central Park.

Since what Alice omits to do is to go for a jog with Beth *in Central Park*, that's the relevant place where she doesn't go for a jog with Beth, and so her omission is (allegedly) located there, and not in High Park.[1] Now, according to realizer-functionalism, Alice's omission is identical to her ψ-ing, for some ψ which ensures that she doesn't go for a jog with Beth. Most plausibly, this is the way in which she *walks* at the relevant time (or some maximally specific behaviour which is 'included' in that way of walking, in the sense explained in Section 5.3.5). But Alice's walk is located in High Park, not in Central Park. So, her omission *can't* be identical to this event, since they have different spatial locations.

Generalizing, suppose we accept the following principle:

Spatial Location of Negative Actions (First Pass)
'x NEG-(φ at r)' is true iff x's NEG-(φ at r)-ing is located at r.

Since, in general, x can NEG-(φ at r) without doing anything *else* at r, there may be no token positive behaviour of x's which is located at r. In such a case, to identify x's negative behaviour with some positive behaviour of hers is to identify it with something that isn't located at r, in violation of Leibniz's Law.[2]

---

[1] '*Where* in Central Park is Alice's omission located?' Presumably, unless Alice and Beth were supposed to take a specific path, there's no more specific answer to the question, 'Where were they supposed to go for their jog?' than 'Central Park'. In that case, it seems, my opponent should claim that, if Alice's omission has a spatial location at all, it occupies the entirety of the park. Compare the discussion of temporally extended negative actions in Section 8.2.2.

[2] See Clarke (2011: 602–603) for a variant on this argument. Silver (2018: 37, 43) raises the concern that we have contradictory intuitions about where negative actions are located, although he seems to recognize that a view like mine can be paired with (something like) the response I give below.

Perhaps unsurprisingly, I reject the *Spatial Location* principle on which this argument rests. There are two reasons to reject it, independent of the problem it raises for realizer-functionalism.

First, consider (2), on its wide-scope reading:

> (2) David saw Alice omit to go for a jog with Beth in Central Park.

If (2) is true, then David must have perceptual access to the spatial location of Alice's omission. According to the *Spatial Location* principle, that omission is located in Central Park. But it seems that (2) can be true even if David lacks perceptual access to that location. In order to see Alice omit to go for a jog with Beth in Central Park, David needs to see *Alice*, and she needn't be in Central Park, in order for (2) to be true. Indeed, in Clarke's example, she's located in High Park, and so it seems that David must have perceptual access to *that* location, in order to see her omission, and hence for (2) to be true. Thus, attention to the interaction of negative action sentences and perceptual locutions suggests that the principle gets the spatial locations of at least some negative actions wrong.

(This argument, of course, echoes an argument against treating negative actions as absences, given in Section 6.2.3. This shouldn't be surprising. The *Spatial Location* principle fits nicely with that treatment since, as I noted there, it's plausible that an absence of *F*s, if it has a spatial location at all, is located at the relevant place where there are no *F*s.)

Second, in cases where 'x NEG-φ-s at r' is given the narrow-scope reading, it makes sense to locate x's NEG-φ-ing at the place given by the locative adverb 'at r'; locative adverbs behave, in those cases, just as they do in positive action sentences (recall Section 6.3.1). But now, if we say that the location of a negative action is given by a locative adverb, whether it occurs within the scope of 'NEG' or not, then we must supplement the *Spatial Location* principle as follows:

Spatial Location of Negative Actions (Second Pass)
(i)   'x NEG-(φ at r)' is true iff x's NEG-(φ at r)-ing is located at r.
(ii) 'x NEG-(φ) at r' is true iff x's NEG-(φ)-ing is located at r.

This principle leads to inconsistent results about the spatial location of omissions, independently of realizer-functionalism. In Clarke's case, while (1) is true on the wide-scope reading, (3) is true on the narrow-scope reading:

> (1) Alice omitted to go for a jog with Beth in Central Park.
> (3) Alice omitted to go for a jog with Beth in High Park.

Thus, even ignoring the issue of whether Alice's omission is identical to some positive behaviour of hers, our supplemented *Spatial Location* principle locates that omission in two different places.

We have independent reason to deny that, if '*x* NEG-(φ at *r*)' is true, then *x*'s token negative behaviour is located at *r*. Thus, we can deny that Alice's omission to go for a jog with Beth is located in Central Park, and affirm that it's located in High Park, where realizer-functionalism says it is.

You might worry that co-locating negative actions and positive events will lead to further, troublesome results. Suppose that as Alice and Charlie walk, they carve a zig-zag path through High Park. It seems that Alice's walk must also take a zig-zag path. But it sounds wrong to say that Alice's *omission* takes a zig-zag path (Clarke 2014: 37–38).

Here, I bite the bullet and insist that Alice's omission *does* take a zig-zag path. To see that the bullet is worth biting, suppose that, as Alice and Charlie go for their walk, they engage in conversation. Then there exists an event that is their conversation, and which is located roughly where they are at the time at which it occurs (its more specific location is given by the locations of the body parts involved in it). Since Alice and Charlie take a zig-zag path through the park as they talk, it follows that their conversation also takes a zig-zag path. That might seem like an odd result, but it's simply a consequence of realism about conversations *qua* events. The claim that omissions can take zig-zag paths is no more objectionable than the claim that conversations can. Thus, we can confidently reject the *Spatial Location* principle.[3]

---

[3] It's worth noting that some opponents of realizer-functionalism – in particular, proponents of role-functionalist and constitutionalist views of the sort sketched in Section 7.2 – face analogous problems with spatial location, which are also best answered by rejecting *Spatial Location*. Consider the following principle:

Inheritance of Spatial Location

If *x* realizes/constitutes *y* at *t*, then *x* is located at *r* at *t* iff *y* is located at *r* at *t*.

This principle strikes me as highly plausible – indeed, Palmer (2020: 746–747) explicitly endorses it when defending his constitutionalist view – but if it's true, then proponents of these views face the exact same objections as the realizer-functionalist. According to the *Spatial Location* principle, Alice's omission is located in Central Park, not in High Park. But if Alice's omission is realized or constituted by Alice's walk, and that event is located in High Park, then by the *Inheritance* principle, Alice's omission is located in High Park, not Central Park. Moreover, if Alice's walk carves a zig-zag path through space, then by the *Inheritance* principle, her omission *also* carves a zig-zag path, since it's co-located with her walk at each point.

The obvious solution is to reject the *Spatial Location* principle. But then, proponents of these views are no better off than the realizer-functionalist. (In fact, they're slightly worse off. As I argued in Section 7.2, this theory has trouble accommodating the data regarding the interaction of negative action sentences and perceptual locutions. Thus, one of my arguments against the *Spatial Location* principle is unavailable to them.)

8.2.2   *Time*

It seems that, if x's NEG-φ-ing is located in time at all, then it must be located at the relevant time (if any) that x doesn't φ. That is, when 'x NEG-φ-s at t' is given the wide-scope reading, the temporal location of x's NEG-φ-ing (if it can be said to have such a location at all) is given by the adverb 'at t'.

Temporal Location of Negative Actions
'x NEG-(φ at t)' is true iff x's NEG-(φ at t)-ing is located at t.

This principle doesn't make the same kind of trouble for realizer-functionalism as the analogous *Spatial Location* principle. Suppose that Alice promised to go for a jog with Beth from 1:00pm to 2:00pm. Then the one-hour interval between 1:00pm and 2:00pm is the relevant time at which she doesn't jog with Beth, and so the *Temporal Location* principle locates Alice's omission in that interval. But this is no problem for the realizer-functionalist, since she shouldn't be tempted to identify Alice's omission with any token behaviour of hers that occurs outside that interval (e.g. an act of eating breakfast which occurs between 8:00am and 8:30am). Due to the presupposition carried by 'omit', nothing Alice does before 1:00pm or after 2:00pm counts as *omitting* to go for a jog with Beth in this case (recall Section 4.5.2). Moreover, it's built into my account of ensuring events that, if what x omits to do (refrains from doing, etc.) is φ *at t*, then nothing x does before or after t counts as *ensuring* that x doesn't φ at t (recall Section 5.3.1). Thus, the realizer-functionalist shouldn't be tempted to attribute distinct temporal locations to Alice's omission.

Nonetheless, some worries about temporal location have been raised in the literature. The time referred to in the adverb 'at t' needn't be (and, in most ordinary negative action sentences, won't be) a single instant; it may be a long interval, made up of many instants. Bernstein (2014b, 2015) worries that, in such cases, it's difficult to determine to which positive event the negative action is identical.

Suppose that Alice is an airplane technician. She's supposed to perform a safety check on one of the planes on the tarmac, but omits to do so. Suppose further that it would have taken 30 minutes to perform the check, and that Alice could have performed it during any half-hour interval between 1:00pm and 2:00pm, but that there's no specific half-hour interval such that she was supposed to do it *then*. Then, we apparently have a problem. It's not clear at which half-hour interval Alice's omission is to be located (The interval between 1:00pm and 1:30pm? The interval between 1:15pm and 1:45pm?) and so it's not clear to which positive behaviour it is identical.[4]

Generalizing: since '*x* NEG-(φ at *t*)' can be true in cases where (i) *t* is a long interval and (ii) if *x* had φ-ed, *x*'s φ-ing wouldn't have occupied that entire interval, we apparently have a problem determining which sub-interval is occupied by *x*'s NEG-(φ at *t*)-ing and hence by that positive event to which it is (allegedly) identical.

Of course, this objection, if successful, doesn't *merely* raise a problem for the identity claims to which the realizer functionalist is committed; it raises a problem for *any* view on which negative actions are temporally located particulars. Even if we don't claim that Alice's omission is identical to some positive behaviour of hers, the question can still be asked, '*When*, in that one-hour interval, does Alice's omission occur?' The problem of locating the relevant positive event is parasitic on this problem.

You might think that a realizer-functionalist should answer the objection by rejecting the *Temporal Location* principle. But I think that principle is *true*: on my sophisticated Neo-Davidsonian approach to negative action sentences, '*x* NEG-(φ at *t*)' quantifies over an event which ensures that *x* doesn't φ at *t*, an event which is itself located at *t*. Fortunately, there's another response available.

Bernstein assumes that, if *x*'s φ-ing wouldn't have occupied the entire interval *t*, but only a sub-interval of a certain length, then *x*'s NEG-(φ at *t*)-ing must *also* occupy a sub-interval of that length (e.g. since it would have taken Alice 30 minutes to perform the safety check, her omission must last 30 minutes). That assumption is questionable. We could say, instead (and it's perfectly compatible with the *Temporal Location* principle to say) that if what *x* omits to do (refrains from doing, etc.) is φ at *t*, then *x*'s omission (refrainment, etc.) occupies the entire interval *t*. Thus, in Bernstein's example, Alice's omission exactly occupies the one-hour period from 1:00pm to 2:00pm, rather than any half-hour sub-interval.[5]

---

[4] (Bernstein 2014b: 4; 2015: 209). Bernstein makes an analogous argument regarding spatial location. Supposing there's no more-specific location on the tarmac such that Alice was supposed to perform the safety check *there*, there are many candidate locations for Alice's omission (2014b: 4). My reply: the spatial location of an omission to φ isn't given by the relevant place (if any) that *x* was supposed to φ, but by the location of the ensuring-event (see Section 8.2.1).

[5] This claim isn't forced on us by the *Temporal Location* principle, since the adverb 'at *t*' needn't be taken to give a negative action's *exact* temporal location, anymore than 'at *r*' need be taken to give an event's exact spatial location (Section 4.2.2). The point is that the claim is consistent with the principle; we needn't assume, in any given case, that a negative action has a temporal location more precise than that given by 'at *t*'.

Indeed, given that Bernstein's example is cast using the language of 'omissions', this is the more natural thing to say. Omissive sentences carry the presupposition that the agent was supposed to do the relevant thing. More specifically, 'x omitted to (φ at t)' carries the presupposition that x was supposed to φ at t. Now, there's no half-hour interval such that Alice is supposed to perform the safety check *then*; she's simply supposed to do it at some point between 1:00pm and 2:00pm. Thus, the relevant time at which Alice doesn't perform the check is that one-hour interval, and so it's natural to say that the time during which she omitted to do the check was 1:00pm–2:00pm. It's odd to suppose, instead, that her omission must occupy one of the many half-hour intervals during which she might have performed the check.[6]

You might worry that allowing negative actions to fully occupy extended intervals will lead to further, troublesome results. Borrowing an example from Clarke (2011: 603; 2014: 21), suppose that Alice was supposed to pull the weeds in her front yard at some point during the month of June; there's no more-specific time in June such that she was supposed to do it *then*, she was simply supposed to do it at *some* point. Now, suppose that Alice omitted to pull the weeds. In my view, her omission lasts the entire month. This seems like an odd result. There's *something* odd about saying that Alice omitted to pull the weeds for the whole month.[7]

---

[6] I've rejected the assumption that, if x's φ-ing wouldn't have occupied the entire interval t, but only a sub-interval of a certain length, then x's NEG-(φ at t)-ing must *also* occupy a sub-interval of that length. It's worth noting that at least some opponents of realizer-functionalism must *also* reject this assumption, in order to answer analogous arguments.

Consider, again, role-functionalist and constitutionalist views of the sort sketched in Section 7.2. If proponents of these views claim that negative actions are located in time, they must reject Bernstein's crucial assumption. Otherwise, they'll have just as much trouble as anyone else in locating Alice's omission to perform the safety check at some half-hour interval between 1:00pm and 2:00pm.

Perhaps more surprisingly, Bernstein's own metaphysical view faces a version of her objection. In her (2014b) view, x's omission to φ (refrainment from φ-ing, etc.) is a *tripartite entity*, comprised of (i) some actually occurring event of which x is the agent, but which isn't a φ-ing, (ii) a merely possible φ-ing by x, and (iii) a counterpart relation which holds between them, the holding of which makes it correct to say that the first event *might have been a φ-ing*. (This view is meant to be combined with, and perhaps motivated by, Bernstein's semantics; recall Section 6.4.2.) Thus, when Alice omits to perform the safety check, her omission is composed of an actual event which isn't a performance of the safety check (e.g. an act of eating a sandwich, if that's what Alice does instead), together with a merely possible performance of the safety check. Since, *ex hypothesi*, it would only take Alice 30 minutes to perform the safety check, there are many merely possible events which could serve as constituents of Alice's omission, and which occur at different 30-minute intervals. Which of these is *really* a constituent of Alice's omission? Bernstein doesn't say, and her view provides no obvious resources for an answer. (Likewise, *mutatis mutandis*, for the spatial version of Bernstein's argument, sketched in note 4.)

[7] Clarke originally directs this argument against views on which negative actions are *constituted* by, though not *identical* to, positive events. Palmer (2020) attempts to respond to Clarke's argument on those terms; see Payton (2020) for criticism.

I agree that there's something odd about saying this, but the reason is pragmatic, not metaphysical. '*x* omitted to φ at *t*' carries the presupposition that *x* was supposed to φ at *t*. Since there's no specific time in June such that Alice was supposed to pull the weeds *then*, there's no such time with respect to which 'Alice omitted to pull the weeds at *t*' is true. *That's* why it sounds odd to say that she omitted to pull the weeds for the whole month: nothing she did, at any time during the month, counted as *omitting* to pull the weeds. We can avoid this oddness by distinguishing the true claim that Alice omitted to pull the weeds in June (in the sense that some behaviour of hers which occupied the whole month was an omission to pull the weeds) from the false claim that she omitted to pull the weeds *throughout* June (in the sense that, at every time in June, some behaviour of hers which occupied that time was an omission to pull the weeds *then*).

8.3 Modal Profiles

8.3.1 The Argument

Let an object or event's 'modal profile' be the set of world-time pairs with respect to which it exists. If the events e_1 and e_2 are identical – if they're really *one* event, not two – then they must have the same modal profile, since nothing can both exist and fail to exist in the same world at the same time. This fact motivates one of the most popular arguments against the identification of negative actions with positive events: it seems that negative actions, often if not always, have distinct modal profiles from the positive events with which they're allegedly identical.

Recall the case in which I abstain from voting by omitting to raise my arm. Suppose that, as a matter of fact, I keep both arms in my lap, so that the event which ensures that I don't raise my arm consists in me keeping my arms in my lap in the specific way I do, or perhaps in my doing something which is included in that behaviour. On the realizer-functionalist view, my abstention is identical to this ensuring-event, and so they must have the same modal profile. But, it seems, they *don't* have the same modal profile. For, I might have omitted to raise my arm without keeping my arms in my lap in the specific way I did: I might have placed them slightly differently. And I might have omitted to raise my arm without keeping both arms in my lap at all: I might have drummed my fingers on the table, or fiddled with a pen, or taken the opportunity to type something into my phone, etc. Thus, it seems, my omission to raise my arm occurs in worlds, and at times, that my act of keeping my arms in my lap in a specific way doesn't occur. Therefore, they can't be identical.

The voting case is just one example, and the point easily generalizes. In many cases, an agent who NEG-φ-s has many ways of NEG-φ-ing available to them: although x actually NEG-φ-s by ψ-ing, they could easily have NEG-φ-ed without ψ-ing. Thus, it seems, x's NEG-φ-ing can't be identical to x's ψ-ing, since the former can exist in the absence of the latter.[8]

8.3.2   Doings, Things Done, and Modality

It's worth noting that, in general, the fact that I could have done one thing without doing another doesn't imply that my doings of those things are distinct. To think that it does is to think that the following is a valid argument form:

(α) Possibly, x φ-s and x doesn't ψ.
(β) ∴ Possibly, x's φ-ing exists and x's ψ-ing doesn't exist.
(γ) ∴ x's actual φ-ing is distinct from x's actual ψ-ing.

There's nothing wrong with the move from (β) to (γ), of course; nothing can both exist and not exist, so if x can exist without y, they must be distinct. But the move from (α) to (β) isn't generally valid. 'x φ-s' and 'x ψ-s' are schematic action sentences, and action sentences express existential quantifications over events; they neither contain, nor function as, names for particular events. Thus, (α) doesn't report that there's some world in which x's φ-ing exists but x's ψ-ing doesn't; rather, it reports that there's some possible world in which an event of x φ-ing exists but no event of x ψ-ing exists. Letting 'a' denote x's actual φ-ing and 'b' denote x's actual ψ-ing, we can regiment (α) and (β) as follows:[9]

(α*) $\Diamond(\exists e(Agent(x)(e)\ \&\ \varphi_{ND}(e))\ \&\ \sim\exists e'(Agent(x)(e')\ \&\ \psi_{ND}(e')))$
(β*) $\Diamond(\exists e(e = a)\ \&\ \sim\exists e'(e' = b))$

---

[8] See Bernstein (2014b: 4; 2015: 209), Sartorio (2009: 518), Silver (2018: 36), and Tiehen (2015: 507–508).

   Although Bernstein endorses this argument, it's not clear that it can be taken to support her view of omissions as tripartite entities (see note 6). The intuition behind the argument is supposed to be that, no matter what I did in the voting case, I would have performed the exact same omission (Silver 2018: 36). But Bernstein's view doesn't secure this result. Consider the omission which is partly composed of a merely possible arm-raising, call it 'e_1', and my actual act of keeping my arms in my lap, call it 'e_2'. Now, I could have done many different things while omitting to cast a vote, so Bernstein presumably thinks that e_1 is a counterpart, not just of e_2, but of each possible doing of one of these things; call them e_3–e_n. But it seems that the sum of e_1 and e_2 (and the counterpart relation) is numerically distinct from the sum of e_1 and e_3 (and the counterpart relation), which in turn is numerically distinct from the sum of e_1 and e_4 (and the counterpart relation), and so on. So, rather than a single omission which occurs in many possible worlds, what we have are many distinct omissions, made up of distinct pairs of events. Thus, it's not true, on this view, that the exact same omission occurs regardless of what I do with my arms.

[9] Here, I understand '$\Diamond$' as a function which takes '$p(w)(t)$' to '$\exists w'(p(w')(t))$'.

But, granting that (α*) is true, it simply doesn't follow, as a matter of logic, that there's some possible world in which x's *actual* φ-ing exists but x's *actual* ψ-ing doesn't. For all (α*) says, the possible world which witnesses (α*) might be one in which x's *actual* φ-ing doesn't exist, and a numerically distinct φ-ing occurs in its place, which is perfectly consistent with the hypothesis that x's actual φ-ing is identical to x's actual ψ-ing.

Putting the point differently, the move from (α) to (β) ignores the distinction drawn in Chapter 1 between the things we do and our doings of those things. The things we do, I argued there, are higher-level properties which we possess by virtue of being suitably related to certain events: the property of φ-ing is the property of being an x such that, for some event e, x is the agent of e and e is a φ-ing. Crucially, the property of φ-ing is the property of being the agent of *some φ-ing event or other*; it's not the property of being the agent of any *particular* φ-ing event. Thus, I can possess that very same property across possible worlds in which I'm the agent of numerically distinct φ-ing events, and so the fact that I possess that property in both the actual world and some merely possible world doesn't show that the very same φ-ing event occurs in both worlds.

This point shouldn't be surprising. It's essentially an extension, to possible worlds, of a point I made with respect to times in Section 1.2.2. The things we do are repeatable across times: I can exemplify the property of *walking* at different times, by virtue of being the agent of numerically distinct walks which occur at those times. This makes perfect sense, given my understanding of the distinction between the things we do as higher-level properties. And it shouldn't be surprising that the point extends to possible worlds: I can exemplify the property of *walking* in different possible worlds, by virtue of being the agent of numerically distinct walks which occur in those worlds. (This is just a more philosophically perspicuous way of saying that I might still have walked, even if I hadn't taken *this particular* walk.)

Indeed, the invalidity of the move from (α*) to (β*) has nothing in particular to do with actions and events at all. In general, the fact that there might have been Fs even if there had been no Gs doesn't imply that *this F* might have existed even if *this G* hadn't, since the object which witnesses '$\Diamond \exists x F x$' might be numerically distinct from any actually existing F. That's why we can't generally infer – using an argument like the argument from modal profiles – that no particular F is identical to any particular G, from the fact that there might have been Fs even if there had been no Gs, that no particular F is identical to any particular G (e.g. we can't infer that no wolf is a mammal from the fact that there might have been mammals even if there had been no wolves).

In general, the fact that an agent could have done one thing without doing another doesn't imply that her doings of those things are distinct. Thus, the fact that I might have omitted to raise my arm, without keeping my hands in my lap in the specific way that I actually did, doesn't show that my *actual* omission might have existed, even if I had drummed my fingers on the table, fiddled with a pen, or taken the opportunity to type something into my phone. Generalizing: the fact that x could have NEG-φ-ed without ψ-ing doesn't imply that x's NEG-φ-ing could have occurred in the absence of x's ψ-ing, and so it doesn't show that those doings of hers are distinct.

Of course, this response to the argument assumes that negative action sentences quantify over events, as positive action sentences do. If Deflationism were correct, and negative action sentences expressed negative existentials, then the move from 'x could have NEG-φ-ed without ψ-ing' to 'x's actual NEG-φ-ing and x's actual ψ-ing are distinct' would be better represented as an instance of the move from (α^{**}) to (β^*), where 'a' denotes x's actual NEG-φ-ing and 'b' denotes x's actual ψ-ing:

(α^{**}) $\Diamond(\neg\exists e(Agent(x)(e)$ & $\varphi_{ND}(e))$ & $\neg\exists e'(Agent(x)(e')$ & $\psi_{ND}(e')))$
(β^*) $\Diamond(\exists e(e = a)$ & $\neg\exists e'(e' = b))$

You might think that the move from (α^{**}) to (β^*) is licensed as a matter of substantive metaphysics, if not as a matter of logical form. Suppose you think that negative actions are absences, realistically construed. Then it seems plausible that, in most cases, *the very same* NEG-φ-ing might have occurred, even if x hadn't ψ-ed. For example, then the very same absence of events in which I raise my arm would have existed whether I kept my arms in my lap or not; for, the very same negative fact would have been obtained in that case, and indeed in *any* case where I don't raise my arm. And if you construe absences non-seriously, you can present a slightly different version of the argument: *if there were* such a thing as the absence of φ-ings by x, it would be distinct from x's φ-ing, since the former could exist without the latter.

The problem, of course, is that Deflationism is *false*, and negative action sentences *do* quantify over events, just as positive ones do. So, this attempt to make the argument more compelling fails.

You might think that we can discern a difference in the modal profiles of negative actions and positive events without relying on any dubious inference. For, you might think, we don't need to *infer* that this difference exists at all: we can simply *tell*, in certain cases, that x's actual NEG-φ-ing could have occurred in the absence of her actual ψ-ing; e.g. we can simply *tell* that, even if I hadn't kept my arms in my lap, and so that very event hadn't occurred, the very same omission to raise my arm would have occurred.

I, for one, have no such modal intuitions. Compare cases in which we (or at least *I*) want to say that two positive actions are identical. If I raise my arm in order to cast a vote, it seems that my act of raising my arm and my act of voting are identical – these are *one* event, not two. You might think that this identity claim is undermined by a difference in the modal profiles of these events: surely, my voting could have occurred even if my arm-raising didn't. But, on reflection, this thought is uncompelling. While it's obvious that I could have voted without raising my arm (since the voting procedures are contingent), it's *not* obvious that the *very same* action of voting would have occurred if I hadn't raised my arm. That is, once we clearly distinguish the things we do from our doings of them, and distinguish action sentences (which neither contain nor function as names for events) and derived nominals (which *do* function as names for events), the appearance of a direct insight to the effect that my voting and my arm-raising have different modal profiles should vanish. Likewise, *mutatis mutandis*, for negative actions and positive events.

8.4 Causal Roles

8.4.1 *The Argument*

Let an event's 'causal role' be the complete set of its causes and effects. If e_1 and e_2 are identical – if they're really *one* event, not two – then they must have the same causal role, since x can't both stand in a causal relation and not stand in that relation.[10] But it seems that negative actions often, and perhaps always, have distinct causal roles from the positive events with which I claim they're identical.

There are four varieties of cases which may be appealed to, to demonstrate this difference:

(a) Cases in which x's NEG-φ-ing causes something that x's ψ-ing doesn't cause.

(b) Cases in which x's ψ-ing causes something that x's NEG-φ-ing doesn't cause.

---

[10] This is true even if causation is context-sensitive in some way, so that x can't be said to cause y *simpliciter*, but only relative to some chosen set of facts Γ. The point is then that, if x causes y relative to Γ, it can't also be the case that x *doesn't* cause y relative to Γ (although it may be that x doesn't cause y relative to some *other* set of facts).

(c)   Cases in which x's NEG-φ-ing is caused by something that doesn't cause x's ψ-ing.

(d)   Cases in which x's ψ-ing is caused by something that doesn't cause x's NEG-φ-ing.

I'll focus on cases of the first variety. My remarks can be applied, *mutatis mutandis*, to cases of the other three varieties as well.

Two general points are in order before I present the argument against realizer-functionalism in more detail. First, cases of the (a) and (c) varieties are meant to show that a certain negative action has causes or effects that a certain positive action doesn't; thus, they assume that negative actions actually *have* causes and effects. By contrast, cases of the (b) and (d) varieties can get by without this assumption, and so arguments which appeal to them are, in principle, available to those who are independently skeptical of causation by and of 'omissions' (where, in the relevant literature, *any* failure of an event to occur counts as an 'omission').[11] I won't address this skeptical position in detail (although see note 12), but will simply assume, for the sake of argument, that negative actions have causes and effects.

Second, cases of the (a) and (c) varieties don't merely assume that negative actions have causes and effects; they also make assumptions about *which* causes and effects certain negative actions have. Of course, if the argument from causal roles is to have any persuasive force at all, these assumptions must at least be *prima facie* plausible, but they can, in principle, be called into question; even if you believe in causation by and of 'omissions', your theory of causation might dictate that a certain 'omission' has different causes and effects than we ordinarily take it to

---

[11]   See, e.g. Beebee (2004) and Dowe (2000, 2004) for recent examples of skepticism about causation of and by omissions. Mellor (1995: 132–134; 2004: 314–315) takes his argument against 'negative events' – which I addressed in Sections 4.4.3 and 5.2.3 – as evidence that causation by omission, while genuine, can't be accommodated by views on which causation relates particulars like events; in his view, causation relates *facts*.

  Note that, in the present dialectical context, such a skeptic can't *justify* their claim that, e.g. x's ψ-ing has an effect that x's NEG-φ-ing doesn't, on the ground that causation by omission is impossible, without risk of begging the question. Skepticism about causation by omission is typically motivated (at least in part) by the thought that omissions aren't the sort of thing that can stand in a causal relation at all – e.g. if causation is thought to be a relation between *events*, then omissions aren't events, but rather absences thereof. But then, we can't use the claim that x's ψ-ing has an effect that x's NEG-φ-ing doesn't as independent reason to deny their identity; we will have *assumed* their non-identity, since if x's NEG-φ-ing *were* identical to x's ψ-ing, it *would* be the sort of thing that can stand in a causal relation. The dispute would need to be about the *other* reasons we (supposedly) have for thinking that x's NEG-φ-ing isn't an event.

have.[12] Again, however, I'll leave these issues aside and simply assume, for the sake of argument, that negative actions have the causes and effects they seem to.

Turning now to the argument, recall Sartorio's (2009) example, discussed in Section 3.3.2, in which I omit to save a child who is drowning in a nearby pond, choosing to sit on the shore eating ice cream instead. She considers whether we might identify my omission with my act of eating ice cream, and argues that we shouldn't, on the ground that they have different effects. In particular, my omission causes the child's death while my act of eating ice cream doesn't.

> On the assumption that omissions can be causes and effects, it seems clear that [my omission] was a cause of the child's death: the child died because I omitted to jump into the water to save him. Should we think that [my eating of ice cream] also caused it? Presumably not. For, intuitively, the child died because of what I didn't do, not because of what I did in its place. It seems, in fact, irrelevant that I was eating ice cream on the shore (as opposed to, say, reading a book, or doing anything else but jumping in): all that matters is that I failed to jump in to save him. (Sartorio 2009: 519, slightly modified)

As with the parallel argument discussed in Section 3.3.2, the reasoning here is naturally understood in counterfactual terms. The fact that I was eating ice cream seems irrelevant to the fact that the child drowned because it's not true that, had I not eaten ice cream, the child wouldn't have drowned. Likewise, the fact that I omitted to jump into the pond seems highly relevant to the fact that the child drowned because, had I not omitted to jump into the pond – that is, if I had jumped in – the child wouldn't have drowned. Thus, Sartorio's argument is naturally understood as having the following structure: my omission and my eating of ice cream appear to have different effects – this is captured by (4) and (5) – and this appearance is motivated by the counterfactuals (6) and (7):

(4) My omission causes the child's death.

(5) My eating of ice cream doesn't cause the child's death.

(6) If I hadn't omitted to jump into the pond (i.e. if I *had* jumped in), the child wouldn't have died.

(7) If I hadn't eaten ice cream, the child might still have died.

Thus, my omission and my eating of ice cream can't be identical.

---

[12] For example, Dowe (2010) considers (but doesn't endorse) an extension of Yablo's (1992a, 1992b) proportionality theory of causation to causation by omission. On this view, ordinary omissions don't have the causal roles we take them to have, because they lack the right amount of detail. For example, my omission to water my plants didn't cause their death, because it didn't matter whether *I* watered them, or even whether any *person* watered them; what mattered was just that the plants didn't receive water (from any source).

(The realizer-functionalist view developed in previous chapters doesn't actually commit me to identifying my omission with my eating of ice cream, since it's not obvious that the latter event is what plays the ensuring role: the relevant event may be my doing of some φ which properly includes, or is properly included in, the behaviour of eating ice cream, or rather, the specific way in which I eat my ice cream. However, I assume that a parallel version of the argument could be given, whatever my view requires me to identify my omission with, so I'll ignore this issue in what follows.)

Of course, this is just one example, but the point generalizes. In many cases, an agent who NEG-φ-s has many ways of NEG-φ-ing available to them: although x actually NEG-φ-s by ψ-ing, they could easily have NEG-φ-ed without ψ-ing. As a consequence, it seems, x's NEG-φ-ing and x's ψ-ing will have different effects, since the obtaining of some fact or state of affairs may counterfactually depend on whether x NEG-φ-s and not on whether x ψ-s.[13]

8.4.2   Doings, Things Done, and Counterfactuals

The problem with the argument concerns the analysis of counterfactuals like (6) and (7). Lewis (1973b) treats the counterfactuals we ordinarily appeal to, in our day-to-day causal reasoning, as reports to the effect that one particular event depended on another for its occurrence (or not), and the subsequent literature on counterfactuals and causation has largely followed him in this.[14] On this approach, a claim with the surface form 'If x hadn't φ-ed then y wouldn't have ψ-ed' is taken to have the logical form '-$\mathbf{O}(e)$ □→ -$\mathbf{O}(e')$', where '$\mathbf{O}(e)$' says that the particular event e occurs. Likewise, a claim with the surface form 'If x hadn't φ-ed then y might still have ψ-ed' is taken to have the logical form '-$\mathbf{O}(e)$ ◊→ $\mathbf{O}(e')$'.

[13] See Bernstein (2014b: 5), Clarke (2014: 19), Silver (2018: 36), and Tiehen (2015: 507).

As with the argument from modal profiles, it's not clear how strongly this argument supports Bernstein's view, on which omissions are tripartite entities (see note 8). Consider: (7) is witnessed by worlds in which, although I don't eat ice cream, I still omit to jump into the pond; or, as the proponent of the argument has it, they're worlds in which my actual eating of ice cream doesn't occur but my actual omission still does. But in Bernstein's view, my actual omission is partly composed of my actual eating of ice cream, and so it seems that the former can only be said to 'occur' in a world where the latter does, too. Thus, she isn't entitled to claim that the worlds which witness (7) are worlds in which my actual omission still occurs, and so isn't entitled to claim that my actual omission and my actual eating of ice cream stand in different counterfactual dependence relations.

[14] See, e.g. Paul and Hall's (2013) survey of issues in the metaphysics of causation, and practically every essay collected in Collins et al. (2004).

Singular causal claims – i.e. claims to the effect that one particular event causes another (or not) – are taken to be supported by such counterfactuals. The evidence that one event causes another (or not) is taken to be that one event counterfactually depends on another (or not).

If this approach were correct, then (6) and (7) would be analyzed as follows:

(6$_L$) $\sim$**O**(omission) $\square\rightarrow$ $\sim$**O**(death)
(7$_L$) $\sim$**O**(eating) $\lozenge\rightarrow$ **O**(death)

(Here, 'eating', 'omission', and 'death' denote my act of eating ice cream, my omission to jump into the pond, and the child's death, respectively.) Notice that (6$_L$) and (7$_L$) are *already* inconsistent with realizer functionalism, regardless of how strongly we take those counterfactuals to relate to singular causal claims: '$\sim$**O**(e) $\lozenge\rightarrow$ **O**(e')' is simply the negation of '$\sim$**O**(e) $\square\rightarrow$ $\sim$**O**(e')', so they can't both be true for a single choice of values for 'e' and 'e'''. Thus, it can't be true, of a single event e, *both* that the child's death wouldn't have occurred if e hadn't, *and* that the child's death might still have occurred if e hadn't.

The problem is that this Lewisian approach is *not* correct, and the reader can anticipate why. While it's undeniable that we *can* frame counterfactuals of the sort Lewis envisions, these aren't the sorts of counterfactuals on which we rely in our day-to-day causal reasoning. When we say things like, 'The light wouldn't have turned on if I hadn't flipped the switch', 'The vase wouldn't have broken if you hadn't dropped it', or 'The child wouldn't have drowned if you'd jumped in and saved him' – we aren't making claims to the effect that one particular event depended on another. The sentences which figure as antecedent and consequent in these conditionals neither function as, nor contain, proper names or definite descriptions which refer to particular events. Rather, these sentences express existential quantifications over events. A claim with the surface form 'If x hadn't φ-ed then y wouldn't have ψ-ed' has the logical form '$\sim\exists eFe \square\rightarrow \sim\exists e'Ge'$', and a claim with the surface form 'If x hadn't φ-ed then y might still have ψ-ed' has the logical form '$\sim\exists eFe \lozenge\rightarrow \exists e'Ge'$'. That is, these counterfactuals report not that one particular event depends on another, but that the exemplification of one event-type depends on the exemplification of another.

Thus, (6) and (7) are properly analyzed as (something like) (6$_{SND}$) and (7$_{SND}$):

(6$_{SND}$) $\sim\exists e(Agent(\text{Jonathan})(e)$ & $Ensure(e)(\sim\exists e'(Agent(\text{Jonathan})(e')$
 & $Jump(e')))) \square\rightarrow \sim\exists e''(Agent(\text{child})(e'')$ & $Death(e''))$
(7$_{ND}$) $\sim\exists e(Agent(\text{Jonathan})(e)$ & $Jump(e)) \lozenge\rightarrow \exists e'(Agent(\text{child})(e')$ & $Death(e'))$

In English: no event of the child dying would have occurred if no event of me omitting to jump into the pond had occurred (that is, if some event of me jumping in *had* occurred); and some event of the child dying might still have occurred, if no event of me eating ice cream had. The exemplification of *death of the child* depends on the exemplification of *omission to jump into the pond*, but not on the exemplification of *eating of ice cream*.

But now, we can't infer from (6_{SND}) and (7_{ND}) that my omission and my eating of ice cream have different effects. For, we can't infer the Lewisian counterfactual (6_L) from the Neo-Davidsonian counterfactual (6_{SND}), and so we can't infer that the child's death depends on my omission but not on my eating of ice cream.

Worlds which witness (6_{SND}) are worlds in which I don't omit to jump into the pond (i.e. worlds in which I jump in), and so the child doesn't die. But there might still be worlds in which, although my *actual* omission doesn't occur, the child's death still does, falsifying (6_L). Suppose that my omission is identical to my eating of ice cream, so that neither can occur without the other, and consider a world in which I still omit to jump into the pond, but instead of eating ice cream, I read a book. This is a world in which a distinct event plays the ensuing role, and so, according to realizer-functionalism, it's a world in which my actual omission doesn't occur. Not only does the child still die in such a world, it's plausible that his *actual* death still occurs there. For, this death differs from the actual one only in highly extrinsic respects which aren't plausibly essential to it. Thus, even if (6_{SND}) is true, there might be nearby worlds in which my actual omission doesn't occur, but the child's actual death still does, falsifying (6_L).

You might think that, even though the death which occurs in this merely possible world differs from the actual one only in highly extrinsic respects, it's nonetheless a distinct death, and so (6_L) is still true. But this claim would be of no help to the opponent of realizer-functionalism. For, to insist that (6_L) is true on those grounds is to undermine the support for (7_L). Worlds which witness (7_L) are meant to be worlds in which, while I still omit to jump into the pond, I do some positive thing other than eat ice cream, and so the child's actual death still occurs. But it's only plausible that the child's actual death still occurs in such worlds because it's plausible that changes in highly extrinsic respects don't force that event out of existence. If my opponent insists that such changes *do* force the child's actual death out of existence, in order to preserve (6_L), it's difficult to see how they can also maintain (7_L).

We can't infer (6_L) from (6_{SND}). Thus, even if (7_L) is true – which, I grant, seems plausible – we can't infer that the child's death depends on my omission but not on my eating of ice cream. For, we can't infer that the child's death depends on my *actual* omission at all.

It's perhaps worth emphasizing a more general point. (6_{SND}) and (7_{ND}), if true, reveal a difference between the event types *omission to jump into the pond* and *eating of ice cream*: the exemplification of *death of the child* depends on the exemplification of the former, but not the latter. These counterfactuals should not be confused with the Lewisian counterfactuals (6_L) and (7_L) which, if true, would reveal a difference between my token omission and my token eating of ice cream. As emphasized in Section 8.4.1, we shouldn't confuse claims about what I do in other possible worlds, i.e. claims about which event *types* are exemplified in those worlds, with claims about which event *tokens* occur in those worlds.

This point has nothing in particular to do with negative actions, and applies quite generally. Quite generally, that *p* would have been false if there had been no *F*s, but might still have been true if there had been no *G*s, doesn't show that no particular *F* is identical to any particular *G*, since the worlds which witness the latter counterfactual (i.e. worlds in which there are *F*s but no *G*s) might be worlds in which all actual *F*s are absent, and are replaced by distinct ones.

Of course, as with the argument from modal profiles, my response assumes that negative action sentences quantify over events, just as positive ones do, and hence that (6) is best analyzed as (6_{SND}). I've argued that this is, in fact, the case, but you might think that causal counterfactuals provide reason to doubt this.

Consider (6) again:

(6) If I hadn't omitted to jump into the pond (i.e. if I *had* jumped in), the child wouldn't have died.

The parenthetical remark seems highly natural: in general, it seems that to suppose that *x* didn't omit to φ is to suppose that *x* φ-ed. Indeed, the equivalence between '*x* didn't omit to φ' and '*x* φ-ed' seems to be what licenses the thought that, if I hadn't omitted to jump into the pond, then the child wouldn't have died. But, as I noted in Section 5.4, '~(*x* NEG-φ)' and '*x* φ' aren't equivalent, in my sophisticated Neo-Davidsonian view. You might think, then, that I can't give my response to the argument from causal roles without undermining the intuitive truth of (6).

Fortunately, we don't need '~(*x* NEG-φ)' and '*x* φ' to be equivalent in order to account for the intuitive truth of (6). In general, '$p \,\square\!\!\rightarrow r$' and '$q \,\square\!\!\rightarrow r$' can be equivalent, even if *p* and *q* aren't: all that's required is that '$p \,\square\!\!\rightarrow q$' and '$q \,\square\!\!\rightarrow r$' are equivalent; that is, all that's required is that the closest p-worlds be the closest q-worlds, and vice-versa (Lewis 1973a: 33). I argued in Section 5.4 that, in ordinary cases, '$\sim(x\,\mathrm{NEG}\text{-}\varphi)\;\Box\rightarrow x\,\varphi$' holds. Applied to Sartorio's case:

(8) If I hadn't omitted to jump into the pond, then I would have jumped into the pond.

The closest worlds in which I don't omit to jump into the pond are worlds in which I exist, and am the agent of some event(s), but in which no such event ensures that I don't jump into the pond. The obvious way for this requirement to be met is for me to jump into the pond. It's also true that, in ordinary cases, '$x\,\varphi\;\Box\rightarrow\;\sim(x\,\mathrm{NEG}\text{-}\varphi)$' holds. Applied to Sartorio's case:

(9) If I'd jumped into the pond, then I wouldn't have omitted to jump into the pond.

For, if I jump into the pond in w, then no behaviour of mine in w could be such that, if I'd done that, then I wouldn't have jumped into the pond. Thus, there's no objection to analyzing (6) as (6_{SND}).

8.4.3 An Alternative Argument

I've argued that we can't infer claims of counterfactual dependence between tokens from claims of counterfactual dependence between types. You might hope to establish a difference in the causal roles of my omission and my eating of ice cream without relying on such shaky inferences. For, you might think, the fact that the event types *omission to jump into the pond* and *eating of ice cream* stand in different dependence relations shows that my omission and my eating of ice cream have different causal roles, even if the child's death depends on them both.

Unfortunately, it's not clear how such an argument might be spelled out. What's required is a set of principles which connect singular causal claims to claims of counterfactual dependence between event types. The most plausible such principles are as follows:

Singular Causation and Neo-Davidsonian Counterfactuals

(i) We're *prima facie* justified in believing that e_1 causes e_2 if, for some event types F and G: (a) e_1 exemplifies F; e_2 exemplifies G; and $\sim\exists eFe$ $\Box\rightarrow\;\sim\exists e'Ge'$.

(ii) We're *prima facie* justified in believing that e_1 doesn't cause e_2 if there are no event types F and G such that: (a) e_1 exemplifies F; e_2 exemplifies G; and $\sim\exists eFe$ $\Box\rightarrow\;\sim\exists e'Ge'$.

In short, we're *prima facie* justified in believing that one event causes another (or not) if those events fall under types which exhibit counterfactual dependence (or not).[15]

Given clause (i), we can infer from (6_{SND}) that my omission causes the child's death; for, the exemplification of *death of the child* depends on the exemplification of *omission to jump into the pond*. But clause (ii) doesn't allow us to infer from (7_{ND}) that my eating of ice cream doesn't cause the child's death. True, the exemplification of *death of the child* doesn't depend on the exemplification of *eating of ice cream*. But clause (ii) requires that there be *no* event type which my eating of ice cream exemplifies, and on which the exemplification of *death of the child* depends. And we can't assume *that* without assuming that realizer-functionalism is false. For, if realizer-functionalism is true, there *is* such a type: the type *omission to jump into the pond*.

8.5 Some Lingering Arguments

8.5.1 The Arguments

So far, I've addressed arguments against realizer-functionalism which appeal to the spatiotemporal locations, modal profiles, and causal roles of negative actions and positive events. There are, however, arguments in the literature which make no appeal to these sorts of properties.

Recall the case in which Alice omits to go for a walk with Beth, and instead goes for a jog with Charlie. I've defended the identity of Alice's omission with her jog (or perhaps with a token of some behaviour of Alice's which is included in the way she jogs). But now, suppose that Alice jogs quickly, and hence that her jog is quick. If the jog is identical to the omission, then the omission must be quick as well. But that seems wrong: there seems to be something deeply wrong with describing an *omission* as 'quick'. Therefore, it seems, we must reject the identity-claim. Likewise, *mutatis mutandis*, if Alice jogged slowly: describing an omission as 'slow' seems no better than describing it as 'quick' (Clarke 2012: 363).

Being quick and *being slow* aren't the only properties that seem to distinguish negative actions from positive events. Suppose that, instead of going for a walk with Charlie, Alice goes to a dance class. Suppose, further, that Alice dances elegantly, and hence that her dance is elegant. If

[15] Compare Davidson's (1967b) view that (roughly) e_1 causes e_2 just in case these events exemplify types F and G which stand in law-like relations.

the dance is identical to the omission, then the omission must be elegant as well. But that seems wrong: there seems to be something deeply wrong with describing an *omission* as 'elegant'.

No doubt, other arguments of this sort could be generated. What unites them, for our purposes, is that they appeal to 'scalar adverbs' and 'gradable adjectives' (I'll explain what this means in Section 8.5.2). My response will aim to address any argument which appeals to these constructions.

Before I give my response, a point about these arguments is in order. On the surface, they're appeals to Leibniz's Law: $a = b \models (Fa \equiv Fb)$ – or, contrapositively, $(Fa \,\&\, {\sim}Fb) \models a \neq b$. But consider the argument with which I began:

(10) Alice's jog is quick.
(11) Alice's omission to go for a walk isn't quick.
(12) Alice's jog isn't identical to her omission to go for a walk.

The motivation for (11) is that (13) is not just *false*, but *meaningless*.

(13) Alice's omission to go for a walk is quick.

But if that's right, then (11) doesn't express a proposition of the form '${\sim}Fb$', since it doesn't express a proposition at all: the negation of nonsense is also nonsense. That makes it difficult to understand the argument as an appeal to Leibniz's Law.

A plausible solution to this problem is that (11) expresses a kind of meta-linguistic negation. In Section 2.2.2, I discussed cases in which a sentence which at first seems to have the form ${\sim}p$ is best interpreted, not as rejecting the proposition p – since the speaker allows that p is true – but rather as rejecting the choice of a certain vehicle for that proposition (e.g. 'Alice isn't a secretary; she's an administrative assistant'). Here, it seems, we have a case in which a sentence is rejected on the ground that it lacks any content at all.[16]

---

[16] Almotahari (2014a: 394–396) proposes that, if 'Not-S_1' receives a meta-linguistic interpretation, and 'S_2' serves as a corrective, then on an *object-level* reading of 'Not-S_1', the content of that sentence is incompatible with the content of 'S_2'. If this principle were correct, then we could twist the argument against realizer-functionalism into an argument *for* realizer-functionalism: from the fact that 'Alice's *jog* is quick' is a corrective to 'Alice's omission isn't quick', where the latter is interpreted meta-linguistically, we could infer that the content of 'Alice's omission isn't quick', on an object-level reading, is incompatible with the content of 'Alice's jog is quick'; and it seems that those contents would only be incompatible if the omission and the jog were identical. (See Almotahari (2014a: 396–404) for a version of this argument, applied to material objects and their matter.)

Unfortunately, Almotahari's principle is false. It assumes that, if 'Not-S_1' has a meta-linguistic reading, then it has an object-level reading, too, and this is false. 'Not-S_1' can have a meta-linguistic

Thus, the argument is best construed as follows: because I identify Alice's omission with her jog (or perhaps with a token of some behaviour of Alice's which is included in the way she jogs; as in Section 8.4.1, I leave this issue aside), I'm apparently committed to thinking that (13) expresses a true proposition, which it apparently doesn't. As I'll now argue, however, I'm *not* committed to thinking that 'Alice's omission is quick' ('Alice's omission is elegant', etc.) expresses a true proposition.

8.5.2 *Scalar Adverbs, Gradable Adjectives*

Recall from Section 4.2.2 that 'quickly' is a scalar adverb. 'F-ly' is a scalar adverb if to say that x φ-s F-ly is to say that x's φ-ing possesses a certain quality (or qualities) to a certain degree, or to say that, by virtue of possessing that quality (or qualities) to a certain degree, x's φ-ing meets the threshold for F-ness. Thus, to say that x φ-s quickly is to say that x's φ-ing meets a certain threshold for quickness.

Scalar adverbs are closely related to 'gradable adjectives'. 'F' is a gradable adjective if to say that x is F is to say that x possesses a certain quality (or qualities) to a certain degree, or to say that, by virtue of possessing that quality (or qualities) to a certain degree, x meets the threshold for F-ness. 'Tall' and 'short' are classic examples. 'Tall' is a gradable adjective because to say that x is tall isn't to attribute any specific height to x, but rather to say that x possesses a sufficient height to meet the threshold for tallness. Likewise, *mutatis mutandis*, for 'short'. Some gradable adjectives are cognates of scalar adverbs. For example, the adjective 'quick' is a cognate of the adverb 'quickly', and so to say that x's φ-ing is quick is to say that x's φ-ing meets a certain threshold for quickness.

Crucially, when 'F' is a gradable adjective, there's no universal, context-insensitive standard or criterion with respect to which objects can be evaluated as being F or not-F. Rather, the standards can shift from context to context, and so the very same object can count as F in one context but not in another.

There are (at least) two ways the standards for F-ness can change from context to context. First, it may be that the quality (or qualities) which are taken to be relevant to evaluations of F-ness remains the same, but the threshold x must meet, in order to count as F, shifts. Suppose that Alice is four feet tall in the third grade. It would be correct to say of Alice, at that

reading in cases where 'S₁' lacks a content, and so 'Not-S₁' doesn't have an object-level reading. Thus, I won't mount this sort of argument for realizer-functionalism.

age, that she's tall. Now, suppose that Alice ceases to grow any taller after the third grade. In respect of height Alice remains unchanged. Nonetheless, soon it will no longer be correct to say that she's tall: a four-foot-tall third grader is tall; a four-foot-tall ninth grader isn't. This is because the threshold will shift: it takes more height to count as tall in the ninth grade than it does in the third grade.

Second, it may be that the quality (or qualities) which are taken to be relevant to evaluations of F-ness shifts from context to context. Consider the adjectival phrase 'well-made'. It's clear that evaluations of craftsmanship aren't universally sensitive to a single set of qualities, but can be sensitive to different qualities in different contexts – e.g. the qualities that make for a well-made car (the ability to run effectively for a certain amount of time, or for a certain number of kilometres, the ability to effectively withstand certain kinds of impact, etc.) are very different from those that make for a well-made coffee cup.

The same remarks apply, *mutatis mutandis*, to scalar adverbs. When 'F-ly' is a scalar adverb, there is no universal, context-insensitive standard with respect to which x can be evaluated as having φ-ed F-ly or not, and hence no such standard with respect to which x's φ-ing can be evaluated as being F or not-F. The very same event can count as F in one context but not in another.

Davidson (1967a: 106–107) makes this point with respect to 'quickly' and 'slowly'. Suppose that Alice swims across the Channel in 15 hours. By most standards, Alice would need to be swimming quite quickly in order to accomplish this, so it seems correct to say that she swam across the Channel quickly, and hence that her swimming across the Channel was quick. Now, given that there are much faster ways to cross the Channel, it also seems correct to say that Alice crossed the Channel slowly, and hence that her crossing was slow. If we thought that 'quickly' and 'slowly' were non-scalar, and hence that 'quick' and 'slow' are non-gradable, we'd have to conclude that Alice's act of swimming across the Channel was distinct from her act of crossing the Channel, which is highly implausible. The more natural thing to say is that a single event can be quick by some standards and not by others, and whether it's correct to say that x φ-ed quickly depends, not just on the intrinsic features of x's φ-ing, but on which standards are in place.

So far, the discussion has been fairly informal. To see how it affords a response to the arguments against realizer-functionalism, however, it will be useful to sketch a more formal picture of the semantics of scalar adverbs and gradable adjectives.

Throughout this book, I've referred to the meaning of a declarative sentence as its 'content'. This was a harmless simplification, but in the present context, it's important to distinguish the *content* of such a sentence from its *character*. The content of a declarative sentence is a function from 'circumstances of evaluation' – typically, world-time pairs – to truth-values. A content represents things as being a certain way, and it maps a world w and a time t to truth just in case things are that way in w at t. Thus, on at least one useful understanding of what a proposition is, the content of a declarative sentence is a proposition: it represents things as being a certain way, and is true just in case they are that way.

The character of a declarative sentence, by contrast, is a function from 'indexes' – what Kaplan (1989) calls 'contexts' – to contents. The elements of an index – the 'indices' – serve to fix the referents of certain kinds of terms – most notably indexicals like 'I', 'here', and 'now' – and are typically thought to include, in addition to a possible world w, a designated speaker a (the referent of 'I'), a designated location r (the referent of 'here'), and a designated time t (the referent of 'now'). Specifying the character of the sentence reveals how its content depends on certain factors. For example, the character of the sentence 'I'm hungry' is (something like) a function from an index i to the proposition a_i *is hungry*, where a_i is the designated speaker of i. The sentence's *character* is the same no matter who utters it, but its *content* shifts. For example, when Alice says, 'I'm hungry', her utterance is naturally interpreted with respect to an index which contains Alice as the designated speaker. Thus, the sentence, in her mouth, has the content that *Alice* is hungry. By contrast, when Beth says, 'I'm hungry', the sentence has the content that *Beth* is hungry, for analogous reasons.

I've said that gradable adjectives like 'tall/short' and 'well-/poorly-made' are standard-relative: no one is tall or short *simpliciter*, but only with respect to some chosen standards or criteria. A plausible semantic theory of how this is achieved is that the standard is supplied by an index: just as an index can provide referents for 'I', 'here', and 'now', it can provide standards with respect to which objects can be evaluated as tall or short, well made or poorly made, etc. Thus, the denotation of 'tall' may be given in (something like) the following way:

$$[\![\text{tall}]\!]_{<w,\ t,\ s>} = \lambda x.(Tall(x)(w)(t)(s))$$

Here, s is a standard of evaluation for tallness. Just as with worlds and times, there's a variable for such standards in the intension of 'tall' which gets saturated by a standard supplied by the index. (I ignore any other indices for simplicity.) Likewise, *mutatis mutandis*, for other gradable adjectives.

Likewise also for scalar adverbs like 'quickly/slowly'. In Chapters 4–6, I made use of a simple picture on which 'quickly' contributes a predicate of events, '*Quick*', which applies (or fails to apply) to an event irrespective of any standard of evaluation. We can now complicate that picture slightly, and give the denotation of 'quickly' in something like the following way:

$$[\![\text{quickly}]\!]_{<w,\ t,\ s>} = \lambda e.(Quick(e)(w)(t)(s))$$

Thus (ignoring worlds and times for simplicity), the logical form of, e.g. (14) is (14$_{\text{ND}}$):[17]

(14)   Alice kissed Beth quickly.

(14$_{\text{ND}}$) $\exists e(Agent(\text{Alice})(e)(s)$ & $Patient(\text{Beth})(e)(s)$ & $Kiss_{\text{ND}}(e)(s)$ & $Quick(e)(s))$

Given this framework, there are two ways in which a Leibniz's Law argument of the sort we've been considering can fail. First, it may be that distinct values for 's' are supplied for the distinct occurrences of 'F-ly'/'F', and hence that 'a is F' and 'b is not-F' have distinct contents, despite the fact that $a = b$. This is arguably what happens in Davidson's example of Alice crossing the Channel. Suppose we're confronted with the following argument:

(15)   Alice's swim across the Channel was quick.

(16)   Alice's swim across the Channel = Alice's crossing of the Channel.

(17)   ∴ Alice's crossing of the Channel was quick.

As noted, there are natural readings in which (15) is true and (17) is false. On one natural reading of (15), it says that Alice's swim was quick *for a swim across the Channel*; the relevant standard is tied to the comparison class of (actual or merely possible) swims across the Channel, and Alice's swim is evaluated as quick because, roughly, it took less time than most of those events. By contrast, on one natural reading of (17), it says that Alice's crossing of the Channel was quick *for a crossing of the Channel*; a different comparison class is invoked, and Alice's crossing is evaluated as *not* being quick because, roughly, it took less time than most (actual or merely possible) crossings of the Channel. Formally, we have propositions with

---

[17] Notice that the occurrence of 's' as an argument of '*Agent*', '*Patient*', and '*Kiss*' doesn't imply that whether Alice is the agent of e depends on the choice of a standard of evaluation for speed. Although a straightforward semantic story requires these additional occurrences of 's', '$Quick(e)(s)$' is the only conjunct whose truth is sensitive to our choice of standard.

the same structure, but where distinct standards have been supplied as values for '*s*'. Letting '*a*' denote Alice's swim and '*b*' denote her crossing:

(15_{ND}) $Quick(a)(s_1)$
(17_{ND}) $Quick(b)(s_2)$

As a matter of form, nothing prevents (15_{ND}) from being true and (17_{ND}) false, even if $a = b$.

The second way in which a Leibniz's Law argument involving a scalar adverb or gradable adjective can fail is if, for one of the occurrences of 'F-ly'/'F', no value for '*s*' has been supplied at all, and hence one of '*a* is F' and '*b* is not-F' lacks a content. This is arguably what happens in the example of Alice's jog:

(11) Alice's jog is quick.
(12) Alice's jog is identical to Alice's omission to go for a walk.
(13) ∴ Alice's omission to go for a walk is quick.

On one natural reading of (11), it says that Alice's jog was quick *for a jog*; the relevant standard is tied to the comparison class of (actual or merely possible) jogs. Since we have some idea of how to evaluate jogs for quickness *qua* jogs, it's easy enough to supply a standard with respect to which (11) can be evaluated. By contrast, on the natural reading of (13), it attempts to say that Alice's omission was quick *for an omission to go for a walk*; the intended standard is tied to the comparison class of such (actual or merely possible) omissions. But we typically don't evaluate omissions for quickness or slowness *qua* omissions to φ, and indeed, it's not clear how to do so. Thus, we're arguably confronted with one sentence which expresses a proposition and one which doesn't, due to the absence of one of the required indices. Letting '*a*' denote Alice's jog and '*o*' denote her omission:

(11_{ND}) $Quick(a)(s_1)$
(13_{ND}) $Quick(o)(???)$

This account of why the argument fails does justice to the sense you might have, that (13) is not just false, but meaningless: it's meaningless in the sense that, although it possesses a *character*, it lacks a propositional *content*.

The account also does justice to the sense you might have that an omission just isn't the kind of thing that can be quick. We don't evaluate omissions for quickness *qua* omissions to φ, and it's not clear how we would go about doing so. Thus, if 'Fs are the kind of thing that can be G' means that we can evaluate an individual F as being G or not-G with respect to the comparison class of (actual or merely possible) Fs, then omissions aren't the kind of thing that can be quick. On the other hand, if 'Fs are the kind of thing that can be G' means simply that we can evaluate an individual F as being G or not-G with respect to *some* standard, then, in my view, omissions – and negative actions generally – *are* the kind of thing that can be quick, since they're identical to positive events.

The same remarks apply, *mutatis mutandis*, to the argument from 'Alice's dance was elegant' to 'Alice's omission was elegant'. Thus, the realizer-functionalist isn't committed to thinking that 'Alice's omission was quick' and 'Alice's omission was elegant' express true propositions. In each case, the required standard for quickness or elegance goes missing and so, while these sentences retain their *character*, they lack propositional *contents*. For this reason, the arguments are invalid.

A point about my formal framework is in order. Fine (2003: 195) considers a view of the sort I've just sketched, and describes it informally as the view that 'the apparent difference in properties [between objects or events brought to light by the Leibniz's Law arguments] represents, not a difference in the objects themselves, but a difference in the *descriptions* under which they may be conceived'.[18] He takes this to mean that, at the very least, if an object or event is explicitly described as being an F, then this description automatically and inexorably fixes the standard or criterion by which that object or event is to be judged well- or badly-made, quick or slow, etc. For example, if I say, 'The *statue* is well made', my use of 'statue' automatically and inexorably fixes the interpretation of 'well made' as *well made with respect to the standards appropriate to statues*.

Fine (2003: 212–217) raises several problems for this view, which I won't consider in detail.[19] The important point, for our purposes, is that the framework I've just sketched has no such commitment built into it. The framework requires that standards or criteria of evaluation can be elements of the indexes with respect to which declarative sentences are assigned contents. No commitment is made about how a particular standard or criterion gets selected as the one with respect to which a given sentence is correctly interpreted. This is as it should be, since those standards and criteria can be fixed in a variety of ways.

---

[18] See also Fine (2003: 200).

[19] See Almotahari (2014a, 2014b), Frances (2006), and King (2006) for discussion of these arguments; for replies to Frances and King, see Fine (2006).

True, *one* way of fixing a standard is through the explicit invocation of a comparison class: by explicitly referring to *x* as an *F*, you can indicate that what you mean, in calling *x* tall/short (well-/poorly-made, quick/slow, etc.) is that *x* is tall/short (well-/poorly-made, quick/slow, etc.) with respect to the standards appropriate to *F*s (whatever those might be). We can make this relativization explicit, if we wish: to say that Alice is 'tall for a third-grader' is to say, roughly, that she meets the threshold for tallness which is appropriate for third-graders.

Moreover, this way of fixing a standard is naturally thought to be operative in the Leibniz's Law arguments we've been considering. If 'F' is a gradable adjective, then, when we're confronted with a sentence of the form '*a* is F' divorced from conversational context – e.g. when the sentence appears in an abstract philosophical argument – we'll naturally look for clues as to how the content of 'F' is to be determined. An explicitly invoked comparison class is an obvious clue (although, as Almotahari (2014a: 510–511) convincingly argues, it can be overturned).

Nonetheless, this isn't the *only* way for standards or criteria of evaluation to be fixed. As DeRose notes, there are cases in which it would be very unnatural to take the relevant standard to be fixed by a comparison class.

> Consider a movie director setting up the background for a key scene. 'I need something tall over there on the left, to balance the shot – maybe a tree, or a streetlight or something. Get me something tall!' When asked what she means by 'tall', the natural answer for her to give might well make no reference at all to any comparison class, but might rather simply cite what we may call a 'tape-measure' standard: 'What I mean is something about 14 to 16 feet tall!' (DeRose 2008: 149)

We can, and should, follow DeRose in adopting a 'pluralist' approach to scalar adverbs and gradable adjectives, on which the relevant standard can be fixed in a variety of ways.

8.5.3 Standard-Neutral Readings?

The arguments I've been considering in this section, as well as my reply, have well-known analogues in the literature on material objects. Fine (2003, 2006) argues against the identity of material objects and their constituting matter, e.g. a statue and the clay from which it's made. In his terminology, he defends 'pluralism' about material objects and their matter, against the 'monist' position that, e.g. a clay statue is identical to the clay from which it's made. Fine objects to monism on the ground that material objects possess many properties that their constituting matter doesn't, and perhaps *couldn't*, possess. A clay statue can be *well made* or *poorly made*, *beautiful* or *ugly*, *valuable* or *worthless*, even though the constituting clay isn't, and the statue can be *Romanesque* or *Gothic*, even though it seems that a piece of clay is just the wrong kind of thing to have these properties (2003: 207–208).

King (2006: 1036–1038) notes that many of the adjectives to which Fine appeals in his arguments ('defective', 'substandard', 'well-/poorly-made', 'beautiful/ugly', 'valuable', 'expensive', 'Romanesque/Gothic') appear to be gradable adjectives, and hence that they seem to be most naturally interpreted relative to a standard or criterion for *F*-ness. This, of course, opens up space for the kind of reply I've been developing: the reason 'The statue is well-made' can be true and 'The clay is well-made' false, *even if the statue and the clay are identical*, is that each sentence is naturally read as invoking a different standard of evaluation; and the reason 'The statue is Romanesque' seems sensible while 'The clay is Romanesque' doesn't is that, while there are criteria by which a statue may be judged Romanesque *qua* statue, there are no criteria by which a piece of clay may be judged Romanesque *qua* piece of clay.

Fine thinks this kind of reply is misguided. He allows that his chosen adjectives have a reading on which their extensions can be shifted from context to context. However, he insists that these phrases also have a reading on which their denotations aren't relativized to any standard or criterion, and their extensions can't be shifted. He even claims that this is the *default* reading: 'there appears to be a default understanding of "badly made" in which one can make sense – at least if one is a pluralist – of an object as such being badly made' (2006: 1068).[20] If this claim can be made good, then one might make a similar claim about 'quick/slow' and 'elegant': although there's one reading of these adjectives which is standard-relative, and on which their extensions can be shifted, there's another reading on which this isn't so, and an event *as such* can be quick or slow, elegant or inelegant.

The existence of these standard-neutral readings is questionable. Focusing first on Fine's adjectives, I've already made the point with respect to 'well-/poorly-made': the qualities that make for a well-made car aren't the same as the qualities that make for a well-made coffee cup. Likewise for

---

[20] Fine (2003) seems to suggest that the standard-neutral reading is the *only* reading of his chosen predicative phrases. However, later (2006) he disavows any such denial, since it would run counter to the linguistic evidence that his chosen phrases are gradable adjectives. He claims not that his phrases have no standard-relative reading, but that they also have a standard-neutral one (2006: 1068).

'Romanesque/Gothic': the qualities that make for a Romanesque statue are different from those that make for a Romanesque painting (or a Romanesque piece of architecture, etc.), and are likewise different from those that make for a Gothic statue (painting, piece of architecture, etc.) The point is perhaps clearest for 'expensive'. Fine (2006: 1075) alleges that we can truly say that x is expensive, or not, in cases where no standard has been set, and that this counts in favour of a standard-neutral reading. But it's clear that whether x is expensive or affordable depends, at the very least, on one's budget. To think that there's a standard-neutral reading of 'expensive' is to think that some people's budgets allow them to discern the objective facts about which things are expensive and which things aren't, i.e. that what those people count as expensive is *really* expensive, and anyone who counts those same objects as affordable is simply getting it wrong.

Thus, the existence of standard-neutral readings of Fine's chosen phrases is *prima facie* implausible. Moreover, Fine's own attempt to distinguish these readings from the standard-relative ones fails. He writes that, on the 'default' reading of 'poorly made', 'x is poorly made' means that x is poorly made 'for an object of its kind' (2006: 1069). But this reading, far from exhibiting independence from any standard, seems to involve relativization to standards associated with a comparison class. What makes this reading friendly to the pluralist, and unfriendly to the monist, is the unspoken assumption that x falls under at most one kind (and hence that the phrase 'its kind' has a determinate referent).

The same remarks apply, *mutatis mutandis*, to 'quick'/'slow' and 'elegant'. As noted in Section 8.5.2, it's clear that whether an event counts as quick or slow, elegant or inelegant, depends on both a choice of relevant qualities and a choice of threshold. No clear sense can be made of the claim that an event is quick, not relative to a certain standard, but *simpliciter*. Nor can we clarify the supposedly standard-neutral readings by saying, e.g. that an event is quick *simpliciter* if it's quick for an event of its kind, unless we simply assume that every event falls under at most one kind.

Do we have any good reason to posit standard-neutral readings of scalar adverbs and gradable adjectives, despite these concerns? An argument can be drawn from Fine (2006: 1075–1076). You might have thought that, if 'F' has only a standard-relative, index-sensitive reading, then 'F' must always mean F *with respect to s*, for some choice of s which has been set, in the conversational context, as relevant for evaluations of F-ness – e.g. 'well made' always means *well made with respect to s*, 'quick' always means *quick with respect to s*, etc., where 's' is not an unsaturated variable, but a particular standard which has been set as relevant in the context. That would imply that, if no such standard has been set in a certain context, then while '*a* is F' retains its *character*, it lacks a propositional *content*. We've seen that that's a plausible thing to say in some cases, but there are cases in which '*a* is F' seems to possess clear truth-conditions, and hence a clear content, even though no standard has been set, in context, as the one with respect to which 'F' is to be interpreted.

Consider the following case. Alice is examining various items on Beth's shelf. Charlie and David are in the next room, and are unable to see which item(s) Alice is examining at any given time. As a kind of guessing game, they make a list of sentences like 'The first item Alice examines is blue' and 'The last item Alice examines is made of wood'. Included in the list is the following sentence:

(18) The item Alice admires most is well made.

The items on Beth's shelf are of various kinds, and no single standard or criterion of good craftsmanship applies to them all. Since Charlie and David don't know which item Alice admires most, at the time they write down this sentence, it seems that they can't intend it to express the content *The item Alice admires most is well made with respect to s*, for any particular standard, *s*. Nonetheless, if the item Alice admires most is in fact a state, then (18) seems to have clear truth-conditions: it's true just in case that statue is well made *for a statue*, i.e. by the standards appropriate to statues. The pluralist has an explanation of this: (18) reports that *the statue* is well made, in the allegedly standard-neutral sense (Fine 2006: 1076). But what can the monist say?

Answer: while Charlie and David don't do anything in their conversational context to select a particular index, and hence don't intend a particular propositional content, they needn't do so in order for there to *be* an index which provides the correct interpretation, and hence for (18) to have a propositional content. The selection of an appropriate index can be *deferred*.

The phenomenon of deferred indexing is familiar from the literature on indexicals. On a simple Kaplanian picture, a sentence may only be interpreted with respect to a 'proper' index, where $<a, r, t, w>$ is a proper index only if *a* is located at *r* at *t* in *w* (Kaplan 1989: 544). Given this simple picture, the sentence 'I'm here now' is guaranteed to be true; that is, its character is guaranteed to map a proper index to a true propositional content. The content of 'I'm here now', relative to an index *i*, is that a_i is at r_i at t_i. But it's simply a condition on *i*'s being a *proper* index that a_i be at r_i at t_i, and so, if 'I'm here now' is only assigned a content relative to proper indexes, that content is guaranteed to be true. The problem is that, if 'I'm here now' were guaranteed to be true, then 'I'm not here now' would be guaranteed to be false, and it isn't. Suppose that I leave an outgoing message on my office voicemail, saying, 'I'm not here right now; please leave a message'. It would simply be wrong to interpret me as saying something false when I say, 'I'm not here right now'. For, when I make that utterance, I don't mean that I'm not in my office *at the time that I make my utterance*, and no competent speaker would interpret me that way.[21]

So, what *do* I mean when I say, 'I'm not here right now'? The natural thought is that I mean that I'm not in my office *at the time(s) that someone calls my office and reaches my voicemail*. Notice that, since I don't know in advance when people will call and reach my voicemail, no referent has been assigned to 'now' *at the time of my utterance*. Instead, the assignment of that referent has been deferred, in a reasonably systematic way, to the time(s), if any, at which someone reaches my voicemail.

Something similar is happening in the case of Charlie and David. When they first utter (18), no particular standard for being well made has been selected as the relevant one, and so no content has yet been assigned to the sentence. The selection of a standard which would allow the assignment of a content has been deferred. But, just as with 'I'm not here right now', this is consistent with our having a sense of which assignments would be appropriate, and with our having a strong sense of (18)'s truth-conditions. Indeed, since Charlie and David describe the item simply as 'the item Alice admires most', they're best interpreted as meaning that it's well made with respect to those standards that are relevant for evaluating the craftsmanship of *F*s, where *F* is the type with respect to which she admires the item, whatever that turns out to be. Nothing more is required to explain the intuitive truth-conditions of (18).

8.6 Conclusion

While I can't claim to have anticipated and answered all possible objections to my view, those discussed in this chapter are frequently taken, either individually or collectively, to show that no view which identifies negative actions with positive events can succeed. Since none of the objections is compelling, we can (and, in light of the previous chapters, *should*) identify negative actions with positive events.

---

[21] This problem is anticipated, though not discussed in detail, in Kaplan (1989: 491 n.12). For discussion of the voicemail example, and examples like it, see, e.g. Colterjohn and MacIntosh (1987), Predelli (1998), and Sidelle (1991).

Conclusion

We began with the problem of negative action. The following sentences are individually plausible, but jointly inconsistent:

(PNA 1)   Negative actions – in the sense of things done – are genuine actions; necessarily, if NEG-φ is a negative action for x at t, then if x NEG-φ-s at t, then x acts by NEG-φ-ing at t.

(PNA 2)   Necessarily, if x acts by φ-ing at t, then there exists an event that is x's token φ-ing at t.

(PNA 3)   Possibly, x NEG-φ-s at t, and there exists no event that is x's token NEG-φ-ing at t.

It seems *prima facie* obvious that the ways in which we can exercise our agency include intentionally omitting to do something, refraining from doing it, etc. If we want the standard, event-based theories to accommodate this, then there must be such events as token negative actions (intentional omissions, refrainments, etc.). But to many philosophers of action, this seems impossible. Negative actions seem to be not events, but absences thereof.

I've argued that we can, and should, reject (PNA 3), and claim that negative actions are events, just as ordinary actions are. By rejecting (PNA 3), we can account for the fact that negative actions are genuine exercises of agency, and we can do so without revising or rejecting event-based theories like the Event-Causal and Agent-Causal theories of action. Moreover, I've argued that we needn't posit any metaphysically negative entities, like absences or negative states of affairs. Negative actions are token-identical to ordinary, positive events.

The motivation for (PNA 3), we've seen, comes from Deflationism, a widely assumed yet typically under-developed semantic theory according to which negative action sentences don't report the occurrence of events, like ordinary action sentences do, and instead express negative existentials.

In the central chapters of this book, I undertook a detailed examination of Deflationism and its credentials. While the case for Deflationism is *prima facie* strong – the theory makes the correct predictions about the validity and invalidity of adverb-dropping, adverb-adding, and adverb-conjoining inferences, while a simple Neo-Davidsonian approach makes exactly the wrong predictions – it can be overcome. My 'sophisticated Neo-Davidsonian approach', according to which negative action sentences report the occurrence of ensuring-events, accommodates all the linguistic data Deflationism does, while also accommodating some data that Deflationism doesn't. Thus, when evaluating the linguistic data relevant to (PNA 2) and (PNA 3), we ought to conclude that (PNA 2) is true and (PNA 3) false: *all* action sentences, whether positive or negative, quantify over events.

Token positive actions are those events which are quantified over in positive action sentences: 'Alice kissed Beth' reports the occurrence of an event which is Alice's kissing of Beth. Thus, given my sophisticated Neo-Davidsonian approach to negative action sentences, we ought to think that token negative actions are the events quantified over in *those* sentences – that is, x's NEG-φ-ing is that behaviour of x's which ensures that x doesn't φ (at the relevant time). This leads to my 'realizer functionalist' metaphysics of negative actions: a negative action is simply an event that plays the ensuring role. Since ordinary, positive events play that role, negative actions just *are* those positive events. Thus, negative actions aren't negative in any metaphysically deep sense, as absences or negative states of affairs would be. The 'negativity' of negative actions resides in the description of the ensuring role, and the negative actions themselves are entirely positive in nature.

Many philosophers who have written on the topic of negative action have thought that this sort of view, on which negative actions are token-identical to positive events, simply can't work. In the last two chapters of this book, I've surveyed what I take to be the strongest arguments against identification, and shown how they fail. I've shown that while my realizer functionalist view is incompatible with the standard development of the popular property-exemplification theory of events, that development is faulty. Once the theory is properly developed, the incompatibility with realizer functionalism disappears. I've also shown that a range of popular arguments against identification can be resisted. In some cases (e.g. when discussing the spatiotemporal locations of negative actions), I deployed the specific resources of my realizer functionalist view. In others (e.g. when discussing the modal profiles and causal roles), I showed that the arguments rest on a confusion between the things we do and our doings of those things, and a related confusion between action sentences and terms which denote particular token actions. And in others (e.g. when discussing scalar adverbs and gradable adjectives), I showed that the arguments rely on an overly simple conception of how certain predicates work.

In sum, I've surveyed what I take to be the dominant and most powerful reasons for thinking that negative actions are absences rather than events, and argued against them. Negative action sentences are existential quantifications over events, just as ordinary ones are, and so the motivation for thinking that ordinary actions are events extends to negative ones as well. Moreover, my realizer functionalist view allows us to identify negative actions with ordinary, positive events, and has the resources to resist common arguments against the identification. Thus, we can solve the problem of negative action by retaining (PNA 1) and (PNA 2) and rejecting (PNA 3). The result is a satisfying and comprehensive picture of the nature of negative actions, our thought and talk about them, and their place in a theory of agency.

References

Almotahari, Mahrad. (2014a) Metalinguistic negation and metaphysical affirmation. *Philosophical Studies* 167(3):497–517.

(2014b) The identity of a material thing and its matter. *Philosophical Quarterly* 64(256):387–406.

Alvarez, Maria. (2009) Actions, thought-experiments, and the 'principle of alternative possibilities'. *Australasian Journal of Philosophy* 87(1):61–81.

(2013) Agency and two-way powers. *Proceedings of the Aristotelian Society* 113:101–121.

Alvarez, Maria and John Hyman. (1998) Agents and their actions. *Philosophy* 73 (2):219–245.

Anscombe, G. E. M. (1963) *Intention*, 2nd ed. Cambridge, MA: Harvard University Press.

Armstrong, D. M. (1989) *Universals: An Opinionated Introduction*. Boulder, CO: Westview Press.

(1997) *A World of States of Affairs*. New York: Cambridge University Press.

(2004) *Truth and Truthmakers*. New York: Cambridge University Press.

Audi, Robert. (1994) Dispositional beliefs and dispositions to believe. *Noûs* 28 (4):419–434.

Azzouni, Jody. (2004) *Deflating Existential Consequence: A Case for Nominalism*. New York: Oxford University Press.

Bach, Kent. (2010) Refraining, omitting, and negative acts. In Timothy O'Connor and Constantine Sandis (eds.) *A Companion to the Philosophy of Action*. Malden: Blackwell, 50–57.

Barker, Stephen and Mark Jago. (2012) Being positive about negative facts. *Philosophy and Phenomenological Research* 85(1):117–138.

Bayer, Samuel Louis. (1997) *Confessions of a Lapsed Neo-Davidsonian: Events and Arguments in Compositional Semantics*. New York: Routledge.

Beebee, Helen. (2004) Causing and nothingness. In John Collins, Ned Hall, and L. A. Paul (eds.) *Causation and Counterfactuals*. Cambridge, MA: The MIT Press, 291–308.

Bennett, Jonathan. (1988) *Events and Their Names*. Indianapolis: Hackett Publishing Company.

(1995) *The Act Itself*. New York: Oxford University Press.

Bentham, Jeremy. (1780) *Introduction to the Principles of Morals and Legislation.* Reprinted 2007. Minneola, NY: Dover Publications.

Bernstein, Sara. (2014a) Two problems for proportionality about omissions. *Dialectica* 68(3):429–441.

(2014b) Omissions as possibilities. *Philosophical Studies* 167(1):1–23.

(2015) The metaphysics of omissions. *Philosophy Compass* 10(3):208–218.

Berto, Franceso, Rohan French, Graham Priest, and David Ripley. (2018) Williamson on counterpossibles. *Journal of Philosophical Logic* 47(4):693–713.

Bird, Alexander. (2007) *Nature's Metaphysics: Laws and Properties.* New York: Oxford University Press.

Bishop, John. (1989) *Natural Agency: An Essay on the Causal Theory of Action.* New York: Cambridge University Press.

Bohn, Einar Duenger. (2018) Panpsychism, the combination problem, and plural collective properties. *Australasian Journal of Philosophy* 97(2):383–394.

(2019) Composition as identity: Pushing forward. *Synthese.* doi: 10.1007/s11229-019-02193-x.

Borg, Emma. (2004) *Minimal Semantics.* New York: Oxford University Press.

(2012) *Pursuing Meaning.* New York: Oxford University Press.

Brand, Myles. (1971) The language of not doing. *American Philosophical Quarterly* 8(1):45–53.

Bratman, Michael. (1987) *Intentions, Plans, and Practical Reason.* Cambridge, MA: Harvard University Press.

Buckareff, Andrei A. (2018) I'm just sitting around doing nothing: On exercising intentional agency in omitting to act. *Synthese* 195(10):4617–4635.

Burgess, John P. and Gideon Rosen. (1999) *A Subject with No Object: Strategies for Nominalistic Interpretation of Mathematics.* New York: Oxford University Press.

Calosi, Claudio and Jessica Wilson. (2019) Quantum metaphysical indeterminacy. *Philosophical Studies* 176(10):2599–2627.

Cameron, Ross P. (2008) Truthmakers and ontological commitment: Or how to deal with complex objects and mathematical ontology without getting into trouble. *Philosophical Studies* 140(1):1–18.

Campbell, Keith. (1990) *Abstract Particulars.* Malden: Blackwell.

Castañeda, Hector-Neri. (1967) Comments on D. Davidson's 'The logical form of action sentences'. In Nicholas Rescher (ed.) *The Logic of Decision and Action.* Pittsburgh: University of Pittsburgh Press, 104–112.

Cheyne, Colin and Charles Pigden. (2006) Negative truths from positive facts. *Australasian Journal of Philosophy* 84(2):249–265.

Clarke, Randolph. (2010a) Intentional omissions. *Noûs* 44(1):158–177.

(2010b) Reply to Sartorio. In Jesús H. Aguilar and Andrei A. Buckareff (eds.) *Causing Human Actions: New Perspectives on the Causal Theory of Action.* Cambridge, MA: The MIT Press, 161–165.

(2011) Omissions, responsibility, and symmetry. *Philosophy and Phenomenological Research* 82(3):594–624.

(2012) Absence of action. *Philosophical Studies* 158(2):361–376.

(2014) *Omissions: Agency, Metaphysics, and Responsibility.* New York: Oxford University Press.

Collins, John, Ned Hall, and L. A. Paul. (eds.) (2004) *Causation and Counterfactuals.* Cambridge, MA: The MIT Press.

Colterjohn, Julia and Duncan MacIntosh. (1987) Gerald Vision and indexicals. *Analysis* 47(1):58–60.

Danto, Arthur. (1973) *Analytical Philosophy of Action.* New York: Cambridge University Press.

(1965) Basic actions. *American Philosophical Quarterly* 2(2):141–148.

Davidson, Donald. (1963) Actions, reasons, and causes. Reprinted in his (2001) *Essays on Actions and Events,* 2nd ed. New York: Oxford University Press, 3–19.

(1967a) The logical form of action sentences. Reprinted in his (2001) *Essays on Actions and Events,* 2nd ed. New York: Oxford University Press, 105–122.

(1967b) Causal relations. Reprinted in his (2001) *Essays on Actions and Events,* 2nd ed. New York: Oxford University Press, 149–162.

(1969) The individuation of events. Reprinted in his (2001) *Essays on Actions and Events,* 2nd ed. New York: Oxford University Press, 163–180.

(1970a) Events as particulars. Reprinted in his (2001) *Essays on Actions and Events,* 2nd ed. New York: Oxford University Press, 181–187.

(1970b) Action and reaction. *Inquiry* 13(1–4):140–148.

(1971) Agency. Reprinted in his (2001) *Essays on Actions and Events,* 2nd ed. New York: Oxford University Press, 43–61.

(1985a) Reply to Bruce Vermazen. In Bruce Vermazen and Merrill B. Hintikka (eds.) *Essays on Davidson: Actions and Events.* New York: Oxford University Press, 217–221.

(1985b) Reply to Quine on events. Reprinted in his (2001) *Essays on Actions and Events,* 2nd ed. New York: Oxford University Press, 305–311.

(1999) Reply to Jennifer Hornsby. In Lewis Edwin Hahn (ed.) *The Philosophy of Donald Davidson.* Chicago and La Salle: Open Court, 623–640.

(2005) *Truth and Predication.* Cambridge, MA: Harvard University Press.

Demos, Raphael. (1917) A discussion of a certain type of negative proposition. *Mind* 26 (102):188–196.

DeRose, Keith. (2008) Gradeable adjectives: A defense of pluralism. *Australasian Journal of Philosophy* 86 (1):141–160.

Dowe, Phil. (2000) *Physical Causation.* New York: Cambridge University Press.

(2004) Causes are physically connected to effects: Why preventers and omissions are not causes. In Christopher Hitchcock (ed.) *Contemporary Debates in Philosophy of Science.* Malden: Blackwell, 189–196.

(2010) Proportionality and omissions. *Analysis* 70(3):446–451.

Dyke, Heather. (2008) *Metaphysics and the Representational Fallacy.* New York: Routledge.

Ehring, Douglas. (1997) *Causation and Persistence: A Theory of Causation.* New York: Oxford University Press.

(2011) *Tropes: Properties, Objects, and Mental Causation*. New York: Oxford University Press.

Enç, Berent. (2003) *How We Act: Causes, Reasons, and Intentions*. New York: Oxford University Press.

Fine, Kit. (2003) The non-identity of a material thing and its matter. *Mind* 112 (446):195–234.

(2006) Arguing for non-identity: A response to King and Frances. *Mind* 115 (460):1059–1082.

(2009) The question of ontology. In David Chalmers, David Manley, and Ryan Wasserman (eds.) *Metametaphysics: New Essays on the Foundations of Ontology*. New York: Oxford University Press, 157–177.

Frances, Bryan. (2006) The new Leibniz's Law argument for pluralism. *Mind* 115 (460):1007–1021.

Frankfurt, Harry G. (1969) Alternate possibilities and moral responsibility. *Journal of Philosophy* 66(23):829–839.

Funkhouser, Eric. (2006) The determinable-determinate relation. *Noûs* 40 (3):548–569.

(2014) *The Logical Structure of Kinds*. New York: Oxford University Press.

Goldman, Alvin I. (1970) *A Theory of Human Action*. Englewood Cliffs, NJ: Prentice Hall.

Grice, H. P. (1975) Logic and conversation. Reprinted in his (1989) *Studies in the Way of Words*. Cambridge, MA: Harvard University Press, 22–40.

Hale, Bob. (2013) *Necessary Beings: An Essay on Ontology, Modality, and the Relations between Them*. New York: Oxford University Press.

Hale, Bob and Crispin Wright. (2012) Horse sense. *Journal of Philosophy* 109(1–2):85–131.

Hanser, Matthew. (2008) Actions, acting, and acting well. In Russ Shafer-Landau (ed.) *Oxford Studies in Metaethics*, Vol. 3. New York: Oxford University Press, 271–298.

Heim, Irene and Angelika Kratzer. (1998) *Semantics in Generative Grammar*. Malden: Blackwell.

Horn, Laurence R. (1989) *A Natural History of Negation*. Chicago: University of Chicago Press.

Hornsby, Jennifer. (1980) *Actions*. London: Routledge & Keagan Paul.

(1986) Bodily movements, actions, and epistemology. Reprinted in her (1997) *Simple Mindedness: In Defense of Naïve Naturalism in the Philosophy of Mind*. Cambridge, MA: Harvard University Press, 93–102.

(1993) Agency and causal explanation. Reprinted in her (1997) *Simple Mindedness: In Defense of Naïve Naturalism in the Philosophy of Mind*. Cambridge, MA: Harvard University Press, 129–153.

(1997) Action and the mental-physical divide. In Jennifer Hornsby (ed.) *Simple Mindedness: In Defense of Naïve Naturalism in the Philosophy of Mind*. Cambridge, MA: Harvard University Press, 83–92.

(1999) Anomolousness in action. In Lewis Edwin Hahn (ed.) *The Philosophy of Donald Davidson*. Chicago and La Salle: Open Court, 623–635.

(2004) Agency and actions. *Royal Institute of Philosophy Supplement* 55:1–23.

(2005) Truth without truthmaking entities. In Helen Beebee and Julian Dodd (eds.) *Truthmakers: The Contemporary Debate.* New York: Oxford University Press, 33–47.

(2010) The standard story of action: An exchange (2). In Jesús H. Aguilar and Andrei A. Buckareff (eds.) *Causing Human Actions: New Perspectives on the Causal Theory of Action.* Cambridge, MA: The MIT Press, 57–68.

Hyman, John. (2015) *Action, Knowledge, and the Will.* New York: Oxford University Press.

Jago, Mark. (2014) *The Impossible: An Essay on Hyperintensionality.* New York: Oxford University Press.

Kaplan, David. (1989) Demonstratives: An essay on the semantics, logic, metaphysics, and epistemology of demonstratives and other indexicals. In Joseph Almog, John Perry, and Howard Wettstein (eds.) *Themes from Kaplan.* New York: Oxford University Press, 481–563.

Karttunen, Lauri. (1974) Presupposition and linguistic context. *Theoretical Linguistics* 1(1–3):181–194.

Kim, Jaegwon. (1973) Causation, nomic subsumption, and the concept of an event. Reprinted in his (1993) *Supervenience and Mind: Selected Essays.* New York: Cambridge University Press, 3–21.

(1976) Events as property exemplifications. Reprinted in his (1993) *Supervenience and Mind: Selected Essays.* New York: Cambridge University Press, 33–52.

(1991) Events: Their metaphysics and semantics. *Philosophy and Phenomenological Research* 51(3):641–646.

King, Jeffrey C. (2006) Semantics for monists. *Mind* 115(460):1023–1058.

Kukso, Boris. (2006) The reality of absences. *Australasian Journal of Philosophy* 84 (1):21–37.

Landman, Fred. (2000) *Events and Plurality: The Jerusalem Lectures.* Norwell: Kluwer Academic Publishers.

Lewis, David. (1968) Counterpart theory and quantified modal logic. Reprinted in his (1983) *Philosophical Papers,* Vol. 1. New York: Oxford University Press, 26–39.

(1973a) *Counterfactuals.* Malden: Blackwell.

(1973b) Causation. Reprinted in his (1986) *Philosophical Papers,* Vol. 2. New York: Oxford University Press, 159–172.

(1979) Counterfactual dependence and time's arrow. Reprinted in his (1986) *Philosophical Papers,* Vol. 2. New York: Oxford University Press, 32–52.

(1980) Index, context, and content. Reprinted in his (1998) *Papers in Philosophical Logic.* New York: Cambridge University Press, 21–44.

(1983) New work for a theory of universals. Reprinted in his (1998) *Papers in Metaphysics and Epistemology.* New York: Cambridge University Press, 8–55.

(1992) Many, but almost one. Reprinted in his (1998) *Papers in Metaphysics and Epistemology.* New York: Cambridge University Press, 164–182.

(1998) A world of truthmakers? Reprinted in his (1998) *Papers in Metaphysics and Epistemology.* New York: Cambridge University Press, 215–220.

(2001) Truthmaking and difference-making. *Noûs* 35(4):602–615.

(2003) Things *qua* truthmakers. In Hallvard Lillehammer and Gonzalo Rodriguez-Pereyra (eds.) *Real Metaphysics: Essays in Honour of D. H. Mellor*. New York: Routledge, 25–38.

Liebesman, David. (2015) Predication as ascription. *Mind* 124(494):517–569.

Lombard, Lawrence B. (1986) *Events: A Metaphysical Study*. London: Routledge & Keagan Paul.

Lowe, E. J. (1989a) What is a criterion of identity? *Philosophical Quarterly* 39 (154):1–21.

(1989b) Impredicative identity criteria and Davidson's criterion of event identity. *Analysis* 49(4):178–181.

(2002) *A Survey of Metaphysics*. New York: Oxford University Press.

(2010a) Action and ontology. In Timothy O'Connor and Constantine Sandis (eds.) *A Companion to the Philosophy of Action*. Malden: Blackwell, 3–9.

(2010b) On the individuation of powers. In Anna Marmodoro (ed.) *The Metaphysics of Powers: Their Grounding and Their Manifestations*. New York: Routledge, 8–26.

Ludwig, Kirk. (2010) Adverbs of action and logical form. In Timothy O'Connor and Constantine Sandis (eds.) *A Companion to the Philosophy of Action*. Malden: Blackwell, 40–49.

(2016) *From Individual to Plural Agency: Collective Action*, Vol. 1. New York: Oxford University Press.

MacBride, Fraser. (2005) Lewis's animadversions on the truthmaker principle. In Helen Beebee and Julian Dodd (eds.) *Truthmakers: The Contemporary Debate*. New York: Oxford University Press, 117–140.

MacDonald, Cynthia and Graham MacDonald. (2006) The metaphysics of mental causation. *Journal of Philosophy* 103(11):539–576.

MacFarlane, John. (2014) *Assessment Sensitivity: Relative Truth and Its Applications*. New York: Oxford University Press.

Martin, C. B. (1994) Dispositions and conditionals. *Philosophical Quarterly* 44 (174):1–8.

(1996) How it is: Entities, absences, and voids. *Australasian Journal of Philosophy* 74(1):57–65.

Mayr, Erasmus. (2011) *Understanding Human Agency*. New York: Oxford University Press.

McKitrick, Jennifer. (2010) Manifestations as effects. In Anna Marmodoro (ed.) *The Metaphysics of Powers: Their Grounding and Their Manifestations*. New York: Routledge, 73–83.

Melia, Joseph. (2005) Truthmaking without truthmakers. In Helen Beebee and Julian Dodd (eds.) *Truthmakers: The Contemporary Debate*. New York: Oxford University Press, 67–84.

Mellor, D. H. (1995) *The Facts of Causation*. New York: Routledge.

(2004) For facts as causes and effects. In John Collins, Ned Hall, and L. A. Paul (eds.) *Causation and Counterfactuals*. Cambridge, MA: The MIT Press, 309–323.

Merricks, Trenton. (2007) *Truth and Ontology*. New York: Oxford University Press.

Molnar, George. (2000) Truthmakers for negative truths. *Australasian Journal of Philosophy* 78(1):72–86.

(2003) *Powers: A Study in Metaphysics*. Edited by Stephen Mumford. New York: Oxford University Press.

Moore, Michael S. (1993) *Act and Crime: The Philosophy of Action and Its Implications for Criminal Law*. New York: Oxford University Press.

(2009) *Causation and Responsibility: An Essay in Law, Morals, and Metaphysics*. New York: Oxford University Press.

(2010) Renewed questions about the causal theory of action. In Jesús H. Aguilar and Andrei A. Buckareff (eds.) *Causing Human Actions: New Perspectives on the Causal Theory of Action*. Cambridge: The MIT Press, 27–43.

Moya, Carlos. (1990) *The Philosophy of Action: An Introduction*. Cambridge: Polity Press.

Mulligan, Kevin, Peter Simons, and Barry Smith. (1984) Truth-makers. *Philosophy and Phenomenological Research* 44(3):287–321.

Mumford, Stephen. (1998) *Dispositions*. New York: Oxford University Press.

Mumford, Stephen and Rani Lill Anjum. (2011) *Getting Causes from Powers*. New York: Oxford University Press.

Nolan, Daniel. (1997) Impossible worlds: A modest approach. *Notre Dame Journal of Formal Logic* 38(4):535–572.

O'Brien, Lucy and Matthew Soteriou. (eds.) (2009) *Mental Actions*. New York: Oxford University Press.

O'Shaughnessy, Brian. (1980) *The Will: A Dual Aspect Theory*, Vol. 2. New York: Cambridge University Press.

(2008) *The Will: A Dual Aspect Theory*, Vol. 2, 2nd ed. New York: Cambridge University Press.

Palmer, David. (2020) Omissions: The constitution view defended. *Erkenntnis* 85 (3):739–756.

Parsons, Josh. (2004) Distributional properties. In Frank Jackson and Graham Priest (eds.) *Lewisian Themes: The Philosophy of David K. Lewis*. New York: Oxford University Press, 173–180.

(2007) Theories of location. In Dean Zimmerman (ed.) *Oxford Studies in Metaphysics*, Vol. 3. New York: Oxford University Press, 201–232.

Parsons, Terence. (1990) *Events in the Semantics of English*. Cambridge, MA: The MIT Press.

Paul, L. A. and Ned Hall. (2013) *Causation: A User's Guide*. New York: Oxford University Press.

Paul, Sarah K. (2009) Intention, belief, and wishful thinking: Setiya on 'practical knowledge'. *Ethics* 119(3):546–557.

Payton, Jonathan D. (2020) Two problems for the constitution view of omissions: A reply to Palmer. *Erkenntnis*. doi: 10.1007/s10670-020-00237-0.

Perovic, Katarina. (2018) What is a fourdimensionalist to do about temporally extended properties? *European Journal of Philosophy* 27(2):1–12.

Predelli, Stefano. (1998) 'I am not here now'. *Analysis* 58(2):107–115.

Quine, W. V. O. (1948) On what there is. Reprinted in his (1980), *From a Logical Point of View*, 2nd ed. Cambridge, MA: Harvard University Press, 1–19.

(1951) Ontology and ideology. *Philosophical Studies* 2(1):11–15.

(1969) Existence and quantification. Reprinted in his (1969) *Ontological Relativity and Other Essays*, New York: Columbia University Press, 91–113.

Ramsey, Frank P. (1927) Facts and propositions (1). *Proceedings of the Aristotelian Society*, Supplement 7:153–170.

Rayo, Agustín. (2002) Words and objects. *Noûs* 36(3):436–464.

(2007) Ontological commitment. *Philosophy Compass* 2(3):428–444.

Recanati, François. (2004) *Literal Meaning*. New York: Cambridge University Press.

(2010) *Truth-Conditional Pragmatics*. New York: Oxford University Press.

Rieppel, Michael. (2016) Being something: Properties and predicative quantification. *Mind* 125(499):643–689.

Rodriguez-Pereyra, Gonzalo. (2002) *Resemblance Nominalism: A Solution to the Problem of Universals*. New York: Oxford University Press.

(2005) Why truthmakers. In Helen Beebee and Julian Dodd (eds.) *Truthmakers: The Contemporary Debate*. New York: Oxford University Press, 17–31.

Ruben, David-Hillel. (2003) *Action and Its Explanation*. New York: Oxford University Press.

(2013) Trying in some way. *Australasian Journal of Philosophy* 91(4):719–733.

Sandis, Constantine. (2012) *The Things We Do and Why We Do Them*. New York: Palgrave Macmillan.

(2017) The doing and the deed: Action in normative ethics. *Royal Institute of Philosophy Supplement* 80:105–126.

Sartorio, Carolina. (2009) Omissions and causalism. *Noûs* 43(3):513–530.

(2015) Sensitivity to reasons and actual sequences. In David Shoemaker (ed.) *Oxford Studies in Agency and Responsibility*, Vol. 3. New York: Oxford University Press, 104–119.

Savellos, Elias E. (1995) Supervenience and the essences of events. In Elias E. Savellos and Umit D. Yalcin (eds.) *Supervenience: New Essays*. New York: Cambridge University Press, 244–263.

Schaffer, Jonathan. (2009) On what grounds what. In David Chalmers, David Manley, and Ryan Wasserman (eds.) *Metametaphysics: New Essays on the Foundations of Ontology*. New York: Oxford University Press, 347–383.

(2012) Disconnection and responsibility. *Legal Theory* 18(4):399–435.

Setiya, Kieran. (2007) *Reasons without Rationalism*. Princeton: Princeton University Press.

(2008) Practical knowledge. Reprinted in his (2017) *Practical Knowledge: Selected Essays*. New York: Oxford University Press, 39–61.

(2009) Practical knowledge revisited. Reprinted in his (2017) *Practical Knowledge: Selected Essays*. New York: Oxford University Press, 62–72.

(2010) Sympathy for the devil. Reprinted in his (2017) *Practical Knowledge: Selected Essays*. New York: Oxford University Press, 73–106.

Shanon, Benny. (1976) On the two kinds of presupposition in natural language. *Foundations of Language* 14(2):247–249.

Shepherd, Joshua. (2014a) The contours of control. *Philosophical Studies* 170 (3):395–411.

(2014b) Causalism and intentional omission. *American Philosophical Quarterly* 51(1):15–26.

Sidelle, Alan. (1991) The answering machine paradox. *Canadian Journal of Philosophy* 21(4):525–539.

Sider, Theodore. (2011) *Writing the Book of the World*. New York: Oxford University Press.

Silver, Kenneth. (2018) Omissions as events and actions. *Journal of the American Philosophical Association* 4(1):33–48.

Smith, Michael. (2010) The standard story of action: An exchange (1). In Jesús H. Aguilar and Andrei A. Buckareff (eds.) *Causing Human Actions: New Perspectives on the Causal Theory of Action*. Cambridge, MA: The MIT Press, 45–55.

Sprigge, Timothy L. S. (1970) *Facts, Words, and Beliefs*. London: Routledge & Kegan Paul.

Stalnaker, Robert. (1968) A theory of conditionals. In Nicholas Rescher (ed.) *Studies in Logical Theory*. Oxford: Blackwell, 98–112.

(1970) Pragmatics. Reprinted in his (1999) *Context and Content*. New York: Oxford University Press, 31–46.

(1987) *Inquiry*. Cambridge, MA: The MIT Press.

(2014) *Context*. New York: Oxford University Press.

Steward, Helen. (1997) *The Ontology of Mind: Events, States, and Processes*. New York: Oxford University Press.

(2000) Do actions occur inside the body? *Mind & Society* 1(2):107–125.

(2009) Sub-intentional actions and the over-mentalization of agency. In Constantine Sandis (ed.) *New Essays on the Explanation of Action*. New York: Palgrave Macmillan, 295–312.

(2012a) *A Metaphysics for Freedom*. New York: Oxford University Press.

(2012b) Actions as processes. *Philosophical Perspectives* 26:373–388.

(2013) Processes, continuants, and individuals. *Mind* 122(487):781–812.

Stroud, Douglas Aikenhead. (1914) *Mens Rea: Or, Imputability under the Law of England*. London: Sweet & Maxwell, Ltd.

Taylor, Barry. (1983) Events and adverbs. *Proceedings of the Aristotelian Society, New Series* 84:103–122.

(1985) *Modes of Occurrence*. Malden: Blackwell.

Taylor, Richard. (1952) Negative things. *Journal of Philosophy* 49(13):433–449.

(1966) *Action and Purpose*. New York: Humanities Press.

Thompson, Judith Jarvis. (1971) The time of a killing. *Journal of Philosophy* 68 (5):115–132.

(2003) Causation: Omissions. *Philosophy and Phenomenological Research* 66 (1):81–103.

Tiehen, Justin. (2015) The role functionalist theory of absences. *Erkenntnis* 80 (3):505–519.

Unger, Peter. (1980) The problem of the many. *Midwest Studies in Philosophy* 5 (1):411–468.

van Inwagen, Peter. (1981) Why I don't understand substitutional quantification. Reprinted in his (2001) *Ontology, Identity, and Modality: Essays in Metaphysics*. New York: Cambridge University Press, 32–36.

  (1998) Meta-ontology. Reprinted in his (2001) *Ontology, Identity, and Modality: Essays in Metaphysics*. New York: Cambridge University Press, 13–31.

  (2009) Being, existence, and ontological commitment. In David Chalmers, David Manley, and Ryan Wasserman (eds.) *Metametaphysics: New Essays on the Foundations of Ontology*. New York: Oxford University Press, 472–506.

Vendler, Zeno. (1967) *Linguistics and Philosophy*. Ithaca, NJ: Cornell University Press.

Vermazen, Bruce. (1985) Negative acts. In Bruce Vermazen and Merrill B. Hintikka (eds.) *Essays on Davidson: Actions and Events*. New York: Oxford University Press, 93–104.

von Fintel, Kai. (2004) Would you believe it? The King of France is back! (Presuppositions and truth-value intuitions). In Marga Reimer and Anne Bezuidenhout (eds.) *Descriptions and Beyond*. New York: Oxford University Press, 315–341.

Williams, Donald C. (1953a) On the elements of being: I. *Review of Metaphysics* 7 (1):3–18.

  (1953b) On the elements of being: II. *Review of Metaphysics* 7(2):171–192.

Williamson, Timothy. (2000) *Knowledge and Its Limits*. New York: Oxford University Press.

  (2007) *The Philosophy of Philosophy*. Malden: Blackwell.

  (2013) *Modal Logic as Metaphysics*. New York: Oxford University Press.

  (2018) Counterpossibles. *Topoi* 37(3):357–368.

Wilson, Jessica. (2009) Determination, realization, and mental causation. *Philosophical Studies* 145(1):149–169.

  (2011a) Much ado about 'something'. *Analysis* 71(1):172–188.

  (2011b) Non-reductive realization and the powers-based subset strategy. *Monist* 94(1):121–154.

  (2013) A determinable-based account of metaphysical indeterminacy. *Inquiry* 56(4):359–385.

  (2017) Are there indeterminate states of affairs? Yes. In Elizabeth Barnes (ed.) *Current Controversies in Metaphysics*. New York: Routledge, 105–119.

Woollard, Fiona. (2015) *Doing and Allowing Harm*. New York: Oxford University Press.

Wyner, Adam. (1989) The semantics of adverbs and the perception problem. *Proceedings of the 1989 Western States Conference on Linguistics*. Arizona State University, October 13–15, 1989.

Yablo, Stephen. (1992a) Cause and essence. Reprinted in his (2010) *Things: Papers on Objects, Events, and Properties*. New York: Oxford University Press, 59–97.

   (1992b) Mental causation. Reprinted in his (2010) *Thoughts: Papers on Mind, Meaning, and Modality*. New York: Oxford University Press, 222–248.

Index

For EU product safety concerns, contact us at Calle de José Abascal, 56–1°,
28003 Madrid, Spain or eugpsr@cambridge.org.